Get the eBooks FREE!

(PDF, ePub, Kindle, and liveBook all included)

We believe that once you buy a book from us, you should be able to read it in any format we have available. To get electronic versions of this book at no additional cost to you, purchase and then register this book at the Manning website.

Go to https://www.manning.com/freebook and follow the instructions to complete your pBook registration.

That's it!
Thanks from Manning!

Testing Java Microservices

Using Arquillian, Hoverfly, AssertJ, JUnit, Selenium, and Mockito

ALEX SOTO BUENO
ANDY GUMBRECHT
AND JASON PORTER

MANNING

SHELTER ISLAND

For online information and ordering of this and other Manning books, please visit
www.manning.com. The publisher offers discounts on this book when ordered in quantity.
For more information, please contact

> Special Sales Department
> Manning Publications Co.
> 20 Baldwin Road
> PO Box 761
> Shelter Island, NY 11964
> Email: orders@manning.com

Manning Publications Co.
20 Baldwin Road
PO Box 761
Shelter Island, NY 11964

Development editor:	Cynthia Kane
Technical development editor:	Adam Scheller
Project editor:	Tiffany Taylor
Copyeditor:	Tiffany Taylor
Proofreader:	Katie Tennant
Technical proofreader:	Joshua White
Typesetter:	Gordan Salinovic
Cover designer:	Marija Tudor

ISBN 9781617292897
Printed in the United States of America
1 2 3 4 5 6 7 8 9 10 – DP – 23 22 21 20 19 18

To my parents: thanks for the ZX Spectrum.

—A. S.

To my children, Antony and Toriann. They get me,
but they'll never get this book!

—A. G.

To the amazing community of software engineers: together we do amazing things!
And to my family and especially my wife, Tessie: thanks for being with me
on this crazy journey of life.

—J. P.

contents

v

preface

In the early days of programming, there were no frameworks. Tests consisted of ad hoc snippets of code that were put in place to ensure that important software features did roughly what they were supposed to. Storage space was very limited and precious at the time.

Eventually, unit testing progressed from being a buzzword to being the de facto means for thoroughly testing software. Space concerns diminished to the point that they were a lame excuse for not writing test code. Today, it's fair to say that all developers learn and employ the unit-testing methodology early on, and it has become fundamental to successful software development.

Today's enterprise applications require far more than just simple unit tests to maintain their integrity. Customers have become more demanding, and acceptance criteria are generally much higher. Multiple testing strategies must be applied throughout the development process if we're to successfully meet this call.

This book was written not only to address many of today's current enterprise testing needs but also to add significant value by helping you decide how to approach the future testing requirements and challenges posed by the introduction of microservices into your architecture.

It has taken us a long time to write this book: it has gone from being a small, single-chapter booklet on using a specific framework, to a 10-chapter, feature-packed epic that presents multiple testing strategies and options for you to choose from. We have learned much along the way, as this technology continually evolves. To provide as many options as possible, we've tried to focus more on strategies, methodology, and solutions rather than on super-clean code and a stunning, yet ultimately unusable, application. If we can help you walk away with some good ideas for how to test your own applications, then we've achieved our goal.

We hope you enjoy our candid style of writing, and we'd like to thank you for taking the time to read this book.

acknowledgments

This book has had input from three independent developers, and we would first like to thank each other for all the hard work and feedback. Well done, and a pat on the back to each other!

A huge thank you goes out to absolutely everyone involved in the Arquillian project, especially Aslak Knutsen, Dan Allen, Bartosz Majsak, and Matous Jobanek. Once you reach the end of the book, we're sure you'll understand how much effort has been put into this truly amazing project and how it will aid you in testing software.

The Open Source Software (OSS) community provides many extremely useful tools that enable everyone to test efficiently. Much of the work done on these projects is performed through the tireless and often thankless work contributed by dedicated developers during their free time. We thank you wholeheartedly for your valued efforts. We would like to encourage you, the reader, to also thank these incredible people at every opportunity.

A big thank you to Daniel Bryant and Marcin Grzejszczak for their time discussing contract testing.

Cynthia Kane and Tiffany Taylor, our editors, were invaluable in pushing us forward when our motivation lagged. Writing a book in your spare time is challenging, to say the least. Thank you, Cynthia and Tiffany, for putting up with us. We also thank everyone else at Manning who made this book possible: publisher Marjan Bace and the editorial and production teams.

Joshua White provided extensive proof-testing on the technical side: thanks to him for ironing out the glitches. He was our test tester!

To everyone involved in providing feedback, a thank-you for taking the time to read and reread the book in order to help us produce the final material. These include our technical peer reviewers, led by Aleksandar Dragosavljević, Alex Jacinto, Anshuman Purohit, Boris Vasile, Conor Redmond, Eddú Meléndez Gonzales, Ethan A. Rivett, Fabrizio Cucci, Gualtiero Testa, Henrik Løvborg, Jan Paul Buchwald, Jonathan Thoms, José Díaz, Kiran Anantha, Leo van den Berg, Mari Machado, Nilesh Thali, Piotr Gliźniewicz, Robert Walsh, Yagiz Erkan, and Zorodzayi Mukuya.

Last but certainly not least, we thank our wives and families for putting up with the long weekends, late hours, frustrations, and ups and downs of writing a book. We couldn't have done it without their support!

about this book

It's apparent to every developer today that testing applications is a basic requirement of software development. This wasn't always the case, and testing frameworks have come a long way since the early days. This book isn't about the theory of *why* we test, because there's plenty of information on that subject out there already. It was more important for us to figure out *how* to test, and how to convey that information to others. This book is very much focused on that approach, and the included application code provides a hands-on example from the start.

A lot of information is of course available in the cloud, but more often than not, we find that when we actually have time to read, we're not connected to the cloud (or choose not to be connected to it). It's also nice to have a readily available resource that pulls all the useful information into one place—and we hope this book will serve as that type of resource for you.

Testing is a general term, but testing is composed of a patchwork of technologies that you need to combine in order to gain the most benefit. We've collected a wide range of popular topics and components, and presented them in a way we feel makes the most sense for readers.

Who should read this book

We'd love to say "everyone," but this isn't much of a story book. Our target audience members are Java developers of Enterprise Edition (Java EE and Spring) applications. If that's you, then this book will show you how to take unit testing to the next level.

If you aren't specifically a Java developer, this book may still be of interest to you. Much of the information provided is relevant and transferable to any programming language.

As the title suggests, we're targeting the popular transition to a microservice-based architecture. But we also provide a lot of information related to more general EE testing, so don't be concerned that we've left things out—we just cover microservices in more depth.

Roadmap

This book has 10 chapters. Here's a quick guide to what we cover:

- Chapter 1 offers an introduction to and explanation of our preferred microservice terminology.
- Chapter 2 presents our prerequisite expectations for reading this book and building the code, to save you time in the long run.
- Chapter 3 will brush you up on common unit-testing techniques, methodologies, and best practices.
- Chapter 4 takes a deep dive into the Arquillian testing framework.
- Chapter 5 explains how to create integration tests for dependent microservices.
- Chapter 6 discusses consumer-driven and contract testing.
- Chapter 7 explores ad hoc, end-to-end testing techniques and tools.
- Chapter 8 covers creating reproducible testing environments with Docker.
- Chapter 9 explores service-virtualization concepts and implementations.
- Chapter 10 discusses continuous delivery and the Jenkins build pipeline.

The order of the chapters was chosen to introduce the fundamental topics in a natural progression. Each chapter builds on the next, but the book can also be read in your own order of interest. The programming language used in the book is Java, but the principles discussed can be applied to any language and framework.

Code conventions and downloads

This book contains many examples of source code both in numbered listings and inline with normal text. In both cases, source code is formatted in a `fixed-width font like this` to separate it from ordinary text.

In many cases, the original source code has been reformatted; we've added line breaks and reworked indentation to accommodate the available page space in the book. In some cases, even this wasn't enough, and listings include line-continuation markers (➥). Additionally, comments in the source code have often been removed from the listings when the code is described in the text. Code annotations accompany many of the listings, highlighting important concepts.

The source code for the book's examples is available at www.manning.com/books/testing-java-microservices.

Book forum

Purchase of *Testing Java Microservices* includes free access to a private web forum run by Manning Publications where you can make comments about the book, ask technical questions, and receive help from the author and from other users. To access the forum, go to https://forums.manning.com/forums/testing-java-microservices. You can also learn more about Manning's forums and the rules of conduct at https://forums.manning.com/forums/about.

Manning's commitment to our readers is to provide a venue where a meaningful dialogue between individual readers and between readers and the authors can take place. It isn't a commitment to any specific amount of participation on the part of the authors, whose contribution to the forum remains voluntary (and unpaid). We suggest you try asking them some challenging questions lest their interest stray! The forum and the archives of previous discussions will be accessible from the publisher's website as long as the book is in print.

about the authors

ALEX SOTO is a Java Champion and software engineer working at Red Hat on developing new tools to make better testing experiences. He enjoys the Java world, as well as software automation, and believes in the open source software model. Alex is the creator of the NoSQLUnit project, a member of the JSR374 (Java API for JSON Processing) Expert Group, and an international speaker.

Alex began programming with ZX Spectrum (in the good old days, using the POKE command) and had several different computers, such as an 80286. (He's grateful to his parents, Mili and Ramon, for buying them.) After graduating as a computer engineer from La Salle Universitat Ramon Llull, he started his professional career in Aventia, developing a platform for generating and validating electronic signatures. Then he moved to Grifols to develop diagnostic medical devices; strict testing was an important part of the lifecycle of the software. Later, he worked for Everis, in the banking sector; Scytl, developing electronic voting systems; and CloudBees.

Alex likes to spend his free time with his wife Jessica and his two daughters, Ada and Alexandra (*ninetes dels meus ulls*).

ANDY GUMBRECHT is a senior software engineer at Tomitribe. He's been interested in anything "computer" since around the age of 12, when he was fortunate to get his hands on a Sinclair ZX81 with a whopping 1 KB of memory. Many of the early examples available were long lists of binary that needed to be typed in by hand. Sometimes that worked out, but Andy soon employed his brother John as his QA tester to ensure he'd gotten it right. That was when he first learned the value of testing code.

Dabbling in machine code and BASIC continued to improve Andy's skills at optimizing code. Later, and after a short spell as a Royal Engineer on operations in the British army, he returned to college in Germany to gain some paper qualifications. He interned at PROVOX Sytemplanung GmbH and stayed for many years, working on government software.

Andy started to work on open source software around 2007 and has been involved in the Apache OpenEJB/Apache TomEE Application Server project since 2009, where he's now a member of the Project Management Committee.

JASON PORTER has been crafting software since he was 12. A couple of years before that, he discovered the amazing world of computers and programming on an old 80286 while looking through games written in BASIC. His interest in programming led him to Java and then C/C++. He became involved in web development in the early days, with Netscape Navigator and Internet Explorer. Fighting with things like DHTML and layers occupied his time. At the venerable age of 15, Jason got a job with a local web development company and spent time coding websites and writing CGI scripts in Perl. (He tries to forget those days, though.) Since that time, he's worked in various industries, coding in Java, PHP, Ruby, C#, and JavaScript. He primarily considers himself a backend developer, but the entire coding landscape is his playground.

At Red Hat, Jason has worked on various frameworks, websites, and integrations. He's spoken in the United States and internationally and is tickled every time he can help someone better understand a programming concept or new technology. Jason lives in Utah with his lovely wife and five children, whom he can't program as easily as a computer.

about the cover

The figure on the cover of *Testing Java Microservices*, titled "Visitor to the Tuileries Gardens," is a hand-colored woodcut from a drawing by Eugène Lami (1800-1890). The illustration was included in an essay in vol. 3 of *Les Français peints par eux-mêmes: Encyclopédie morale du dix-neuvième siècle* ("The French painted by themselves: moral encyclopedia of the nineteenth century"), a multivolume work by Louis Curmer, published in Paris in the early 1940s. This work presented a fascinating picture of French society through representative characters and was particularly interested in popular types and small trades. Five volumes were devoted to Parisians and three to the French provinces and colonies.

The diversity of the figures in this collection reminds us vividly of the uniqueness and individuality of the world's towns and regions just 200 years ago. This was a time when the dress codes of two regions separated by a few dozen miles identified people uniquely as belonging to one or the other. The collection brings to life a sense of isolation and distance of that period—and of every other historic period except our own hyperkinetic present.

Dress codes have changed since then, and the diversity by region, so rich at the time, has faded away. It's now often hard to tell the inhabitant of one continent from another. Perhaps we've traded a cultural and visual diversity for a more varied personal life—or a more varied and interesting intellectual and technical life.

We at Manning celebrate the inventiveness, the initiative, and the fun of the computer business with book covers based on the rich diversity of regional life of two centuries ago.

An introduction
to microservices

1

This chapter covers

- Why move toward a new microservice architecture?
- What microservices are today, and where the future may lead
- The basic component makeup of a microservice
- Testing strategies

Traditional monolithic applications are deployed as a single package, usually as a web or enterprise-archive file (WAR or EAR). They contain all the business logic required to complete multiple tasks, often alongside the components required to render the *user interface* (UI, or GUI for *graphical user interface*). When scaling, this usually means taking a complete copy of that entire application archive onto a new server node (basically, deploying it to another server node in a cluster). It doesn't matter where the load or bottleneck is occurring; even if it's only in a small cross section of the application, scaling this way is an all-or-nothing approach. Microservices are specifically designed to target and change this all-or-nothing aspect by allowing you to break your business logic into smaller, more manageable elements that can be employed in multiple ways.

This book isn't intended to be a tutorial on the varied microservice architectures that are available today; we'll assume you have some understanding of the subject. Rather, we're going to help you overcome the challenges involved in *testing* the common features that all microservice applications share. In order to do that, in this chapter we'll establish some common ground about what a microservice is, so that you can relate to where we're coming from when we discuss these topics in later chapters.

Shifting toward the ever-more-popular microservice architecture means you need to adopt new strategies in development, testing, and restructuring/refactoring and move away from some of the purely monolithic-application practices.

Microservices offer you the advantage of being able to scale individual services, and the ability to develop and maintain multiple services in parallel using several teams, but they still require a robust approach when it comes to testing.

In this book, we'll discuss various approaches for using this new, more focused way of delivering tightly packaged "micro" services and how to resolve the complex testing scenarios that are required to maintain stability across multiple teams. Later chapters will introduce an example application and how to develop testing strategies for it; this will help you better understand how to create your own test environments.

You'll see and use many features of the Arquillian test framework, which was specifically designed to tackle many of the common testing challenges you'll face. An array of mature extensions have been developed over the years, and although other tools are available, Arquillian is our tool of choice—so expect some bias. That said, Arquillian also provides close integration with many testing tools you may already be familiar with.

A note about software versions

This book uses many different software packages and tools, all of which change periodically. We tried throughout the book to present examples and techniques that wouldn't be greatly affected by these changes. All examples require Java 8, although when we finished the book, Java 10 had been released. We haven't updated the examples because in terms of testing microservices, the release doesn't add anything new. Something similar is true for JUnit 5. All of the examples are written using JUnit 4.12, because when we started writing the book, JUnit 5 wasn't yet in development. At the time we finished the book, not all of the frameworks explained here have official support for JUnit 5, so we decided to skip updating the JUnit version. Other libraries, such as Spring Boot and Docker (Compose), have evolved as well during the development of the book, but none of these changes have a significant impact on how to write tests.

1.1 What are microservices, and why use them?

In this section, we present what we believe is a reasonably good interpretation of the currently available answers to these questions. What you learn will provide a solid basis for understanding the microservice architecture, but expect innovation over time. We won't make any predictions: as stated, our principle focus for the book is testing microservices, which is unlikely to change in any significant way.

It isn't important that you fully understand the microservice architecture at this point. But if, after reading this chapter, the term *microservice* is still a dark void for you, we encourage you to gather more information from your own sources.

> **TIP** You may find it useful to join the open discussions at MicroProfile (http:// microprofile.io). This is an initiative by the likes of IBM, London Java Community (LJC), RedHat, Tomitribe, Payara, and Hazelcast to develop a shared definition of Enterprise Java for microservices, with the goal of standardization.

1.1.1 Why use microservices?

Before we delve into the nature of microservices, let's answer the "why" question. Until recently, it's been commonplace to develop monolithic applications, and that's still perfectly acceptable for any application that doesn't require scaling. The problem with scaling any kind of monolithic application is straightforward, as shown in figure 1.1. Microservices aren't here to tell you that everything else is bad; rather, they offer an architecture that is far more resilient than a monolith to changes in the future.

Microservices enable you to isolate and scale smaller pieces of your application, rather than the *entire* application. Imagine that you've extracted some core business logic in your application to services A and B. Let's say service A provides access to an inventory of items, and B provides simple statistics. You notice that on average, service A

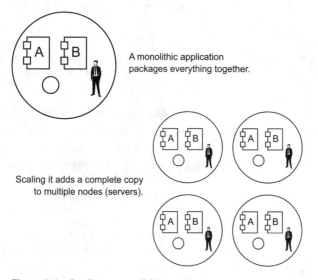

A monolithic application packages everything together.

Scaling it adds a complete copy to multiple nodes (servers).

Figure 1.1 Scaling a monolithic application

is called one million times per hour and service B is called only once per day. Scaling a monolithic application would mean adding a new node with the application that includes both services A and B.

Wouldn't it be better if you only needed to scale service A? This is where the potential of microservices becomes apparent: in the new architecture, shown in figure 1.2, services A and B become microservices A and B. You can still scale the application, but this additional flexibility is the point: you can now choose to scale where the load is greatest. Even better, you can dedicate one team of developers to maintaining microservice A and another to microservice B. You don't need to touch the application to add features or fix bugs in either A or B, and they can also be rolled out completely independently of each other.

The application calls services A and B.

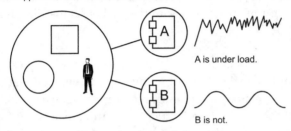

A is under load.

B is not.

Scale A to distribute the load.

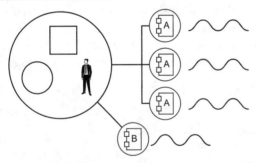

Figure 1.2   Scaling a microservice independently of the main application

Companies like Netflix, Google, Amazon, and eBay have based much of their platforms on a microservice architecture, and they've all been kind enough to share much of this information freely. But although considerable focus is placed on web applications, you can apply a microservice architecture to any application. We hope this whets your appetite!

1.1.2   *What are microservices?*

At first glance, the term *micro* may conjure up images of a tiny application with a small footprint. But regarding application size, there are no rules, other than a rule of thumb. A microservice may consist of several, several hundred, or even several thousand lines of code, depending on your specific business requirements; the rule of thumb is to keep the logic small enough for a single team to manage. Ideally, you should focus on a single endpoint (which may in turn provide multiple resources); but again, there's no hard-and-fast rule. It's your party.

The most common concept is that a single application should be the uppermost limit of a microservice. In the context of a typical application server running multiple applications, this means splitting applications so they're running on a single application server. In theory, think of your first microservice as a single piece of a jigsaw puzzle, and try to imagine how it will fit together with the next piece.

You can break a monolithic application into its logical pieces, as shown in figure 1.3. There should be just enough information within each piece of the puzzle to enable you to build the greater picture. In a microservice architecture, these pieces are much more loosely coupled; see figure 1.4.

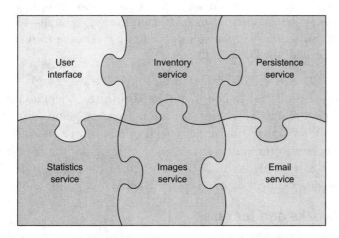

Figure 1.3   Each service is part of the big picture.

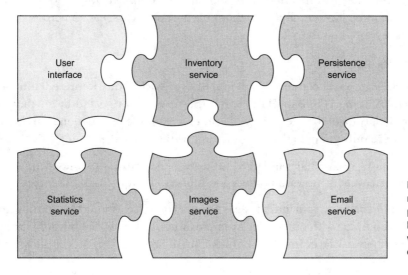

Figure 1.4   Each microservice is still part of the picture but is isolated within a separate environment.

1.1.3 Continuous integration, deployment, and Docker

The *decoupling* of application elements into scalable microservices means you'll have to start thinking about the *continuous integration (CI)* and *continuous delivery (CD)* pipelines from an early stage. Instead of one build script and one deployment, you'll need multiple independent builds that must be sewn together for integration testing and deployment to different hosts.

You'll find that far less work is involved than you may think. This is largely due to the fact that a microservice is, for all intents and purposes, an application like any other. The only difference is that a microservice packages the application together with its runtime environment. The easiest and most recognized way to do this today is to create and deploy a microservice as a Docker image (www.docker.com).

> **NOTE** Docker is the world's leading software-containerization platform. If you're not sure what Docker is, then at some point please visit www.docker .com and follow the "What is Docker?" tutorial. Don't worry, though—we'll guide you through this pipeline when we put all the microservice elements together toward the end of the book.

The heavyweight CI/CD contenders are Travis (https://travis-ci.org), Bamboo (https://de.atlassian.com/software/bamboo), and Jenkins (https://jenkins.io). They all provide great support for microservices and deployment pipelines for Docker images; but in this book, we'll use Jenkins, because it's open source and has a huge community. It's not necessarily the easiest to use, but it offers by far the most features via plugins. In chapter 8, we'll highlight all the involved technologies in detail and guide you through the development of a viable CI/CD pipeline.

1.2 Microservice networks and features

Microservices are *loosely coupled*, which leads to new questions. How are microservices coupled, and what features does this architecture offer? In the following sections, we'll look at some answers. But for all intents and purposes, each microservice is isolated by a network boundary.

1.2.1 Microservice networks

Microservices are most commonly integrated over a RESTful (Representational State Transfer) API using HTTP or HTTPS, but they can be connected by anything that's considered a protocol to access an endpoint to a resource or function. This is a broad topic, so we're only going to discuss and demonstrate Java REST using JAX-RS.

> **TIP** If you're unfamiliar with RESTful web services using JAX-RS (https:// jax-rs-spec.java.net), now would be a good time to read up on these topics.

With this information, your initial ideas for microservices should be starting to take form. Let's continue with our earlier example. Microservice A, the inventory service, is isolated by a network layer from the UI and from microservice B, the statistics service. B

> ## Hypermedia
>
> Services should be developed with *hypermedia* in mind. This is the latest buzzword; it implies that services should be self-documenting in their architecture, by providing links to related resources in any response. Currently there's no winner in this category, and it would be unfair to start placing bets now, but you can take a look at the front runners and make an educated guess: JSON-LD (http://json-ld.org), JSON Hypertext Application Language (HAL, https://tools.ietf.org/html/draft-kelly-json-hal-08), Collection+JSON (https://github.com/collection-json/spec), and Siren (https://github.com/kevinswiber/siren).

communicates with A to collect statistics using the defined request-and-response protocols. They each have their own domain and external resources and are otherwise completely separate from each other. The UI service is able to call both A and B to present information in a human-readable form, a website, or a heavy client, as shown in figure 1.5.

Tests must be designed to cover comprehensively any and all interaction with external services. It's important to get this right, because network interaction will always present its own set of challenges. We'll cover this extensively in chapter 5.

By now it should be clear that a microservice can be large in terms of application size, and that "micro" refers to the public-facing surface area of the application. Cloud space is cheap today, so the physical size of a microservice is less relevant than in the past.

Another concern that we often hear mentioned is, "What about network speed?" Microservices are generally hosted in the same local network, which is typically Gigabit Ethernet or better. So, from a client perspective, and given the ease of scaling microservices, response times are likely to be much better than expected. Again, don't take our word for it; think of Netflix, Google, Amazon/AWS, and eBay.

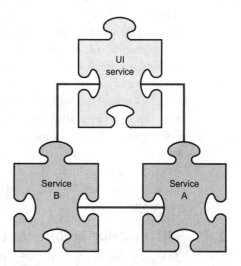

Figure 1.5   Each service communicates by defined protocols.

1.2.2   *Microservice features*

In our example, both microservices A and B can be developed independently and deployed by two entirely different teams. Each team only needs to understand the resource-component layer of the microservice on which they're working, rather than the entire business-domain component. This is the first big win: development can be much faster and easier to understand in the given context.

JavaScript Object Notation (JSON, www.json.org) and Extensible Markup Language (XML, www.w3.org/XML) are the common resource languages, so it's easy to write clients for such services. Some cases may dictate a different approach, but the basic scenarios remain essentially the same: the endpoints are accessible from a multitude of devices and clients using defined protocols.

Multiple microservices form a network of connected applications, where each individual microservice can be scaled independently. Elastic deployment on the cloud is now commonplace, and this enables an individual service to scale *automatically* up or down—for example, based on load.

Some other interesting benefits of microservices are improved fault isolation and memory management. In a monolithic application, a fault in a single component can bring down an entire server. With resilient microservices, the larger part of the picture will continue to function until the misbehaving service issue is resolved. In figure 1.6, is the statistics service really necessary for the application to function as a whole, or can you live without it for a while?

Of course, as is the nature of all good things, microservices have drawbacks. Developers need to learn and understand the complexities of developing a distributed application, including how best to use IDEs, which are often orientated toward monolithic development. Developing use cases spanning multiple services that aren't included in distributed transactions requires more thought and planning than for a monolith. And testing is generally more difficult, at least for the connected elements, which is why we wrote this book.

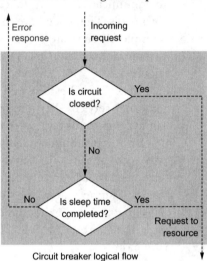

Figure 1.6   Resilient design using circuit breakers

1.3   *Microservice architecture*

The anatomy of a microservice can be varied, as shown in figure 1.7, but design similarities are bound to occur. These elements can be grouped together to form the application-component layers. It's important to provide test coverage at each layer, and you'll likely be presented with new challenges along the way; we'll address these challenges and offer solutions throughout the book.

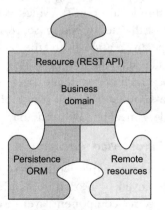

Figure 1.7   The basic microservice components

Let's look at these microservice component layers from the top down.

NOTE A microservice should encapsulate and expose a well-defined area of logic as a service. That doesn't mean that you can't allow interaction from other systems by other means. For example, your service may expose specific documents that are stored in Elasticsearch (ES). In such a case, it's perfectly legitimate for other applications to talk natively to ES in order to seed the documents.

1.3.1 Resource component

Resources are responsible for exposing the service interaction via a chosen protocol. This interaction occurs using mapped objects, usually serialized using JSON or XML. These mapped objects represent the input and/or output of the business domain. Sanitization of the incoming objects and construction of the protocol-specific response usually occur at this layer; see figure 1.8.

Figure 1.8 The resource component publicly exposes the service.

> **NOTE** Now that we're here, it's worth mentioning that the resource-component layer is the layer that puts the *micro* in *microservice*.

For the rest of this book, and for the sake of simplicity, we'll focus on the most common form of resource providers today: *RESTful endpoints.*[1] If you aren't familiar with RESTful web services, please take the time to research and understand this important topic.

1.3.2 Business-domain component

The business-domain component is the core focus of your service application and is highly specific to the logical task for which the service is being developed. The domain may have to communicate with various other services (including other microservices) in order to calculate a response or process requests to and from the resource component; see figure 1.9.

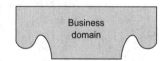

Figure 1.9 The business-domain component is your service's business logic.

A bridge is likely to be required between the domain component and the resource component, and possibly the remote component. Most microservices need to communicate with other microservices at some point.

1.3.3 Remote resources component

This component layer is where your piece of the jigsaw puzzle may need to connect to the next piece, or pieces, of the picture. It consists of a client that understands how to send and receive resource objects to and from other microservice endpoints, which it

---

[1] See "What Are RESTful Web Services?" in the Java EE 6 tutorial, http://mng.bz/fIa2.

then translates for use in the business component layer; see figure 1.10.

Due to the nature of remote resources, you must pay special attention to creating a resilient design. A resilient framework is designed to provide features such as circuit breakers and timeout fallbacks in the event of a failure. Don't try to reinvent the wheel: several resilient frameworks are available to choose from, including our top pick,

Figure 1.10   The remote resources component is the gateway to other services.

Hystrix (https://github.com/Netflix/Hystrix/wiki), which is open source and contributed by Netflix.

A gateway service should act as a bridge between the domain component and the client component. It's responsible for translating request-and-response calls to and from any remote resource via the client. This is the best place to provide a graceful failure if the resource can't be reached.

The client is responsible for speaking the language of your chosen protocol. Nine times out of ten, this will be JAX-RS (https://jax-rs-spec.java.net) over HTTP/S for RESTful web services.

We highly recommend the open source services framework Apache CXF (http://cxf.apache.org) for this layer, because it's fully compliant with JAX-WS, JAX-RS, and others, and it won't tie you down to a specific platform.

1.3.4   *Persistence component*

More often than not, an application requires some type of persistence or data retrieval (see figure 1.11). This usually comes in the form of an object-relational mapping (ORM)[2] mechanism, such as the Java Persistence API (JPA),[3] but could be something as simple as an embedded database or properties file.

Figure 1.11   The persistence component is for data storage.

1.4   *Microservice unit testing*

Chapter 3 will take a deep dive into real unit-testing scenarios. The next few paragraphs are an introduction to the terminology we'll use and what to expect as you develop your testing strategies.

A typical unit test is designed to be as small as possible and to test a trivial item: a *unit of work*. In the microservice context, this unit of work may be more difficult to represent, due to the fact that there's often much more underlying complexity to the service than is apparent at first glance.

Unit testing can often lead to the conclusion that you need to refactor your code in order to reduce the complexity of the component under test. This also makes testing useful as a design tool, especially when you're using test-driven development

---

[2]   See "Hibernate ORM: What Is Object/Relational Mapping?" http://hibernate.org/orm/what-is-an-orm.

[3]   See "Introduction to the Java Persistence API" in the Java EE 6 tutorial, http://mng.bz/Cy69.

(TDD). A beneficial side effect of unit testing is that it lets you continue developing an application while detecting regressions at the same time.

Although you're likely to encounter more-detailed scenarios along the way, there are basically two styles of unit testing: *sociable* and *solitary*. These styles are loosely based on whether the unit test is isolated from its underlying collaborators. Both styles are nonexclusive, and they complement each other nicely. You should count on using both, depending on the nature of the testing challenge. We'll expand on these concepts throughout the book.

1.4.1 Solitary unit tests

Solitary unit testing should focus on the interaction around a single object class. The test should encompass only the class's own dependents or dependencies on the class. You'll usually test resource, persistence, and remote components using solitary tests, because those components rarely need to collaborate with each other; see figure 1.12.

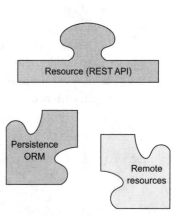

You need to isolate individual classes for testing by stubbing or mocking all collaborators within that class. You should test all the methods of the class, but not cross any boundaries to other concrete classes. Basically, this means all injected fields should receive either a mock or stubbed implementation that only returns canned responses. The primary aim is for the code coverage of the class under test to be as high as possible.

Figure 1.12 Predominantly solitary unit-test components

1.4.2 Sociable unit tests

Sociable unit testing focuses on testing the behavior of modules by observing changes in their state. This approach treats the unit under test as a black box tested entirely through its interface. The domain component is nearly always a candidate for sociable testing, because it needs to collaborate in order to process a request and return a response; see figure 1.13.

Figure 1.13 Predominantly sociable unit-test component

You may still need to stub or mock some complex collaborators of the class under test, but this should be as far along as possible within the hierarchy of collaborating objects. You shouldn't only be testing that a specific class sends and receives correct payloads, but also that the class collaborators are operating as expected *within* the class. The test coverage should ideally include all models, variables and fields as well as the class collaborators. It's also important to test that the class can correctly handle any response, including invalid responses (negative testing).

Summary

- A microservice is a part of a monolithic application that has been dissected into a smaller logical element.
- Microservices benefit your application by allowing targeted scaling and focused development.
- Microservices offer a logical way to meet scalability requirements by providing the ability to scale not only *where* performance is required, but also *when.*
- You can break monolithic applications into smaller elements that can be used as microservices.
- Microservices allow several teams to focus on individual, nonconflicting tasks that make up the bigger picture.
- Solitary unit tests are used for components that don't store state or don't need to collaborate in order to be tested.
- Sociable unit tests are used for components that must collaborate or store state in order to be tested.

Application under test

2

This chapter covers

- Exploring a sample application
- Understanding critical parts of the code
- Developing microservices with Java EE and Spring Boot

The previous chapter introduced you to microservices, including their basic anatomy and architecture. This introduction was intended to give you insight into the kinds of tests you might need to write for a microservice-based architecture.

This chapter introduces the application that will be used throughout the book to demonstrate the development and testing of a microservices architecture. Our goal is to provide an easy-to-follow example that will help you understand the relevance of each kind of test that will be applied. We try to follow best practices for a microservices architecture, but we make some design choices for the sake of simplicity and also purely for educational purposes. For instance, we may use more technologies than necessary, or simplify the number of layers used in a microservice because they don't add value from a testing point of view. In such cases, we point out the reason for a particular approach and discuss how to perform these tasks in real-world programming. It's ultimately your responsibility as a developer to choose the appropriate tools to use, but we always offer a recommended approach.

2.1   Getting started

The example application, Gamer, is a simple software portal for gamers. Its purpose is to expose information about software games and to let gamers not only read important facts about games and watch videos of games being played, but also comment on and leave a star rating for played games. Although this application is intentionally simple, it covers all the main topics needed to showcase the microservices architecture. Throughout the book, we'll guide you through the various kinds of tests to be written for a microservices-based application.

We'll start by providing some use cases for the Gamer app, to get a high-level view of the actions a gamer can take. Gamers want to be able to do these things:

- Search for games by name, so they can see a list of games that match their interests
- Read about important aspects of a game, such as its publication date and which platforms are supported
- Read other gamers' comments about a game, to help them decide whether they'll enjoy it and want to buy it
- Write comments about a game, so other gamers can benefit from their evaluation of it
- Assign a star rating to a game and quickly see the games with the highest ratings
- Watch game-related videos such as trailers, tutorials, and real in-game play

Let's begin by defining the data required for this application. We won't focus on technical details just yet—this section only describes the conceptual data model.

The main entity is a *game*. Table 2.1 shows the parts that make up a game.

Table 2.1   The parts of a game

Field	Description
title	String representing the name of the game
cover	URL of an image of the game cover
ReleaseDate	The game's release date
Publisher	The game's publisher
Developer	The game's developer

Table 2.2 shows the parts that make up a *release date*.

Table 2.2   Parts of a release date

Field	Description
platform	Platform name under which the game was released
date	Date (day, month, and year) when the game was released for a platform

Table 2.3 shows the parts that make up a *comment*.

Table 2.3 Parts of a comment

Field	Description
comment	String containing the comment message
rate	Star rating from 1 to 5, indicating the overall quality of the game

Now that you understand the kinds of data the Gamer app will manage, we can go a little deeper and inspect the architecture of the application.

2.2 Prerequisites

This book isn't a Java tutorial. If you're not already familiar with Java as a language, then you're highly unlikely to have an enjoyable read. That said, we hope to present information that's of use to readers with all levels of interest. The Java tutorials at https://docs.oracle.com/javase/tutorial are outstanding resources for any aspiring Java developer and a fantastic reference for everyone who uses Java.

The book also isn't an academic masterpiece. The authors are primarily developers, and English isn't the first language for some of us. We like getting our hands dirty, and we hope you do too. We expect you to bring an open mind and understand that not everyone may share our opinions. There's never one way that's entirely right or entirely wrong, and our suggestions are presented as food for thought for your creative mind.

> **NOTE** Much of the source code is formatted based on the restrictions of presenting it on a printed page. This can lead to verbose layout. Feel free to adjust the code formatting to your own preferences.

2.2.1 Java Development Kit

You'll need at least version SE (Standard Edition) 8 of the Java Development Kit (JDK) to compile and run the code in this book. You can always find the latest Oracle JDK (recommended) at http://mng.bz/83Ct or the OpenJDK at http://openjdk.java.net.

To test for Java, run the following command, which should display results similar to the following, depending on your installed version:

```
$ java -version

java version "1.8.0_121"
Java(TM) SE Runtime Environment (build 1.8.0_121-b13)
Java HotSpot(TM) 64-Bit Server VM (build 25.121-b13, mixed mode)
```

2.2.2 Build tools

We're using both Apache Maven (https://maven.apache.org) and Gradle (https://gradle.org) to build several of the project modules. Make sure you've installed both of these tools by following the instructions provided on the corresponding websites.

To test for a correct Maven installation, run the following command:

```
$ mvn -version

Apache Maven 3.3.9
...
```

For Gradle, run this command:

```
$ gradle -v

------------------------------------------------------------
Gradle 3.2.1
------------------------------------------------------------
```

2.2.3 *Environment variables*

The full application requires two API keys in order to access some remote resources. The API keys are registered to individual user accounts, so we can't provide shared keys here.

It's *not* necessary to obtain these keys in order to run most of the test examples provided in this book. But if you wish to experiment with the code, we suggest that you obtain the keys and create the corresponding environment variables. To obtain an API key for YouTube, visit https://developers.google.com/youtube/v3/getting-started and follow the instructions in the Before You Start section. To obtain an API key for the Internet Game Database (IGDB), visit https:// igdb.github.io/api/about/welcome or go directly to https://api.igdb.com to register for access.

Once you have your own API keys, add them to your environment variables. On Linux, add the following in /home/profile:

```
...
export YOUTUBE_API_KEY="Your-Key"
export IGDB_API_KEY="YourKey"
```

Windows users may find the following link useful for configuring environment variables: http://mng.bz/1a2K.[1]

2.2.4 *Integrated development environment (IDE)*

None of the application code *requires* you to use an IDE. Notepad will do.

Of course, feel free to open the projects using your favorite IDE (that supports Maven- and Gradle-based projects). If you want to add breakpoints in the code in order to follow the execution path (highly recommended), then we suggest using an IDE.

---

[1] William R. Stanek, "Configuring System and User Environment Variables," MSDN, from *Microsoft Windows 2000* (Microsoft Press, 2002).

We've tested the code in the following IDEs, in no particular order of preference:

- *IntelliJ IDEA* (www.jetbrains.com/idea)
- *NetBeans* (https://netbeans.org)
- *Eclipse* (www.eclipse.org/downloads)

2.3 *Architecture*

As mentioned at the beginning of the chapter, the Gamer app follows a microservices architecture. The first thing to do is identify which services make up the application. For this app, we concluded that splitting the domain into four distinct microservices was required:

- *Game service*—Provides all the information related to games. It includes queries for obtaining a game ID by a specific name, or returns information for a specific game ID.
- *Comments service*—Adds star ratings and comments for a specific game, as well as retrieves them.
- *Video service*—Returns the location of the three most prominent videos for a game.
- *Aggregator service*—Calls the aforementioned named services, and aggregates the data of each service into a single response.

The application schema is shown in figure 2.1.

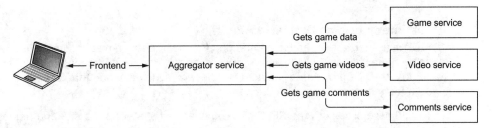

Figure 2.1 Gamer application schema

As you can see, a frontend (typically a browser) consumes the information provided by the Gamer API. The point of entry is the aggregator service, which communicates with the game, video, and comments services to get or insert required data for games. The aggregator service compiles all the data into a single response and returns this to the frontend. You can now understand the application architecture and the technical reasons behind the decisions that were made for each service.

> **NOTE** At first, please skip the tests when you build the application from the command line or IDE. To demonstrate a point, and also to provide exercises, some of the tests won't complete as provided. As your knowledge builds throughout the book, you'll be in a better position to play with and expand the sample code.

2.3.1 The game service

Install the game service using the following code:

```
cd ./game
mvn install -DskipTests
```

The game service is a Java EE 7 application running on WildFly Swarm that's responsible for providing all the information related to games. It provides two operations to retrieve this information:

- Getting a list of games by title (multiple games can have the same title). The information provided for this endpoint must be minimal: for example, only the identifier and/or title of the game.
- Returning detailed information about a game by specifying a known game identifier.

You might have noticed that there's no operation for inserting games. This is because the game service acts as a proxy/cache to an external service API. An *external service* is a service that's out of the current application scope, that's developed and maintained by a third party, and to which you're merely a subscriber. Typical examples of these services are search engines, weather forecasts, and geospatial calculations.

This service example relies on the Internet Game Database website (www.igdb .com) to provide all of the required game data.

> **The Internet Game Database API**
>
> IGDB is a video game database, intended for use by both game consumers and video game professionals. In addition to serving as a portal for getting information about games, the site provides a public REST API (www.igdb.com/api) that lets you access data for games registered on the site.
>
> To authorize access to the REST API, you need to register on the site and request a new API key. This key must be passed in each call as an HTTP header.
>
> During the course of the book, we provide more information about the IGDB REST API, such as how to authenticate against IGDB, and the required format for resource endpoints.

When you rely on external calls to third-party services, it's always important (if possible) to cache as much data from the external service as you can. This is important for three reasons:

- You avoid round trips to external networks, which is typically a slow operation.
- If you have quota/metered access to the external API, you save on hits to the service.
- In the event the external service experiences an outage, your application can continue to work with cached data.

WARNING Generally, caching is used only in cases where the external data doesn't change often or you can replicate all the data on your systems. To maintain coherence of the external data, you should apply a periodic refresh strategy to the cache so it doesn't become outdated. For the sake of simplicity, no refresh strategy is implemented in the example app, but this is something to take into consideration in a real-world scenario.

In this microservice, a cache-persistence-layer system is implemented using the light SQL database H2 (www.h2database.com/html/main.html). The *entity-relationship* (ER) model used in the game service is composed of four entities, described in tables 2.4–2.7. Figure 2.2 shows this in graphical terms.

Table 2.4 Game table

Field	Data type	Description
id	Long	Game identifier.
version	Int	Internal field for avoiding conflicts in optimistic locking.
title	String	Name of the game. This value is unique.
cover	String	URL of the cover of the game, or null if no cover.
Release dates	ReleaseDate	One-to-many relationship of type ReleaseDate.
Publishers	Collection of Strings	One-to-many relationship between publishers and the name of the game.
Developer	Collection of Strings	One-to-many relationship between developers and the name of the game.

Table 2.5 ReleaseDate table

Field	Data type	Description
OwnerId	Long	Identifier for the game. This field acts as a foreign key.
platformName	String	Platform name under which game was released.
releaseDate	String	Date when the game was released for this platform, in YYYY/MM/DD format.

Table 2.6 Publisher table

Field	Data type	Description
OwnerId	Long	Identifier for the game. This field acts as a foreign key.
publisherName	String	Publisher name.

Table 2.7   `Developer` table

Field	Data type	Description
OwnerId	Long	Identifier for the game. This field acts as a foreign key.
developer	String	Developer name.

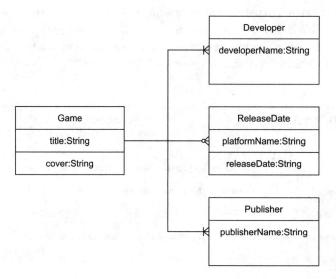

Figure 2.2   Gamer application entity relationship

The entity-relationship schema in figure 2.2 shows that a game is composed of a title and a cover, is made by one-to-*n* (one-to-many) developers, is published by one or many publishers, and has zero or more release dates for each platform.

> **NOTE**   There are other options that are a good fit for caching data for micro-service architectures, such as Infinispan, Hazelcast, and Redis. They not only offer *time-to-live* (TTL) features, which makes the refresh logic much simpler, but also work in distributed (clustered) environments, which is typical in microservice architectures. For teaching purposes, in this book we use a SQL database. This approach is simple and uses a technology that you may be accustomed to. This also allows us to introduce an important feature: persistence testing of the ORM.

On the server layer, the game service runs on the WildFly Swarm application server. An overall schema of this service is shown in figure 2.3. The persistence layer uses an H2 SQL database for storing and retrieving cached data for games. Finally, the service connects to the external site (IGDB.com) to obtain information for games that aren't yet cached on the system.

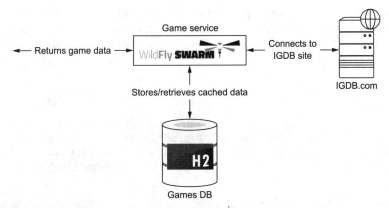

Figure 2.3 Game service overview

> **WildFly Swarm**
>
> WildFly Swarm (http://wildfly-swarm.io) offers an approach to packaging and running Java EE applications by generating an uber-JAR (`java -jar MyApp.jar`), which packages the application with just enough of the server runtime to run.
>
> It also has built-in support for applications and frameworks such as Logstash, Netflix projects like Hystrix and Ribbon, and Red Hat projects like Keycloak and Hawkular.

2.3.2 The comments service

Build and package the comments service using the following code:

```
cd ./comments
./gradlew war -x test
```

The comments service is an EE 7 application running on Apache TomEE. It's responsible for managing comments for a specific game, as well as the game rating. A rating is a number between 1 (the lowest rating) and 5 (the highest rating). Notice that this feature isn't provided by IGDB; it's something you'll add to the portal to make it more participatory. This service provides two endpoints:

- One adding a comment and a game rating
- A second that returns all the comments that have been written for a game, along with the average game rating

The persistence layer for this service uses a document-oriented NoSQL database for storing all the data required by the service. We chose the MongoDB NoSQL database specifically due to its out-of-the-box aggregation framework. It's a perfect solution for calculating the average rating for a given game.

NOTE   Similar logic could be implemented using a traditional SQL database, but nowadays it's not uncommon to use a NoSQL database due to its better performance in certain circumstances. This service uses a NoSQL database to showcase the example.

MongoDB

MongoDB is a document-oriented NoSQL database. Instead of using a relational database structure, MongoDB stores JSON-like documents with dynamic schemas in collections. Documents that have a similar purpose are stored in the same collection. You can think of a collection as being equivalent to an RDBMS table, but without forcing a schema.

In addition to storing documents, MongoDB provides features like indexing, replication, load balancing with horizontal shards, and an aggregation framework.

MongoDB structures documents into *collections*. For the comments service, this collection is named *comments*. Each document that represents a comment has a schema like the following and contains the game's ID, the comment itself, and the game's rating (see figure 2.4):

```
{
  "gameId": 1234,
  "comment": "This game is awesome",
  "rate": 3
}
```

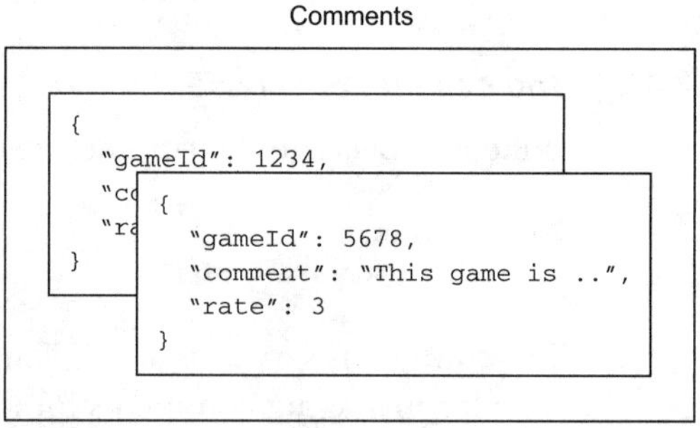

An overall schema of the comments service is shown in figure 2.5. On the server layer, it runs on the Apache TomEE application server (http://tomee .apache.org); and for the persistence layer, it uses the MongoDB NoSQL database for storing and retrieving comments associated with games.

Figure 2.4   Collection of comments

Apache TomEE

Apache TomEE (http://tomee.apache.org), pronounced "Tommy," is an all-Apache Java EE 6 Web Profile–certified and EE 7–enabled stack where Apache Tomcat is top dog. Apache TomEE is assembled from a vanilla Apache Tomcat zip file. Starting with Apache Tomcat, TomEE adds its JARs and zips up the rest. The result is Tomcat with added EE features—hence, the name TomEE.

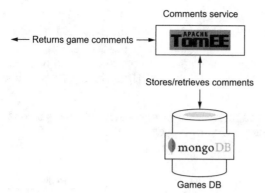

Figure 2.5   Comments service overview

2.3.3   *The video service*

Build the video service using the following code:

```
cd video
./gradlew build -x test
```

The video service is a Spring Boot application that's responsible for retrieving the three most prominent videos related to a given game. Notice that this feature isn't provided by IGDB; it's something you'll add to the portal to make it more attractive to end users. Obviously, this service isn't going to reinvent the wheel by creating a new video-sharing/-streaming site, so it uses YouTube to retrieve videos.

> **YouTube**
>
> YouTube is a global video-sharing website. You can add YouTube functionality to any site and even search for content.
>
> The *YouTube Data API* is the REST API that YouTube provides to users to connect to its system and execute operations like uploading videos, modifying videos, and searching for videos that match specific terms. See the book's appendix for information about how to use the YouTube Data API.

This service provides a single endpoint, which returns the links of the three most prominent videos for the specified game.

This microservice has no persistence layer in the sense of long-lived data stored in the system. For this microservice, a NoSQL in-memory database of key-value pairs is used for caching search results from YouTube. When you're caching distributed data where optional durability is required, key-value databases are the best choice, because they fit this requirement perfectly. With this approach, you save time, because an external network hit is more expensive than an internal one. You also save on the hits quota allotted by the YouTube Data API. In the video service, the key-value database used as a caching system is the Redis database.

Redis

Redis is an in-memory data-structure store that can be used as a database, cache system, or message broker. It supports data structures such as strings, hashes, lists, sets, sorted sets with range queries, bitmaps, HyperLogLogs, and geospatial indexes with radius queries.

Redis offers clustering capabilities, master-slave replication, and transactions, with extremely good performance when not persisting data.

The Redis structure used for this microservice is a *list*. This basic structure holds a list of string values for a given key with an optional TTL. In this case, the key is the game ID, and the value of each element of the list is a URL of the video associated with the game. As you can see in the schema shown in figure 2.6, the Redis structure stores a game ID and a list of three YouTube URLs.

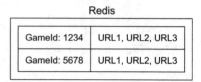

Redis	
GameId: 1234	URL1, URL2, URL3
GameId: 5678	URL1, URL2, URL3

Figure 2.6   Video URLs cached in Redis

Spring Boot

Spring Boot (http://projects.spring.io/spring-boot) makes it easy to create stand-alone, production-grade, Spring-based applications that you can "just run." It follows the uber(fat)-JAR approach by packaging an application into a single JAR file, which contains the runtime (embedded server plus application) and a `Main` class to run it. It integrates well with other products in the Spring ecosystem, like Spring Data and Spring Security.

An overall schema of this service is shown in figure 2.7. You can see that the video service is a Spring Boot application, and the cache layer it uses is Redis. The service connects to the external site (youtube.com) to get video links for a specific game.

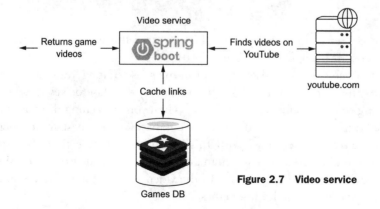

Figure 2.7   Video service

2.3.4   *The aggregator service*

Build and package the aggregator service using the following code:

```
cd aggregator
./gradlew war -x test
```

This service is an EE 7 application that's responsible for creating calls to the game and comments services, merging the results of both calls into a single document, and returning this document to the caller. This service provides three endpoints:

- One for adding a comment and a game rating
- A second that returns all the games that have a specified name
- A third that returns all the data related to a specified game, all user comments and ratings, and the three most important videos for the game

The overall schema of the aggregator service is shown in figure 2.8. It has no persistence layer. The service runs inside the Apache Tomcat server and connects to all other services.

> **Apache Tomcat**
> The Apache Tomcat server is an open source implementation of the Java Servlet, JavaServer Pages, Java Expression Language, and Java WebSocket technologies.

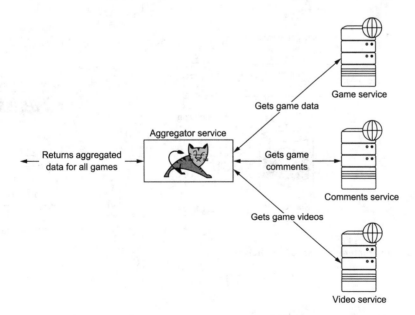

Figure 2.8   Game aggregator service relations to other services

2.3.5   *Overall architecture*

In summary, the Gamer app is made up of three services. Each of these services is deployed in a different platform, from the light application server Apache TomEE to a WildFly Swarm uber-JAR. Two different kinds of database engines are used for the persistence layer: H2, a traditional SQL database, and MongoDB, which belongs to the family of NoSQL databases.

This is a broad range of technologies. We chose to use these various technologies specifically to broaden the scope of this book for the purposes of illustration. In the real world, your applications are likely to be founded on technologies that are more similar to each other. But, as mentioned previously, it's not uncommon for different teams to work on different microservices.

The overall schema of the Gamer app can be seen in the architecture diagram in figure 2.9. It's important to note in the schema diagram how all the pieces are connected to compose a fully functional, microservice-based application.

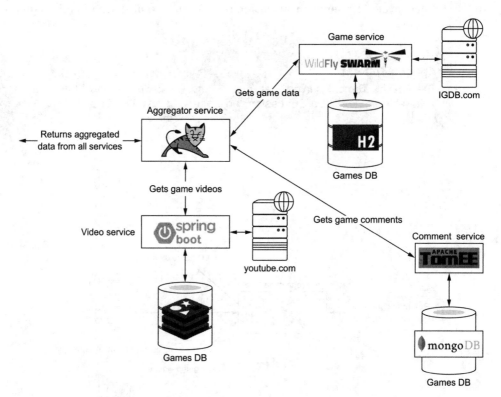

Figure 2.9   Architecture diagram of our project

2.4 Application design patterns

In previous sections, you've read about the Gamer app from a high-level perspective, and we've been paying a lot of attention to the requirements of the application from a business perspective. In the following sections, we'll dig down into the technical side of the application.

2.4.1 Anatomy

The Gamer app follows the microservices architecture by applying the Single Responsibility Principle (SRP) at an architectural level, making each service independent in terms of deployment, technology, and language. In summary, each microservice is structured following the schema shown in figure 2.10. Let's see how each piece is implemented in the Gamer app.

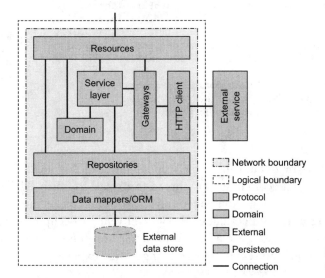

Figure 2.10 Detailed microservice structure

THE RESOURCE COMPONENT

The *resource component* is a thin layer of the application that acts as a mapper between incoming messages (typically JSON documents) and the business logic in the domain component. It also provides a response in accordance with the outcome produced by the business logic, using the desired protocol.

In Java EE, this component is typically implemented using the Java API for RESTful Web Services (JAX-RS), which provides support for creating web services following the REST architectural pattern. An example of a resource component is coded in the comments service (code/comments/src/main/java/book/comments/boundary/CommentsResource.java).

Listing 2.1   Resource component

```
@Path("/comments")
@Singleton
@Lock(LockType.READ)
public class CommentsResource {

    @Inject
    private Comments comments;

    @Inject
    private DocumentToJsonObject transformer;

    @GET
    @Path("/{gameId}")
    @Produces(MediaType.APPLICATION_JSON)
    public Response getCommentsOfGivenGame(@PathParam("gameId")
                                           final Integer
                                               gameId) {
        final Optional<Document>; commentsAndRating = comments
                .getCommentsAndRating(gameId);

        final JsonObject json = transformer.transform
                (commentsAndRating.orElse(new Document()));
        return Response.ok(json).build();
    }
}
```

Sets the relative path for a class or method

Indicates that the method services the HTTP GET request type

Sets the response MIME type

Binds the parameter to a path segment

Returns the content with the HTTP response code OK (200)

Request processing occurs by default in a synchronous fashion; this means a client request is processed by a single container I/O thread from start to finish. This blocking approach is fine for business logic that takes only a short time to execute.

But for long-running tasks, the container thread will remain occupied until the task has been completed. This can have a significant impact on the server's throughput, because new connections can remain blocked longer than expected while waiting for the backlog queue to be processed.

To resolve this problem, JAX-RS has an asynchronous model. This enables the container thread to be released to accept a new connection before the client connection is closed. The lengthy task runs in another thread, and the container I/O thread can be used by another connection that's waiting in the backlog queue.

An example of an asynchronous resource component is coded in the game service (code/game/src/main/java/book/games/boundary/GamesResource.java), because connections to external resources can take a considerable amount of time to complete.

Listing 2.2   Asynchronous resource component

```
@Path("/")
@javax.ejb.Singleton
@Lock(LockType.READ)
public class GamesResource {
```

Resource is marked as Singleton EJB so the endpoint becomes transactional

```
        @Inject
        GamesService gamesService;
```

Injects an executor service provided by the container

```
        @Inject
        ExecutorServiceProducer managedExecutorService;
```

```
        @GET
        @Produces(MediaType.APPLICATION_JSON)
        @javax.ejb.Asynchronous
        public void searchGames(@Suspended final AsyncResponse
                                    response,
                @NotNull @QueryParam("query") final
                String query) {
```

Designates a method as asynchronous. Valid only if it's an EJB.

Instructs the JAX-RS runtime that this method is asynchronous and injects an AsyncResponse

```
        response.setTimeoutHandler(asyncResponse ->; asyncResponse
                .resume(Response.status(Response.Status
                        .SERVICE_UNAVAILABLE).entity("TIME OUT !")
                        .build()));
        response.setTimeout(15, TimeUnit.SECONDS);

        managedExecutorService.getManagedExecutorService().submit(
                () ->; {
            try {

                final Collector<JsonObject, ?, JsonArrayBuilder>;
                        jsonCollector = Collector.of
                        (Json::createArrayBuilder,
                                JsonArrayBuilder::add, (left,
                                                right) ->; {
                    left.add(right);
                    return left;
                });

                final List<SearchResult>; searchResults =
                        gamesService.searchGames(query);

                final JsonArrayBuilder mappedGames = searchResults
                        .stream().map(SearchResult::convertToJson)
                        .collect(jsonCollector);

                final Response.ResponseBuilder ok = Response.ok
                        (mappedGames.build());
                response.resume(ok.build());
            } catch (final Throwable e) {
                response.resume(e);
            }
        });
    }
}
```

Executes logic in a different thread

When the result is ready, the connection is resumed.

In case of an error, communication should also be resumed.

For Spring applications, a resource is implemented using the Spring Web model-view-controller (MVC) framework. This framework is built around the `DispatcherServlet` class and dispatches requests to configured handlers for executing business logic.

An example of a resource written for the Spring Web MVC framework is coded in the video service (code/video/src/main/java/book/video/boundary/VideosResource.java).

Listing 2.3   Spring resource

```
package book.video.boundary;

import book.video.controller.VideoServiceController;
import org.springframework.beans.factory.annotation.Autowired;
import org.springframework.http.ResponseEntity;
import org.springframework.web.bind.annotation.CrossOrigin;
import org.springframework.web.bind.annotation.RequestMapping;
import org.springframework.web.bind.annotation.RequestParam;
import org.springframework.web.bind.annotation.RestController;

import java.util.List;

@CrossOrigin(origins = {"http://localhost:8080",
        "http://localhost:8181", "http://localhost:8282",
        "http://localhost:8383"})
@RestController
public class VideosResource {

    @Autowired
    VideoServiceController videoServiceController;

    @RequestMapping(value = "/", produces = "application/json")
    public ResponseEntity<List<String>>; getVideos(
                    @RequestParam ("videoId") final long videoId,
                    @RequestParam("gameName") final String gameName) {
        final List<String>; linksFromGame = videoServiceController
                .getLinksFromGame(Long.toString(videoId), gameName);
        return ResponseEntity.ok(linksFromGame);
    }
}
```

The resource is marked as a Spring Rest controller.

Injects video-service logic

Configures the endpoint method

DOMAIN MODEL

A *domain model* is a representation or abstraction of real-world concepts belonging to the domain that need to be modeled in software. Each object of the domain incorporates both the data and the behavior of the object.

In Java EE and Spring applications, if the domain is to be persisted to a SQL database, then the domain is annotated with Java Persistence API (JPA) annotations. We'll discuss JPA in depth in chapters 4 and 5.

An example is found in the game service (code/game/src/main/java/book/games/entity/Game.java), where the domain model is Game.

Listing 2.4 Domain model

```java
@Entity
public class Game implements Serializable {

    @Id
    @Column(name = "id", updatable = false, nullable = false)
    private Long id;
    @Version
    @Column(name = "version")
    private int version;

    @Column
    private String title;

    @Column
    private String cover;

    @ElementCollection
    @CollectionTable(name = "ReleaseDate", joinColumns =
    @JoinColumn(name = "OwnerId"))
    private List<ReleaseDate>; releaseDates = new ArrayList<>;();

    @ElementCollection
    @CollectionTable(name = "Publisher", joinColumns = @JoinColumn
            (name = "OwnerId"))
    private List<String>; publishers = new ArrayList<>;();

    @ElementCollection
    @CollectionTable(name = "Developer", joinColumns = @JoinColumn
            (name = "OwnerId"))
    private List<String>; developers = new ArrayList<>;();

    public JsonObject convertToJson() {

        final JsonArrayBuilder developers = Json.createArrayBuilder();
        this.getDevelopers().forEach(developers::add);

        final JsonArrayBuilder publishers = Json.createArrayBuilder();
        this.getPublishers().forEach(publishers::add);

        final JsonArrayBuilder releaseDates = Json
                .createArrayBuilder();
        this.getReleaseDates().forEach(releaseDate -> {
            final String platform = releaseDate.getPlatformName();
            final String date = releaseDate.getReleaseDate().format
                    (DateTimeFormatter.ISO_DATE);
            releaseDates.add(Json.createObjectBuilder().add
                    ("platform", platform).add("release_date", date));
        });

        return Json.createObjectBuilder().add("id", this.getId())
                .add("title", this.getTitle()).add("cover", this
                        .getCover()).add("developers", developers)
                .add("publishers", publishers).add("release_dates",
                        releaseDates).build();
    }
}
```

Domain objects have fields that describe their properties in the system.

Object-manipulation methods should reside within the object.

SERVICE LAYER

The services in the *service layer* are responsible for coordinating the various domain activities and interactions with other subsystems. For example, these services handle database interactions through the persistence component and call external services through the remote-resource component.

In Java EE and Spring, this layer is usually implemented as a simple Java class, which is annotated in order to be eligible for injection either by *context dependency injection* (CDI), or autowiring in Spring components. Services should be injectable in any element that makes up the microservice.

One example of a Java EE service can be found in the game service (code/game/src/main/java/book/games/control/GamesService.java). This service is responsible for checking if a game is cached in the Gamer local database, or if it must first be retrieved from the IGDB API.

Listing 2.5   Java EE service

```java
@Dependent                                          Sets this class eligible
public class GamesService {                         for a CDI container as
                                                    Dependent scoped

    @EJB
    Games games;
                                                    Other elements can be
                                                    injected in a service.
    @EJB
    IgdbGateway igdbGateway;
    public Game searchGameById(final long gameId) throws IOException {

        final Optional<Game>; foundGame = games.findGameById(gameId);
        if (isGameInSiteDatabase(foundGame)) {
            return foundGame.get();                  Finds a game in the database
        } else {
            final JsonArray jsonByGameId = igdbGateway
                    .searchGameById(gameId);
            final Game game = Game.fromJson(jsonByGameId);   If the game isn't found,
            games.create(game);                              gets it from IGDB
            return game;
        }

    }
}
```

A Spring service example can be found in the video service (code/video/src/main/java/book/video/boundary/YouTubeVideos.java).

Listing 2.6   Spring service

```java
package book.video.boundary;

import org.springframework.beans.factory.annotation.Autowired;
import org.springframework.data.redis.core.ListOperations;
```

```
import org.springframework.data.redis.core.StringRedisTemplate;
import org.springframework.stereotype.Service;

import java.util.List;

@Service
public class YouTubeVideos {

    @Autowired
    StringRedisTemplate redisTemplate;

    public void createYouTubeLinks(final String gameId, final
    List<String>; youtubeLinks) {
        final ListOperations<String, String>;
                stringStringListOperations = redisTemplate
                .opsForList();
        stringStringListOperations.leftPushAll(gameId, youtubeLinks);
    }

    public boolean isGameInserted(final String gameId) {
        final ListOperations<String, String>;
                stringStringListOperations = redisTemplate
                .opsForList();
        return stringStringListOperations.size(gameId) >; 0;
    }

    public List<String>; getYouTubeLinks(final String gameId) {
        final ListOperations<String, String>;
                stringStringListOperations = redisTemplate
                .opsForList();
        final Long size = stringStringListOperations.size(gameId);
        return stringStringListOperations.range(gameId, 0, size);

    }

}
```

REPOSITORIES

Repositories act on collections of domain entities and generally act as entry points or bridges to the persistence-component backend.

> **TIP** If you're only going to manage a single entity, we don't recommend adding a repository layer, because it would add unnecessary overhead. There's also no need to pass objects through layers that never interact with them. For educational purposes, we've implemented a simple repository layer that demonstrates how to best test the class in a real-world scenario.

When using a SQL database over JPA in a Java EE container, you should use Enterprise Java Beans (EJBs), because they provide transactional awareness, concurrency management, and security out of the box.

An example repository layer can be found in the game service (code/game/src/main/java/book/games/boundary/Games.java).

Listing 2.7   Repository layer

```
@Stateless                          ◁──┐ EJBs ensure that classes are
public class Games {                    │ transaction aware by default.

    @PersistenceContext             ◁──┐ Injects the EntityManager
    EntityManager em;                   │ for database operations

    public Long create(final Game request) {
        final Game game = em.merge(request);      ◁── Creates a new game
        return game.getId();
    }

    public Optional<Game>; findGameById(final Long gameId) {
        Optional<Game>; g = Optional.ofNullable(em.find(Game.class,
                gameId));

        if (g.isPresent()) {
            Game game = g.get();
            game.getReleaseDates().size();
            game.getPublishers().size();
            game.getDevelopers().size();
            em.detach(game);
        }

        return g;
    }

}
```

When you use Spring, repositories are usually written to use the Spring Data project. This provides a familiar, consistent, Spring-based programming model for data access to relational and non-relational data stores, as well as to map-reduce frameworks and cloud-based data services. An example of a repository utilizing Spring Data can be found in the video service code for accessing Redis.

DATA MAPPERS AND OBJECT-RELATIONAL MAPPING

Just about all microservices need to persist some kind of data to persistent storage. In Java EE, when the persistence backend is a SQL database, the JPA specification is used through an object-relational mapping (ORM) tool. *ORM* is a technique for converting classes of object-oriented programming (OOP) languages into relational tables of relational database systems (RDBSs).

> **TIP** Some vendors also offer object mapping to NoSQL databases, but this feature isn't in the specification.

A JPA data-mapping example that demonstrates this capability can be seen in the game service (code/game/src/main/java/book/games/entity/Game.java).

Listing 2.8 Data mapping

```
@Entity
public class Game implements Serializable {

    @Id
    @Column(name = "id", updatable = false, nullable = false)
    private Long id;
    @Version
    @Column(name = "version")
    private int version;

    @Column                          ◁────┐ Object properties are
    private String title;                  │ mapped to relational
                                           │ table elements.
    @Column
    private String cover;

    @ElementCollection
    @CollectionTable(name = "ReleaseDate", joinColumns =
    @JoinColumn(name = "OwnerId"))
    private List<ReleaseDate>; releaseDates = new ArrayList<>;();

    @ElementCollection
    @CollectionTable(name = "Publisher", joinColumns = @JoinColumn
            (name = "OwnerId"))
    private List<String>; publishers = new ArrayList<>;();

    @ElementCollection
    @CollectionTable(name = "Developer", joinColumns = @JoinColumn
            (name = "OwnerId"))
    private List<String>; developers = new ArrayList<>;();
}
```

GATEWAYS AND THE HTTP CLIENT

When a service collaborates with one or more microservices, logic must be implemented to communicate with these external services. A *gateway* encapsulates all the logic for connecting to a remote service and takes care of the underlying protocol and marshalling/unmarshalling objects to and from domain objects. REST architectures generally use the RESTful-web-services approach, so a gateway will more often than not use an HTTP client to connect to the external service. In Java EE, the JAX-RS specification provides client classes for consuming RESTful web services.

Spring provides a simple but powerful class called RestTemplate, which provides methods for consuming other REST services. An example of a gateway that communicates with another microservice can be found in the aggregator service (code/aggregator/src/main/java/book/aggr/GamesGateway.java).

Listing 2.9   Gateway

```
public class GamesGateway {

    private final Client client;
    private final WebTarget games;
    private final String gamesHost;

    public GamesGateway() {
        this.client = ClientBuilder.newClient();

        this.gamesHost = Optional.ofNullable(System.getenv
                ("GAMES_SERVICE_URL")).orElse(Optional.ofNullable
                (System.getProperty("GAMES_SERVICE_URL")).orElse
                ("http://localhost:8181/"));
        this.games = this.client.target(gamesHost);      ◁─── Creates a client connection
    }                                                         to a given server

    public Future<JsonObject>; getGameFromGamesService(final long
                                                        gameId) {
        return this.games.path("{gameId}").resolveTemplate
                ("gameId", gameId)                              Registers the
                .register(JsonStructureBodyReader.class)   ◁─── unmarshaller
                .request(MediaType.APPLICATION_JSON).async()   ◁───
                .get(JsonObject.class);
    }                                        Usually, aggregators want to execute
                                                 calls in asynchronous mode.
}
```

Defines the endpoint URL (annotation pointing to `.path("{gameId}").resolveTemplate`)

In this section, we've introduced you to the layers of a microservice. Let's now see how to bring each of these elements into the Java space.

2.4.2   ECB pattern

Each microservice developed for the Gamer app follows the entity control boundary (ECB) pattern. ECB is a variant of the well-known MVC pattern, but unlike MVC, it's responsible not only for dealing with user interfaces, but also for applications (in our case, microservices) that don't have a UI.

The ECB pattern is composed of three elements (or key perspectives): *entity, control,* and *boundary.* Each element of a microservice can be assembled into one of these three perspectives:

- *Entity*—An object that represents a domain model. It primarily contains the data (attributes) required by the domain, but also performs behavior operations related to the entity, such as validating data and performing business operations.
- *Control*—An object that acts as the mediator between boundaries and entities. It manages the end-to-end behavior of a scenario.
- *Boundary*—An object that lies on the border of the system. Some boundary objects might be responsible for the frontend of the system: for example, REST endpoints. Others might be responsible for the backend, managing communications to external elements such as databases or other services, for example.

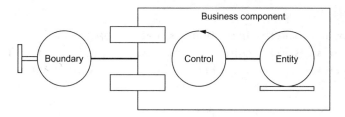

Figure 2.11   ECB pattern

Figure 2.11 shows how these elements fit together.

The three elements can have certain appropriate interactions; others *should not* occur. The relationships between the entity, control, and boundary objects can be summarized as follows:

- An *element* can communicate with other elements of the same kind.
- A *control* can communicate with *entity* and *boundary* elements.
- *Boundary* and *entity* elements shouldn't communicate directly.

Table 2.8 illustrates these relations.

Table 2.8   Communication between entity, control, and boundary objects

	Entity	Boundary	Control
Entity	X		X
Boundary		X	X
Control	X	X	X

You can see that the ECB pattern is perfectly suited to the anatomy of microservices. For example, applying the ECB pattern to the Gamer microservices might look like this:

- *Resources, repositories,* and *gateways* might be placed into *boundaries.*
- The *service layer* might be placed into the *control.*
- The *domain* (and *ORM,* when providing multiple objects) might be placed into the *entity.*

The schema diagram in figure 2.12 shows how each element of a microservice is mapped into an ECB pattern.

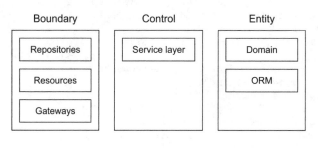

Figure 2.12   Example of the ECB pattern applied to Gamer microservices

2.4.3 *Miscellaneous patterns*

So far, you've seen how patterns like resources, data mappers, and gateways are applied to the microservices architecture, and how these patterns fit into the ECB pattern. The Gamer microservices also use other patterns that are worth mentioning.

AGGREGATOR PATTERN

The *aggregator pattern* is used in the microservices architecture, but it's not something new in software development: it comes from the enterprise-integration-pattern catalog. The goal of this pattern is to act as an aggregator between responses from several services. Once all the responses have been received, the aggregator correlates them and sends them back as a single response to the client for processing, as shown in figure 2.13.

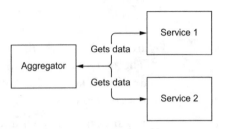

Figure 2.13   Aggregator pattern

An example of this pattern can be found in the Gamer aggregator service (code/aggregator/src/main/java/book/aggr/GamersResource.java). As its name suggests, it's responsible for aggregating all the information a gamer might wanted to see: game data and comments.

Listing 2.10   Aggregator pattern

```
@Inject
private GamesGateway gamesGateway;              ◁── The gateway pattern
                                                    communicates with
@Inject                                             another service.
private CommentsGateway commentsGateway;

private final Executor executor = Executors.newFixedThreadPool(8);

@GET
@Path("{gameId}")
@Produces(MediaType.APPLICATION_JSON)
public void getGameInfo(@Suspended final AsyncResponse
                               asyncResponse, @PathParam
      ("gameId") final long gameId) {

   asyncResponse.setTimeoutHandler(ar ->; ar.resume(Response
          .status(Response.Status.SERVICE_UNAVAILABLE).entity
                 ("TIME OUT !").build()));
   asyncResponse.setTimeout(15, TimeUnit.SECONDS);

   final CompletableFuture<JsonObject>; gamesGatewayFuture =
          Futures.toCompletable(gamesGateway
                 .getGameFromGamesService(gameId), executor);
   final CompletableFuture<JsonObject>; commentsGatewayFuture =
          Futures.toCompletable(commentsGateway
                 .getCommentsFromCommentsService(gameId),
```

```
                        executor);
```

Both responses are merged when available. →
```
gamesGatewayFuture.thenCombine(commentsGatewayFuture,
        (g, c) ->; Json.createObjectBuilder()
                .add("game", g).add("comments", c).build())
        .thenApply(info ->; asyncResponse.resume(Response.ok
                (info).build())
    ).exceptionally(asyncResponse::resume);
```

← Games and comments are retrieved asynchronously.

← **After the response is composed, it's sent back to the caller.**

```
}
```

CLIENT CONNECTIONS AS ENVIRONMENT VARIABLES

It's good practice to configure URLs for client connections via environment variables, and to provide a default/fallback value. Although this can't be considered a pattern, it's a good practice to pick up when you're developing microservices.

In our experience, the best way to configure client connections is to use environment variables, because they're simple to define and are supported by the native OS, build tools, and system-configuration scripts. You don't need to reinvent the wheel.

Anything that simplifies management of the runtime configuration will be useful. Rather than having multiple configuration files with different hardcoded values for each environment spread across the project, you can have one generated configuration that's fed from the environment at build time. For example, when using Docker, you have a docker-composition file. This can be generated from a resource using build-environment properties to set runtime-environment values in the composition. Doing this any other way would mean the system configuration script would have to take care of copying the correct file, with the correct values, to the correct place.

You can take this approach one step further and add fallback support for Java system properties (or vice versa). Java system properties can be set on the command line using -D options: for example, -DmyVey=myValue. This means both options are available for the DevOps team when it comes to configuring the microservices. Using this approach provides complete freedom to tune the microservice configuration during deployment.

An example of this appears, among other places, in the aggregator service (code/aggregator/src/main/java/book/aggr/CommentsGateway.java). This service needs the URLs of the game and comments services under which they're deployed.

Listing 2.11 Environment variables

```
String commentsHost = Optional.ofNullable(System.getenv
        (COMMENTS_SERVICE_URL))
    .orElse(Optional.ofNullable(System.getProperty
        ("COMMENTS_SERVICE_URL")).orElse
        ("http://localhost:8282/comments-service/"));
```

← **Uses the Optional class to set property priorities**

2.5   *Design decisions*

This book is about how to write tests for a microservices architecture. Thus we've simplified many of the examples so they remain as readable as possible. These simplifications mean we haven't followed the best practices for writing microservices:

- In some cases (which are identified and explained), we include as many different technologies as possible in order to demonstrate a principle. We therefore don't always use the best technology for the job at hand.
- Some layers, such as API gateways, load balancing, and caching, have been removed, because they don't offer anything in regard to testing a particular scope.

We strongly recommend that you implement a microservices architecture following the best practices available. We provide relevant notes, insights, and links for further reading when we skip over a topic.

Summary

- We've laid out the business-domain details of the book's example application in an orderly fashion, and you should now understand the application goals.
- We presented the application's technical details, along with the containers and databases it uses; we made these choices in order to present a larger spectrum of differing solutions. We also showed snippets of the application code where it's important to understand why we're using a specific approach when writing a particular test.
- The introduction to microservices patterns in the example application are rudimentary. We'll expand on these patterns in the following chapters as we develop various testing techniques and strategies for each scenario.

Unit-testing microservices 3

This chapter covers

- Applying unit testing techniques in a microservices-based architecture
- Deciding which tools fit best for writing unit tests
- Understanding solitary versus sociable unit tests
- Writing readable, robust unit tests

So far, you've become acquainted with the basic architecture, anatomy, and typical patterns used when developing microservices. You've also been introduced to the Gamer application, which is the reference application used throughout the book and for which we'll now write some tests. In this chapter, you'll learn how to write unit tests for a microservices-based architecture.

3.1 Unit testing techniques

As you now know, *unit testing* is a testing technique where the code of the application under test should be the smallest possible snippet to produce the required behavior. Another main characteristic of unit tests is that they should execute as quickly as possible, so developers get rapid feedback after any addition to or refactoring of the code base.

It's important to remember that unit tests aren't only a testing technique—unit testing is also a powerful design tool when you use a *test-driven-development* (TDD) approach, something we highly recommend.

> **TIP** Writing a unit test should be an easy task. TDD helps with designing classes that are testable; if you find yourself getting into trouble while writing a unit test, then the problem is probably not in the unit test but in the code under test. In such cases, this is usually a sign that your code design should be changed somehow.

The scope of what a unit test should cover has been discussed extensively over the history of unit testing, and the answer is likely to differ depending on the language paradigm. For example, in the case of a procedural language, it's common to see a unit test cover a single function or procedure. For object-oriented languages, unit tests often cover a class. But the scope exposed here is only indicative. Depending on the project, team, code under test, and architecture, you may decide to expand or reduce the scope of a unit test, involving more or fewer business classes in a single test. As always, this is something that will need to be studied, discussed, and agreed on by the entire team.

> **NOTE** Because Java is an object-oriented language, we make an equivalence between the *unit* under test (the generic term) and the *class* under test, which is the concrete unit under test for object-oriented languages.

Naturally, a unit test will look different based on whether the code under test is isolated from its dependencies—testing only the unit under test without taking any of its collaborators into account—or involves the collaborators of the unit as part of the test scope. Jay Fields, author of *Working Effectively with Unit Tests* (Leanpub, 2015), provides names for both approaches to writing unit tests. A test that collaborates with its dependencies is a *sociable unit test*, and an isolated style is appropriately named a *solitary unit test*.

3.1.1 *Sociable unit tests*

Sociable unit tests focus on testing the behavior of the class under test along with its dependencies and collaborators by taking into consideration changes in state. Obviously, when using this approach, you're treating the unit under test as a facade interface where some input is provided. Afterward, the unit under test uses its collaborators to calculate the output, and, finally, the output is validated by an assertion.

Using these kind of tests, you build a *black-box* environment because everything is tested through the class under test. This approach is a great way to test classes belonging to the *business-domain component*, where such classes often expose calculations and state transitions.

Because business-domain objects are representations of real-world concepts, they contain the data of the model and the behavior that changes the state of the model. Domain objects are state-based, and there's no real value in testing them in an isolated way. For this reason, sociable unit tests are best suited for testing business-domain logic.

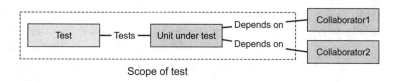

Figure 3.1 Sociable unit test

Figure 3.1 illustrates the makeup of a sociable unit test. You can see that the test class and the class under test are contained within the scope of the test. As in solitary testing, the dependencies (and collaborators) of the class under test are outside that scope. The major difference between sociable testing and solitary testing, in which test doubles are used, is that the dependencies (and collaborators) are real classes.

3.1.2 Test doubles

As you saw in section 3.1, there are two approaches regarding the scope of what a unit test should cover. The first approach is solitary unit testing, where the class under test is isolated from all its dependencies and collaborators, and the second approach is sociable unit testing, where the class under test involves its collaborators.

Maybe you've already started to think about the following question: "If my class under test has a collaborator, and I want to write a unit test using a solitary unit testing approach, how do I isolate the class under test?"

If you don't do anything, then the test will probably complete, at best, on a `Null-PointerException`, because there won't be any collaborator instance available for the test. So, the answer to the question is to use test doubles.

Test double is the generic term used when you replace a production object, usually a collaborator of the class under test, with a simplified class double for testing purposes. Generally speaking, there are five kinds of test doubles, as identified by Gerard Meszaros in *xUnit Test Patterns: Refactoring Test Code* (Addison-Wesley, 2007):

- *Dummies*—A dummy object is passed but never used. It's just used to fill required method parameters.
- *Fakes*—A fake object is an implementation of a collaborator, but it takes some shortcuts to make it more performant. Usually, a fake object isn't suitable for production. A well-known example is the *in-memory database.*
- *Stubs*—A stub provides predefined answers to calls made during the test.
- *Mocks*—A mock is an object with preprogrammed expectations. An expectation can be a discrete value or an exception. Unlike stubs, mocks do runtime behavior verification. No state is stored.
- *Spies*—A spy object is a stub that records information during the calls to it. For example, an email gateway stub might be able to return all the messages that it "sent."

Usually, test doubles are predictable (this is especially true for mocks). This means using test doubles makes your unit tests more robust, because collaborators will behave in exactly the same way during each execution. The execution speed when using test doubles is also a big advantage. They're not real implementations, so they perform well. This makes your test suites performant and also provides quick feedback to developers.

Mocks vs. stubs (and spies)

In our experience, most cases can be tested using *mocks* or *spies*; the only differences are what you assert in the test and the level of confidence that this assertion gives you.

Let's use a concrete example. Suppose you want to test a class, and one of its collaborators is used for sending an email. Here's how you *spy* the collaborator:

```java
public interface MailService {
   void sendEmail(Message msg);
}

public class MailServiceStub implements MailService {

   List<Message> messages = new ArrayList<>();

   void sendEmail(Message msg) {
     messages.add(msg);
   }

   boolean hasSentMessage(Message msg) {
     return messages.contains(msg);
   }

}
```

Now you can write a test using the previous class:

```java
Registration r = new Registration();
MailServiceStub mss = new MailServiceStub();
r.setMailService(mss);

User u = ....
r.register(u);

Message expectedEmailMessage = ...;
assertThat(mss.hasSentMessage(expectedEmailMessage),
                is(true));
assertThat(mss.numberOfSentMessage(), is(1));
```

Notice that this test verifies the state of the spy: in this case, that the expected message has been sent.

In a similar way, *mocking* the collaborator uses a test that looks like this:

```
Registration r = new Registration();
MailService mss = mock(MailService.class);
r.setMailService(mss);

User u = ....
r.register(u);

Message expectedEmailMessage = ...;
verify(mss).sendEmail(expectedEmailMessage);
```

Notice that the biggest difference is that this test only verifies an interaction, so it performs behavior verification. Another big difference is that the test relies on collaborator method calls. Meanwhile, the spies-and-stubs case requires extra methods to help with verification of state changes.

As mentioned earlier, choosing between stubs/spies and mocks depends on what kind of test your unit needs. If you need state verifications or custom test implementations of a collaborator, then spies are the best choice. On the other hand, if you only need behavior verifications without any custom implementation, then mocks are generally the best choice.

Based on our experience and in cases of doubt, the best way to start is by using mocks. It's faster to get started, you only need to record the expectations, and usually it covers the use cases to test.

3.1.3 *Solitary unit tests*

Solitary unit tests focus on testing the unit or work in an isolated and controlled way. The unit's collaborators are replaced by test doubles or mocks.

This approach is a great way to avoid test failures that are unrelated to the class under test, but are related to one of its dependencies. This is usually far outside the scope of the test.

Moreover, solitary unit tests are useful in cases where the class under test has a dependency that requires a physical connection to a network, a database, an email service, or even another microservice. Using real dependencies in these cases is a bad thing for two reasons:

- Access to I/O is a comparatively slow operation, and unit tests should be fast.
- Remote services are prone to failure at any time (due to server outages, network outages, firewall rules, and so on), and this means a test might fail for reasons other than incorrect code.

Hence, you should aspire to use solitary unit tests for the following scenarios:

- *When collaborators of the unit under test are slow*—This can be due to I/O access, but it could also be due to long-running calculations.

- *When collaborators of the unit under test contain logic that may change often*—In this case, the test may fail not because of the class under test, but because one of the collaborators fails.
- *When you want to test corner cases that would be difficult to test using real instances*—For example, a disk-is-full test case.

Figure 3.2 illustrates what a solitary unit test looks like. You can see that the test class and the unit under test are within the scope of the test. The dependencies (and collaborators) of the class being tested are outside of that scope, and they're not the real classes—they're replaced with test doubles.

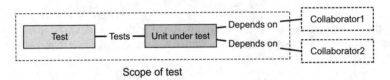

Figure 3.2   Solitary unit test

3.1.4   *Unit testing in microservices*

We've introduced what unit testing is, what different approaches you might take—such as solitary or sociable—and test doubles and how they can help you write better unit tests. In this section, you'll see how to apply unit test concepts to the microservice architecture. Before we look at a concrete example, let's review the anatomy of a microservice.

RESOURCE AND SERVICE COMPONENT LAYERS

Resources and services commonly contain coordination code between gateways, domain objects, and repositories, as well as message conversion between modules. We strongly recommend using solitary unit tests for resources and services. The reason is that collaborators of resources and services are usually slow. This will affect the robustness of the test (for example, the network might be down, leading to a false negative). In the case of gateways, they usually communicate with a service deployed on another server, so this again means touching the network. Use of repositories is a similar story, because disk I/O is virtually analogous with network traffic. For this reason, using test doubles and, to be more concrete, *mock* objects in collaborators is the best choice when working with resources and services.

> **TIP** Sometimes, resources and services act as facades, passing messages between collaborators. In such cases, unit testing may not pay off—other testing levels, such as component testing, may be more worthwhile.

GATEWAY COMPONENT

Gateway component layers contain the logic to connect to an external service, typically using an HTTP/S client. In this case, a solitary unit test using mocks or stubs is the best way to proceed to avoid touching the network from within the unit test.

The items to test in this layer are as follows:

- Mapping logic between the underlying protocol and business objects
- Forcing error conditions that might be difficult to simulate using real services (negative testing)

DOMAIN COMPONENT

We talked about how to test the domain layer in section 3.1.1. *Domain logic* exposes calculations and state transitions. Because domain objects are state-based, there's no value in testing them in an isolated way. For this reason, sociable unit testing is the best strategy for testing domain logic.

REPOSITORY COMPONENTS

A repository usually acts as a "gateway" to a persistence layer by connecting to a database, executing queries, and adapting the output to domain objects. A repository could also be a properties file, or Elasticsearch, for example. The list is endless.

A persistence layer is usually implemented using an ORM such as JPA, so in most cases, this layer just deals with the core class of the system. (In the case of JPA, this is EntityManager.) If you decide that writing unit tests for persistence objects isn't going to pay off, then at least write integration tests for them. But if some logic is encompassed in mapping the response, then a solitary unit test and mocking the core class, such as EntityManager, should be sufficient to provide mapped objects.

SOLITARY OR SOCIABLE?

Table 3.1 summarizes when to use the solitary approach and when to use the sociable one.

Table 3.1 Solitary vs. sociable unit testing

Component	Solitary	Sociable
Resources	X	
Services	X	
Gateways	X	
Domain		X
Repositories	X	

3.2 Tools

We've presented how to best match unit testing styles to each of the components of the microservices architecture. Now, let's look at the tools used for writing unit tests. Many such tools are available, but in our opinion the following are currently the most widely adopted and accepted by the Java community.

3.2.1 *JUnit*

JUnit is a unit testing framework for Java. Currently, it's extended by other tools for writing different levels of tests such as integration and component tests.

A JUnit test is a Java object with special annotations to mark a method as a test. Older versions provided objects to extend, but the annotation approach is more flexible.

The following snippet shows how a typical JUnit test is structured:

```
public class MyTest {

    @BeforeClass                              ←——  The method is executed before
    public static void setUpClass() throws Exception {    the tests defined in the class.
    }
                                                     The method is executed before
    @Before                                   ←——   each test in the class.
    public void setUp() throws Exception {
    }
                              Flags the method as a test method
    @Test                     ←——
    public void testMethod() {
        assertEquals("Hello World", message);    ←——  JUnit provides methods
        assertTrue (17 < age);                         for asserting results.
    }
                              The method is executed
                              after each test in the class.
    @After                    ←——
    public void tearDown() throws Exception {
    }
                                              The method is executed after
                                              execution of all tests in the class.
    @AfterClass                               ←——
    public static void tearDownClass() throws Exception {
    }


}
```

3.2.2 *AssertJ*

Several important features are critical for good unit tests. A unit test should be *fast* and *isolated*; we've talked about this before. But an equally important aspect is that they should be *readable*.

Any reader of the test should be able to identify with a quick glance what the test is about and also what the expected result should be. The snippet in the previous section used clauses like `assertEquals` and `assertTrue`—these are clear statements.

Using these clauses is valid, but they pose challenges regarding readability. Let's explore some of these issues:

- You don't immediately know which parameter is the expected value and which is the result value. Assuming `assertEquals(val1, val2)`, is the first parameter the expected value or the calculated one? It's the expected value. This is important because, in the case of failure, the error message is built using these parameters.

- Asserting simple conditions might be hard to read and write. `assertTrue (17 < age)` seems unnatural to read.

- Usually, methods return more-complex objects or lists of objects. Note that `assertTrue(games.contains(zelda))` has two problems. First, the assertion isn't very readable; and second, what will happen if the `zelda` object doesn't implement `equals`, or implements it in some detrimental way for the assertion logic? The *assertion* may become an *assumption*.

To avoid all these problems, AssertJ (http://joel-costigliola.github.io/assertj) was developed so developers can use fluent assertions in tests. One of the areas where AssertJ shines is in providing a rich set of assertions that facilitate writing assumptions for complex elements, as well as improving readability.

The static import you need to use is `import static org.assertj.core .api.Assertions.*`. You can still use `assertEquals` and `assertTrue` if you prefer, but let's compare using AssertJ with previous examples.

Instead of writing `assertEquals(val1, val2)`, you can write `assertThat(val1) .isEqualTo(val2)` using AssertJ. Notice that now the assertion is explicit for the reader, and there's no ambiguity about what the expected value and the real one should be.

You can use `assertTrue (17 < age)`, but rewriting it with AssertJ looks like `assert-That(age).isGreaterThan(17)`. And you thought we were using a bad example!

Finally, AssertJ can help in the case of complex validations. Instead of using `assertTrue(games.contains(zelda))`, which depends on the `equals` method, you can rewrite it with AssertJ to be something like `assertThat(games).extracting ("name").contains("Zelda")`. This has none of the ambiguity of the `equals` method, and at the same time, it improves readability.

> **NOTE** You may wonder what the difference is between AssertJ and Hamcrest (part of JUnit). Both projects were created for the same purpose: improving the readability of tests. But the most important difference between them is that whereas AssertJ uses fluent assertions, making writing assertions from the IDE an easy task, in Hamcrest you write assertions like the layers of an onion, one inside another, which is less natural to read and write in an IDE.

You might agree that using AssertJ in your tests is a great way to not only improve readability but also avoid having to write cumbersome code in tests. We'll use all of them, leaving the choice up to you as to which one you prefer in your own code.

3.2.3 *Mockito*

In section 3.1.2, you saw different strategies for replacing a production object with a test object. There are five types of test doubles: dummies, fakes, stubs, spies, and mocks.

In unit tests, spies and mocks are by far the most used. Spies are usually implemented as an interface with custom code. For mocks, you need a framework that lets you record the canned answers for the calls.

In Java, there are several mocking frameworks, such as *JMockit*, *EasyMock*, and *Mockito*. In this book, the mocking framework we'll focus on is Mockito (http://site.mockito.org)—using more than one would be too confusing. According to an analysis performed on 30,000+ Java projects, Mockito is the fourth-most-used library in Java projects, so we can consider it a de facto framework for mocking in Java. It's a fast-moving project that will outpace this book, so please be sure to follow the project online. But feel free to analyze and choose your preferred mocking framework.

Mockito is a mocking framework written in Java that allows the creation of test doubles (mock objects) with a clean, simple API. Moreover, one of the features that differentiates Mockito from other mocking frameworks is that you can verify the behavior of the unit under test without defining expectations in advance, making tests simpler and reducing the coupling between test code and the unit under test.

The following snippet shows the typical structure of a Mockito test:

The methods of the mocked object are called like any other method.

Creates a proxy around the interface (or class) that you want to mock

Verifies that an expected interaction has been produced during test execution

Produces an answer when this method is called with the given parameter

Returns "first" as the canned response

```
import static org.mockito.Mockito.*;

List mockedList = mock(List.class);

mockedList.add("one");
mockedList.clear();

verify(mockedList).add("one");
verify(mockedList).clear();

List mockedList2 = mock(List.class);
when(mockedList2.get(0)).thenReturn("first");
System.out.println(mockedList2.get(0));
```

The snippet shows only a basic usage of Mockito; more features are explained in the book as required.

Now that you've been introduced to unit testing tools, let's see what you need to do to start using them.

3.2.4 *Build-script modifications*

In order to use a testing framework like JUnit, AssertJ, or Mockito, you need to define it as a test dependency in your build script. In the case of Maven, this information goes inside the `dependencies` block in pom.xml:

```
<dependency>
  <groupId>junit</groupId>
  <artifactId>junit</artifactId>
  <version>4.12</version>
  <scope>test</scope>            <-- Defines a dependency in the test scope
</dependency>
<dependency>
  <groupId>org.assertj</groupId>
  <artifactId>assertj-core</artifactId>
  <version>3.5.2</version>
```

```
      <scope>test</scope>
  </dependency>
  <dependency>
      <groupId>org.mockito</groupId>
      <artifactId>mockito-core</artifactId>
      <version>2.8.47</version>
      <scope>test</scope>
  </dependency>
```

WARNING Mockito used to erroneously provide a version of the Hamcrest library that clashed with the one that comes with JUnit. Although this has been fixed in Mockito 2, be aware that older projects might need upgrading.

After registering dependencies in the build script, you can start writing unit tests.

3.3 *Writing unit tests for the Gamer app*

After discussing what unit tests are, which tools can be used, some strategies you can follow for each of the microservice layers, and registering the tools in the project, it's time to begin writing unit tests.

Usually, unit tests are created under the de facto test directory named src/test/java. We suggest that you stick to this pattern.

3.3.1 *YouTubeVideoLinkCreator test*

Let's look at how to write a unit test for the YouTubeVideoLinkCreator class (code/video/src/main/java/book/video/controller/YouTubeVideoLinkCreator.java). This is a simple controller class that has no dependency on any other class, so it doesn't require any test doubles. This class is responsible for the creation of the embedded URL of a YouTube video ID.

Listing 3.1 YouTubeVideoLinkCreator class

```
public class YouTubeVideoLinkCreator {

    private static final String EMBED_URL = "https://www.youtube" +
            ".com/embed/";

    public URL createEmbeddedUrl(final String videoId) {
        try {
            return URI.create(EMBED_URL + videoId).toURL();
        } catch (final MalformedURLException e) {
            throw new IllegalArgumentException(e);
        }
    }
}
```

For this class, only one test method is required for testing that the creation of the URL is correct (code/video/src/test/java/book/video/controller/YouTubeVideoLinkCreatorTest.java).

Listing 3.2 Unit test for `YouTubeVideoLinkCreator`

Descriptive test method name: call it what it is.

The test method must be annotated with @Test.

Class under test

Calls createEmbeddedUrl

Asserts that the YouTube link is valid

```
public class YouTubeVideoLinkCreatorTest {

    @Test
    public void shouldReturnYouTubeEmbeddedUrlForGivenVideoId() {
        final YouTubeVideoLinkCreator youTubeVideoLinkCreator = new
            YouTubeVideoLinkCreator();

        final URL embeddedUrl = youTubeVideoLinkCreator
            .createEmbeddedUrl("1234");

        assertThat(embeddedUrl).hasHost("www.youtube.com").hasPath
            ("/embed/1234");

    }
}
```

You can see that the test method is annotated with `@Test`, and it's structured using the well-known Given-When-Then structure, which essentially separates a test case into three sections. The *givens* are the preconditions of the test, the *when* is the stimulus of the test, and the *then* describes the expectations of the test.

TIP Notice that currently the catch code (the `IllegalArgumentException`) isn't tested. The feedback it provides isn't worth the effort of testing it.

3.3.2 *YouTubeLink test*

Let's write a unit test for the `YouTubeLink` class (code/video/src/main/java/book/video/entity/YoutubeLink.java). This class is a domain object that has a collaborator (`YouTubeVideoLinkCreator`) that implements logic with this domain object.

Listing 3.3 `YouTubeLink` class

Behavior logic is implemented as a Java 8 functional interface.

```
public class YouTubeLink {

    private final String videoId;
    Function<String, URL> youTubeVideoLinkCreator;

    public YouTubeLink(final String videoId) {
        this.videoId = videoId;
    }

    public void setYouTubeVideoLinkCreator(final Function<String,
            URL> youTubeVideoLinkCreator) {
        this.youTubeVideoLinkCreator = youTubeVideoLinkCreator;
    }

    public URL getEmbedUrl() {
        if (youTubeVideoLinkCreator != null) {
            return youTubeVideoLinkCreator.apply(this.videoId);
        } else {
            throw new IllegalStateException
```

```
                            ("YouTubeVideoLinkCreator not set");
        }
    }

    public String getVideoId() {
        return videoId;
    }

}
```

Notice that there are two options for writing this test:

- A solitary-testing approach, which means mocking the YouTubeVideoLink-Creator class
- A sociable-testing approach, which means using the real YouTubeVideoLink-Creator class

This case is typical in that it's not worth mocking the dependency, and using the real one is better.

Listing 3.4   Unit test for `YouTubeLink`

```
public class YouTubeLinkTest {

    @Test
    public void shouldCalculateEmbedYouTubeLink() {
        final YouTubeLink youtubeLink = new YouTubeLink("1234");

        final YouTubeVideoLinkCreator youTubeVideoLinkCreator = new
                YouTubeVideoLinkCreator();
        youtubeLink.setYouTubeVideoLinkCreator
                (youTubeVideoLinkCreator::createEmbeddedUrl);

        assertThat(youtubeLink.getEmbedUrl()).hasHost("www.youtube" +
                ".com").hasPath("/embed/1234");
    }

}
```

Creates a real dependency ⤷

Injects the logic

This unit test has the same look as the previous one. But because it's a sociable test, two instances are created: one for the class under test, and another as a dependency of it.

> **NOTE**   In the YouTube link case, the test looks simple, and you might be wondering whether it makes sense to write it: after all, YouTubeVideoLinkCreator was already tested in its own test. What's being tested here isn't the ability to create the YouTube embed link for a video, but that YouTubeLinkTest's domain object is able to generate a correct YouTube embed link with its own data.

3.3.3   *Games test*

So far, we've written unit tests without having to mock any dependencies. Let's write a unit test for a *repository* element. In this case, we'll use the Games class (code/game/src/main/java/book/games/boundary/Games.java).

```
Listing 3.5   Games class
```

```java
@Stateless                              ⊲──┐ EJBs make classes transactional-
public class Games {                       │ aware by default.

    @PersistenceContext             ⊲──┐ EntityManager is injected
    EntityManager em;                  │ for database operations.

    public Long create(final Game request) {
        final Game game = em.merge(request);   ⊲── Creates a new game
        return game.getId();
    }

    public Optional<Game> findGameById(final Long gameId) {
        Optional<Game> g = Optional.ofNullable(em.find(Game.class,
                gameId));

        if (g.isPresent()) {
            Game game = g.get();
            game.getReleaseDates().size();
            game.getPublishers().size();
            game.getDevelopers().size();
            em.detach(game);
        }

        return g;
    }

}
```

One of the most important things in unit tests is maintaining a good pace of execution. Because this repository is implemented using JPA, you need to mock this part.

```
Listing 3.6   Unit test for Games
```

```java
@RunWith(MockitoJUnitRunner.class)  ⊲──┐ The Mockito runner
public class GamesTest {                │ initializes @Mock fields.

    private static final long GAME_ID = 123L;

    @Mock                               ⊲── Marks the field as a mock
    EntityManager entityManager;

    @Test
    public void shouldCreateAGame() {
        final Game game = new Game();
```

```
        game.setId(GAME_ID);
        game.setTitle("Zelda");

        final Games games = new Games();

        when(entityManager.merge(game)).thenReturn(game);
        games.em = entityManager;

        games.create(game);

        verify(entityManager).merge(game);


    }
}
```

Sets a mocked dependency → (points to `games.em = entityManager;`)

Records the answer when the mock is called ← (points to `when(entityManager.merge(game)).thenReturn(game);`)

Normal call to the class under test → (points to `games.create(game);`)

Verifies that the merge method is called with the expected game ← (points to `verify(entityManager).merge(game);`)

This test is slightly different from the previous ones. The first thing to notice is that it uses a custom JUnit runner. This runner is provided by the Mockito framework and is responsible for initializing all fields annotated with @Mock, among other things. You can use Mockito without the JUnit runner by using the Mockito.mock() method, as was shown in the introduction to the Mockito section; but in our opinion, unit tests look clearer when using the runner.

The second difference is that now, in the test method, some canned answers are recorded for the EntityManager class. And finally, in addition to asserting the expected value, the test verifies that the mocked method is called, too. This is important so you can be sure that the class under test calls the expected dependency methods and not another method unrelated to the test.

Something similar can be done for the other methods.

Listing 3.7 Additional test methods in GamesTest.java

```
@Test
public void shouldFindAGameById() {
    final Game game = new Game();
    game.setId(GAME_ID);
    game.setTitle("Zelda");

    final Games games = new Games();
    when(entityManager.find(Game.class, GAME_ID)).thenReturn(game);
    games.em = entityManager;

    final Optional<Game> foundGame = games.findGameById(GAME_ID);

    verify(entityManager).find(Game.class, GAME_ID);
    assertThat(foundGame).isNotNull().hasValue(game)
            .usingFieldByFieldValueComparator();
}
@Test
public void shouldReturnAnEmptyOptionalIfElementNotFound() {
    final Game game = new Game();
    game.setId(GAME_ID);
```

The ID must be the same as the one recorded in the when function.

Verifies that find is called, but also returns the required Optional

```
                game.setTitle("Zelda");

                final Games games = new Games();
                when(entityManager.find(Game.class, GAME_ID)).thenReturn(null);
                games.em = entityManager;
```
Asserts
that
Optional
has no
value
```
                final Optional<Game> foundGame = games.findGameById(GAME_ID);

                verify(entityManager).find(Game.class, GAME_ID);
            ⊳   assertThat(foundGame).isNotPresent();
        }
```

TIP Sometimes it doesn't pay to write a unit test for repositories, because from the point of view of unit tests, they only act as a bridge. In this case, it's worth it to not write a unit test and just write integration tests for the repository layer.

3.3.4 *GamesService test*

You've seen how to use JUnit, AssertJ, and Mockito in simple scenarios. Now, let's write a unit test for the searchGameById(gameId) method, which is a bit more complicated (code/game/src/main/java/book/games/control/GamesService.java). This method is responsible for controlling whether information from a game is present in the database system or whether it needs to be retrieved from the official IGDB site.

Listing 3.8 searchGameById(gameId) method

```
@Dependent                          ◁────┐  Sets this class eligible for a CDI
public class GamesService {              │  container as Dependent scope

    @EJB                    ◁────┐  Other elements can be
    Games games;                 │  injected in a service.

    @EJB
    IgdbGateway igdbGateway;
    public Game searchGameById(final long gameId) throws IOException {
```
Finds the
game in the
database
```
        ⊳   final Optional<Game> foundGame = games.findGameById(gameId)
            if (isGameInSiteDatabase(foundGame)) {
                return foundGame.get();
            } else {
                final JsonArray jsonByGameId = igdbGateway
                        .searchGameById(gameId);                    ◁────┐  If the game isn't
                final Game game = Game.fromJson(jsonByGameId);           │  found, gets it from
                games.create(game);                                     │  the IGDB site.
                return game;
            }
        }

    }
}
```

If you take a careful look at the logic of `GamesService`, you see that the methods `convertToJson` and `fromJson` of the `Game` entity are called. Again, you might wonder if it makes more sense to call these real methods, or to mock the entities as well.

In our experience, if it's not complicated to manage their behavior, the best way to proceed is by using *real* entities (that is, the sociable-testing approach) instead of mocking them. It's important to note that this test doesn't substitute testing the entity object, because it's focused on testing the `GameService` class and not `Game`. As you've seen in the previous section, the `Game` class must have its own test class where you test it deeply.

Let's look at a test that validates that if you have game data in an internal database, it's retrieved from there and not by hitting the IGDB site (code/game/src/test/java/book/games/control/GamesServiceTest.java).

Listing 3.9   Unit-testing the games cache

```
@RunWith(MockitoJUnitRunner.class)
public class GamesServiceTest {

    @Mock
    Games games;

    @Mock
    IgdbGateway igdbGateway;

    @Test
    public void shouldReturnGameIfItIsCachedInInternalDatabase()
            throws IOException {

        final Game game = new Game();
        game.setId(123L);
        game.setTitle("Zelda");
        game.setCover("ZeldaCover");

        when(games.findGameById(123L)).thenReturn(Optional.of(game));

        final GamesService gamesService = new GamesService();        The game returned
        gamesService.games = games;                                  should be the one
        gamesService.igdbGateway = igdbGateway;                      recorded in the
                                                                     mock object.
        final Game foundGame = gamesService.searchGameById(123L);
        assertThat(foundGame).isEqualToComparingFieldByField(game);  ◄──┘
        verify(igdbGateway, times(0)).searchGameById(anyInt());    ◄──┐
        verify(games).findGameById(123L);                            │

                                                   Verifies that no interaction with
                                                        the IGDB site is produced
    }
}
```

This test is very similar to the previous test, but there's one simple but powerful change. Notice that this test verifies not only that something *has* occurred—in this case, that the game was retrieved by calling the search method from the database—

but also that something *has not* occurred, in this case that the IGDB gateway methods weren't called.

In a similar way, you can test the other case: when game data isn't in the internal database and needs to be retrieved from IGDB.

Listing 3.10   Unit-testing game retrieval

```
@Test
public void
shouldReturnGameFromIgdbSiteIfGameIsNotInInternalDatabase()
        throws IOException {

    final JsonArray returnedGame = createTestJsonArray();

    when(games.findGameById(123L)).thenReturn(Optional.empty());
    when(igdbGateway.searchGameById(123L)).thenReturn
            (returnedGame);

    final GamesService gamesService = new GamesService();
    gamesService.games = games;
    gamesService.igdbGateway = igdbGateway;

    final Game foundGame = gamesService.searchGameById(123L);
    assertThat(foundGame.getTitle()).isEqualTo("Battlefield 4");


    Assertions.assertThat(foundGame.getReleaseDates())
            .hasSize(1).extracting("platformName",
            "releaseDate").contains(tuple("PlayStation 3",
            LocalDate.of(2013, 10, 29)));

    assertThat(foundGame.getDevelopers()).hasSize(1).contains
            ("EA Digital Illusions CE");

    assertThat(foundGame.getPublishers()).hasSize(1).contains
            ("Electronic Arts");

    verify(games).create(anyObject());
    verify(igdbGateway).searchGameById(123L);

}
```

Asserts that the release-date tuple is correct → (points to the `Assertions.assertThat(foundGame.getReleaseDates())` block)

Verifies that the game is stored in the internal database → (points to `verify(games).create(anyObject());`)

Verifies that the game is retrieved from IGDB (points to `verify(igdbGateway).searchGameById(123L);`)

But there are cases where things can become more complex. In the next test, we'll introduce the `ArgumentCaptor` feature and exception testing.

3.3.5   *GamesResource test*

As you've seen in previous sections, Mockito is helpful for mocking dependencies of the units under test. But testing can be more complicated in situations such as exception scenarios and special verification cases.

Let's write a unit test for `GamesResource` (code/game/src/main/java/book/games/boundary/GamesResource.java). Remember that this class is the definition of REST endpoints related to game operations.

Listing 3.11 `GamesResource` class

```
@Path("/")
@javax.ejb.Singleton          ◄──┐  Resource is marked as a
@Lock(LockType.READ)             │  Singleton EJB, so the endpoint
public class GamesResource {     │  becomes transactional

    @Inject
    GamesService gamesService;
                                 ┐  Injects an executor service
    @Inject                      │  provided by the container
            ExecutorServiceProducer managedExecutorService;

                                                              @Asynchronous
    @GET                                                      designates a
    @Produces(MediaType.APPLICATION_JSON)                     method as
    @javax.ejb.Asynchronous                                   asynchronous.
    public void searchGames(@Suspended final AsyncResponse    Only valid if it's
                                      response,      ◄──      an EJB.
                        @NotNull @QueryParam("query") final
                        String query) {

        response.setTimeoutHandler(asyncResponse -> asyncResponse
                .resume(Response.status(Response.Status
                    .SERVICE_UNAVAILABLE).entity("TIME OUT !")
                    .build()));
        response.setTimeout(15, TimeUnit.SECONDS);

        managedExecutorService.getManagedExecutorService().submit(
            () -> {
            try {

                final Collector<JsonObject, ?, JsonArrayBuilder>
                        jsonCollector = Collector.of
                        (Json::createArrayBuilder,
                            JsonArrayBuilder::add, (left,
                                                    right) -> {
                    left.add(right);
                    return left;
                });

                final List<SearchResult> searchResults =
                        gamesService.searchGames(query);

                final JsonArrayBuilder mappedGames = searchResults
                        .stream().map(SearchResult::convertToJson)
                        .collect(jsonCollector);

                final Response.ResponseBuilder ok = Response.ok
                        (mappedGames.build());
```

@Suspended instructs the JAX-RS runtime that this method is asynchronous and injects AsyncResponse.

Executes logic in another thread

```
                    response.resume(ok.build());          ◁        Once the result is ready,
                } catch (final Throwable e) {                       the connection is resumed.
                    response.resume(e);              ◁
                }
        });                                                 In case of an error, communication
    }                                                       should also be resumed.
}
```

Notice that this class under test has some elements that are slightly different from other classes. The first item of note is that the method returns void. This doesn't mean that the method doesn't return *anything*, but that it returns the response using an async method, response.resume(). The second difference is that there's special treatment in case an exception is thrown.

To resolve the first problem, you could use the verify method as seen in previous tests, but the verify method just checks the equality of arguments in a natural style by calling the equals method. This is the recommended way to match arguments when you have control of the object under verification, because you decide whether there are changes to the equals method. But when the object isn't under your control, like javax.ws.rs.core.Response, then using the default equals method may not work, and it's worth using ArgumentCaptor, which allows you to assert on certain arguments after verification instead of using the equals implementation.

Listing 3.12   Unit test that uses an `ArgumentCaptor`

```
@RunWith(MockitoJUnitRunner.class)
public class GamesResourceTest {

    @Mock
    GamesService gamesService;

    @Mock
    ExecutorServiceProducer executorServiceProducer;

    @Mock                                                   Creates a mock to provide as an
    AsyncResponse asyncResponse;              ◁             argument to the JAX-RS endpoint

    @Captor                                          ◁      Creates an
    ArgumentCaptor<Response> argumentCaptorResponse;        ArgumentCaptor
                                                            using @Captor
    private static final ExecutorService executorService =
            Executors.newSingleThreadExecutor();     ◁
                                                            Creates a single
    @Before                                                 thread pool
    public void setupExecutorServiceProducer() {
        when(executorServiceProducer.getManagedExecutorService())
                .thenReturn(executorService);
    }
```

```
@AfterClass
public static void stopExecutorService() {          Terminates
    executorService.shutdown();                     ExecutorService
}


@Test
public void restAPIShouldSearchGamesByTheirNames() throws
        IOException, InterruptedException {

    final GamesResource gamesResource = new GamesResource();
    gamesResource.managedExecutorService =
            executorServiceProducer;
    gamesResource.gamesService = gamesService;              Waits until the
                                                            method is
    when(gamesService.searchGames("zelda")).thenReturn      executed at
            (getSearchResults());                           the separated
                                                            thread
    gamesResource.searchGames(asyncResponse, "zelda");
    executorService.awaitTermination(2, TimeUnit.SECONDS);

    verify(asyncResponse).resume(argumentCaptorResponse.capture
            ());

    final Response response = argumentCaptorResponse.getValue()
            ;

    assertThat(response.getStatusInfo().getFamily()).isEqualTo
            (Response.Status.Family.SUCCESSFUL);

    assertThat((JsonArray) response.getEntity()).hasSize(2)
            .containsExactlyInAnyOrder(Json.createObjectBuilder
                    ().add("id", 1).add("name", "The Legend Of " +
                    "" + "Zelda").build(), Json
                    .createObjectBuilder().add("id", 2).add
                            ("name", "Zelda II: The " +
                                    "Adventure of Link").build()
            );

}

}
```

Left margin annotations:
- **Verifies that resume is called, and captures the object that was used during the call**
- **Gets the captured object, and asserts with the expected values**

This test is more complex than the ones you've written for other classes. The first thing to notice is that it uses ArgumentCaptor. It's useful in this case because you're only interested in the family of the response. You don't know how the equals method is implemented and how it might change in the future, so capturing and manipulating the object in the test is the safest way to proceed. A captor is initialized by using the @Captor annotation instead of @Mock. The captor requires you to set the type of data that's going to be captured: in this case, javax.ws.rs.core.Response.

Second, this case uses a sociable test by using the "real" java.util.concurrent .ExecutorService. Mocking an executor service would imply not executing any logic in the test and would make the test useless.

You could argue that logic in the submit method could be added into its own class. In that case, you could write a unit test isolated from ExecutorService. That approach would be valid as well, but the truth is that with the introduction of functional interfaces in Java 8, the approach followed in the example is valid and well accepted.

The last thing to note is the ArgumentCaptor lifecycle, which can be summarized as follows:

1 The captor is initialized, in this test by using the @Captor annotation.
2 The captor captures argument values used in the mocked method. In this test, the important value is the response passed to the resume method of Async-Response. To do this, you need to verify that the method is called, and if it's called, capture its arguments. In the test, this is done by calling verify(async-Response).resume(argumentCaptorResponse.capture()).
3 Get the value captured by the captor. In this test, a Response object is captured. To get it, you call the getValue method.

JSON Processing API dependency

The GamesResource class uses the JSON Processing API, which is provided by the application server. Because unit tests aren't run in an application server, you need to provide an implementation of the JSON Processing Specification. For this example, because you're using WildFly Swarm, you'll add the one used in WildFly:

```
<dependency>
   <groupId>org.jboss.resteasy</groupId>
   <artifactId>resteasy-client</artifactId>
   <version>3.0.21.Final</version>
   <scope>test</scope>
</dependency>
```

In a similar way, you can test the exception scenario.

Listing 3.13   Unit-testing an exception scenario

```
@Test
public void exceptionShouldBePropagatedToCaller() throws
        IOException, InterruptedException {
    final GamesResource gamesResource = new GamesResource();
    gamesResource.managedExecutorService =
            executorServiceProducer;
    gamesResource.gamesService = gamesService;

    when(gamesService.searchGames("zelda")).thenThrow
            (IOException.class);
```

◄─── Throws an IOException when the searchGames("zelda") method is called

```
gamesResource.searchGames(asyncResponse, "zelda");
executorService.awaitTermination(1, TimeUnit.SECONDS);

verify(gamesService).searchGames("zelda");
verify(asyncResponse).resume(any(IOException.class));  ⊲
}
```

Verifies that resume is called with an IOException instance

This is the last unit test we'll show you. The next section suggests some tests you can write to be sure you understand what you've learned.

Exercises

After reading this chapter, you may be ready to write tests for book.video.boundary .YouTubeGateway and book.games.entity.Game classes. In the first test, we suggest using a solitary-testing approach, and using Mockito for dependencies. For the second test, try using a sociable-testing approach.

Summary

- We've started to look at how to apply unit test principles to a microservices architecture and use best strategies to write unit tests.
- It's important to always try to develop unit tests that are as fast, robust, and readable as possible.
- You should know when it's best to use test doubles, following the basic principles covered in the examples.
- The JUnit, AssertJ, and Mockito technologies can be used together to create powerful unit tests.

Component-testing
microservices

This chapter covers

- Introducing the Arquillian testing framework
- Working with Arquillian extensions for RESTful web services and Spring
- Testing resource, domain, and remote components

You've learned about the basic component makeup of a microservice and various basic testing techniques. Now it's time to dig a little deeper into what style of test best suits each component, and how you should implement those tests.

Component tests should be designed to verify the functionality of and between a microservice's internal modules, with one exception: the external public-facing resource component. You want to be sure the public-facing service is accessible to the world in the way that you've planned, so you'll need to define a client-based test that ensures this is the case. A component test shouldn't cross a remote boundary outside the local machine.

You need a good mixture of solitary and sociable tests to cover all the internal interactions of the microservice under test. Tests should use doubles to replace interactions that would normally collaborate with external resources.

We're sure that at some point you've written a test to be sure a piece of code is correct, only to later deploy that code to the staging or production environment and have it fail. That's happened to all of us! It usually has to do with something in the production environment that wasn't apparent at the development stage. Testing components in what we call a *production-near* environment ensures that they react the way you expect. We'll focus on this scenario next: developing production-near testing using the Arquillian test framework.

4.1   *The Arquillian test framework*

Arquillian was originally created for testing applications that run in a Java EE container such as Apache TomEE, JBoss AS, IBM Liberty Profile, Payara, Red Hat WildFly, and many more. The framework has evolved since then to encompass not only Java EE, but also Spring and Docker environments. You can find the full history on the Arquillian website at www.arquillian.org.

> **NOTE** Even though we can often be found evangelizing about Arquillian online or at conferences, we don't want you to think we're promoting this framework because we're being sponsored. We're promoting it because we have, over several years, found it to be the best-of-breed tool for solving many of our personal testing challenges. We hope you'll enjoy learning about it and using it as much as we do.

Arquillian is a framework that can be used for all kinds of software testing. When it comes to testing microservices, Java EE, or Spring Boot, the Arquillian test framework is the best thing since sliced bread. It's important to find a tool that doesn't tie you to a specific product or implementation. If there's one thing we know in software engineering, it's that things change. Arquillian has been designed from the ground up to be as flexible as possible with regard to change, but as simple as possible to use.

The framework can be expanded to meet new demands by using extensions. Thus it can incorporate many other well-known testing components such as Mockito and PowerMock. It doesn't try to compete with these technologies, but rather incorporates their use in a standardized lifecycle.

You already understand unit testing and the `@Test` annotation, so it would be a step in the wrong direction to try to introduce a completely new concept. Arquillian takes what you already know and enriches this common knowledge with new features. As a result, you can be up and running in a few hours, if not minutes.

Before we look at a real test, you should understand the Arquillian test lifecycle. The test itself will look trivial, but under the hood there's a lot going on. It's not essential that you know exactly how it all works, but having a basic understanding may help you in the future if you run into issues. The diagrams in figures 4.1 through 4.6 outline the basic Arquillian automated lifecycle.

NOTE For all intents and purposes, *container* is another word for your application server of choice. Whenever you see the word *container*, just think *application server.*

As previously mentioned, we're not going to tie you down to a specific container. The first phase is to select the container that will be used for the current test (figure 4.1). You can run tests against several containers at the same time, as we'll discuss in chapter 5.

1 Select a container.

Figure 4.1   Selecting the test container

Either the selected container is started by Arquillian, or you can connect to an existing container (figure 4.2). Connecting to a running container means the test can avoid the startup cost of the container. This will be covered later in this chapter, in section 4.6.1.

2 Start or connect to a container.

   The classes under test need to be deployed to the container in some way. Arquillian knows how to take your test classes and deploy them to the selected container to run the tests. The complexity of this task is hidden by the framework. You can use an extremely powerful tool called *ShrinkWrap* to package your test application as the container expects (figure 4.3).

Figure 4.2   Activating the container environment

3 Package the test archive, and deploy it to the container.

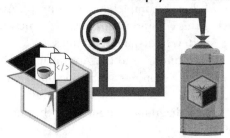

Figure 4.3   Packaging the test application using ShrinkWrap, and deploying to the container

④ Run tests in the container.

Figure 4.4   The deployed test
application runs in the container.

Once ShrinkWrap has packaged your test and deployed it, the tests are run against the container (figure 4.4). Many elements belonging to the test environment are proxied and can be accessed from a local context using CDI. You'll see this extremely powerful feature in action shortly.

⑤ Capture and report the test results.

As the tests run, the results need to be captured and collected. Again, the framework hides this complexity from you and works hand in hand with the common unit test you're familiar with already. The IDE or build environment displays the results in the exact same fashion as a normal test (figure 4.5).

Figure 4.5   Capturing the results and returning them to the test environment

Once all the tests are complete, the resources used throughout the test cycle are disposed of safely (figure 4.6). This may include shutting down the application server, databases, and other remote connections used during the test.

⑥ Undeploy the test archive, and stop or disconnect from the container.

Figure 4.6   Cleaning up resources and shutting down the container

WARNING If the container is started by Arquillian and a test suffers a catastrophic failure, be aware that the server may be left running as a dangling process. This usually manifests itself as a port conflict on the next test run. If this happens, you'll need to locate the errant container process and terminate it manually.

4.2 Introducing the @RunWith(Arquillian.class) annotation

We'll introduce several concepts in this chapter, because they go hand in hand: *build-script* dependencies, the `@RunWith(Arquillian.class)` annotation, and the *arquillian.xml* configuration file. For now, keep in mind that although the Arquillian configuration file is optional to the test, you may eventually need to customize the internally configured default settings. This will become clear after you read this chapter; don't worry just yet about how the container is configured or what build-script modifications are required.

> **NOTE** In this example, we left the `imports` in place so you can see the relevant namespaces. In later examples, we omit most of these for the sake of brevity. All the source code for the demo application is available with the book as a reference; see www.manning.com/books/testing-java-microservices.

The following listing shows a simple Arquillian test (code/game/src/test/java/book/games/arquillian/ArquillianBasicTest.java).

Listing 4.1 Arquillian test

```
package book.games.arquillian;

import book.games.boundary.Games;
import book.games.boundary.IgdbGateway;
import book.games.control.GamesService;
import book.games.entity.Game;
import book.games.entity.ReleaseDate;
import book.games.entity.SearchResult;
import org.jboss.arquillian.container.test.api.Deployment;
import org.jboss.arquillian.junit.Arquillian;
import org.jboss.shrinkwrap.api.ShrinkWrap;
import org.jboss.shrinkwrap.api.asset.EmptyAsset;
import org.jboss.shrinkwrap.api.spec.WebArchive;
import org.junit.Assert;
import org.junit.Test;
import org.junit.runner.RunWith;

import javax.ejb.EJB;
import javax.inject.Inject;
import javax.persistence.EntityManager;
import javax.persistence.PersistenceContext;

@RunWith(Arquillian.class)              ◁──────  Defines this as an
public class ArquillianBasicTest {               Arquillian test

    @Deployment
    public static WebArchive createDeployment() {

        //return ShrinkWrap.create(JavaArchive.class                 Builds an
        //return ShrinkWrap.create(EnterpriseArchive.class           application
        return ShrinkWrap.create(WebArchive.class,                   archive
            ArquillianBasicTest.class.getName() + ".war")
```

Defines the deployment

Adds test-
persistence.xml
to enable JPA

Generates and adds
a beans.xml file to
switch on CDI

```
        .addClasses(IgdbGateway.class, GamesService.class,
            SearchResult.class, Games.class, Game
                .class, ReleaseDate.class)
        .addAsResource("test-persistence.xml",
            "META-INF/persistence.xml")

        .addAsWebInfResource(EmptyAsset.INSTANCE,
            "beans" + ".xml");
    }

    @Inject
    private GamesService service;

    @EJB
    private Games games;

    @PersistenceContext
    private EntityManager em;

    @Test
    public void test() {
        Assert.assertNotNull(this.service);
        Assert.assertNotNull(this.games);
        Assert.assertNotNull(this.em);
    }
}
```

Builds an
application
archive

**Injects the runtime instance of the
GamesService bean into the test class**

**Injects the transaction-aware Games
EJB instance into the test class**

**Injects the runtime JPA EntityManager
instance into the test class at runtime**

Indicates that
the method is
a test

**Asserts to
demonstrate that the
injections worked**

Let's go through all the elements required to build up this Arquillian test. The following steps correspond to the annotations in listing 4.1:

1   You define this test class as an Arquillian test and inform JUnit that there's some
    wiring to do before any test runs.

2   @Deployment defines a deployment of everything you need for the test to run
    in the container. This is the shrink-wrapped application to be physically
    deployed to the container. The defining method must be static.

3   Build an application archive using ShrinkWrap. This may look a little confus-
    ing, but section 4.3 discusses how to use ShrinkWrap to build a deployment
    archive. Here, you're building a WAR file, so ignore the comments. You add
    only the classes that make up the test; the application may be much larger.

4   Add a copy of test-persistence.xml to the application under the META-INF
    directory, to enable JPA. test-persistence.xml resides in the project's
    test/resources directory. It will be copied to the automatically created directory
    and renamed persistence.xml. Your tests may not require persistence, but it's
    easy to add resources here.

5   Generate and add an empty beans.xml file to the archive WEB-INF directory to
    switch on CDI (contexts and dependency injection—EE6). EmptyAsset
    .INSTANCE tells ShrinkWrap to create an empty file, but in step 4 you saw how
    you can add a local file.

6   Inject the runtime instance of the GamesService bean via CDI into the test class when JUnit runs the test. You can call this instance from within the test environment just as you would from your application. How cool is that? This is where you get your first taste of how powerful the Arquillian framework is.

7   Inject the transaction-aware Games EJB instance into the test class at runtime. Similar to CDI, injecting container-hosted EJBs directly into the test class gives you full access to the runtime bean.

8   Inject the runtime JPA `EntityManager` instance into the test class at runtime. This example allows direct access to the application persistence layer from within the test.

9   The usual @Test annotation denotes that the method is to be a test. Several of the previous steps are obviously optional, such as CDI and JPA, and are provided to demonstrate some of what to expect from Arquillian.

10 Simple asserts demonstrate that the injections worked.

Imagine how thorough your microservice tests can now be in a few lines of code. As you can see, adding the `@RunWith(Arquillian.class)`, `@Deployment`, and `@Test` annotations creates a very empowered test environment.

Even if your application is a microservice, it's fair to say that the deployment is unlikely to consist of only a few classes. In this basic test, you add classes individually—and that would be tedious in a larger application. The next section delves into the power of ShrinkWrap; it will enable you to add literally anything you're ever likely to need in your archive—and more!

4.3   *The ShrinkWrap utility class*

Like many components in the Arquillian universe, ShrinkWrap evolved from a basic need into a powerful tool in its own right. Early in the development of Arquillian, it became obvious that a tool was required to build a Java archive containing all the desired dependencies for the test, and also a means to deploy that archive to the application server.

Relying on the build process for the application wouldn't work. The build process could be slow, the resulting deployable archive could be large, and integration with each possible build process would be exceptionally difficult, if not impossible. Arquillian needed something easier, faster, and more isolated. ShrinkWrap achieves this by being the manager of a virtual filesystem that can export as a Java archive. All the possible entry types of that archive are modeled and exposed to you, so you can build up any type of archive containing anything you need for the test.

We're sure you're familiar with the various archive formats common to web deployments, including Java archive (JAR), web archive (WAR), enterprise archive (EAR), and Roshal archive (RAR) files. ShrinkWrap understands these formats exceptionally well, but it can build *any* zip-based archive.

The idea is to take your application and break it down into the smallest possible archive format required to achieve your test goal:

Creates a simple JAR file, and adds a single class

```
Archive jar = ShrinkWrap.create(JavaArchive.class, "service-provider.jar")
    .addClass(MyService.class);
```

```
WebArchive war = ShrinkWrap.create(WebArchive.class, "web-library.war")
    .addClass(MyResource.class)
    .addAsLibrary(jar);
```
Creates a more complex WAR
file format, and adds a JAR file

```
EnterpriseArchive ear = ShrinkWrap
    .create(EnterpriseArchive.class, "application.ear")
    .addAsModule(war);
```
Creates an EAR file, and adds a WAR file

For the purposes of Arquillian, ShrinkWrap is the library used to create *microdeployments* for tests to run against. You could almost call these microdeployments microservices, because this is essentially what they are. But ShrinkWrap can do more and can also be used as a standalone utility. That would be beyond the scope of this book, so we won't cover it; feel free to do some research if you want to learn more (http://arquillian.org/modules/shrinkwrap-shrinkwrap/).

ShrinkWrap essentially manages an in-memory representation of a Java archive, whatever the format. That representation can be modified by adding or removing entries through a powerful API. After the archive is built to your requirements, it can be handed off to Arquillian for deployment to the container. We'll cover adding the required dependencies in section 4.5.1, but it's important to understand what you'll be adding, and why, before you get to that stage.

4.3.1 Building an archive with ShrinkWrap

Creating an archive is simple. You create an empty archive using the static `create()` method of the `org.jboss.shrinkwrap.api.ShrinkWrap` class:

```
Archive jar = ShrinkWrap.create(GenericArchive.class, "my-first-archive.jar");
```

Of course, all this does is create an empty archive with a name, but you've created your first ShrinkWrap archive. Congratulations!

Next, you'll want to add more assets to the archive. Before you do that, you might find this snippet useful, to help you see the contents of the archive during development:

```
System.out.println(jar.toString());
// OUTPUT: my-first-archive.jar: 0 assets
System.out.println(jar.toString(true));
// OUTPUT: my-first-archive.jar:
```
Using toString() is an easy way to
see what your archive contains.
This is a plain Java toString call.

Other forms of toString() can be used,
as well. Use your IDE to discover more.

4.3.2 Adding content to the ShrinkWrap archive

A `GenericArchive` doesn't do much in the way of adding assets to an archive. But ShrinkWrap can create much more than a simple `GenericArchive`!

All you need to do to create a different kind of archive is pass the subclass of Archive you wish to create in the method. When a more specific subtype is used, many more options are available for adding content to the archive.

For example, with a JAR, you can add classes, packages, META-INF resources, and so on. The other types have similar additions: a WAR has methods to add web content, libraries, and web.xml. An EAR can add modules, application resources, and application.xml, as well as libraries and manifest resources. You can learn more by exploring the ShrinkWrap API.

You'll notice that many of these methods have multiple overrides. You may not use all the methods, but each has its purpose. If you find yourself doing something that feels like it could be easier, look at the method overrides you don't often use—something may be available to make your task easier.

The first thing you'll want to do with an archive is add classes to it:

```
ShrinkWrap.create(WebArchive.class, "my-first-archive.jar").
add
addAsDirectories
addAsDirectory
addAsLibraries
addAsLibrary
addAsManifestResource
addAsManifestResources
addAsResource
addAsResources
addAsServiceProvider
addAsServiceProviderAndClasses
addAsWebInfResource
addAsWebInfResources
addAsWebResource          All the add methods are intuitive,
addAsWebResources         but you'll probably want to add
addClass          ◁────┘  classes.
addClasses
addDefaultPackage
addHandlers
addManifest               You may also want
addPackage        ◁────┘  to add packages.
addPackages
...
```

NOTE The plural add methods are vararg versions of the singular versions and can be used to add multiple items at a time: for example, addClasses and addPackages.

The following is an example of using the *singular* addClass method:

```
Archive jar = ShrinkWrap.create(JavaArchive.class, "my.jar").addClass
➥ (HelloWorld.class);

System.out.println(jar.toString(true));
/*
```

```
OUTPUT:
my.jar:
/org/
/org/example/
/org/example/shrinkwrap/
/org/example/shrinkwrap/HelloWorld.class
*/
```

You add the name here: my.jar. If you don't add a name, a name will be generated in the format UUID.jar, so we suggest using descriptive names from the start. They make more sense when you're visually scanning the console output or log files.

> **TIP** Use the test-class name as part of the archive name: this.getClass().get-Name() + .jar. This will help to visually separate test archives in the console output.

Sometimes it's more convenient to add an entire namespace package to the archive. As you should expect by now, there's a simple call for this—addPackages:

```
Archive jar = ShrinkWrap.create(JavaArchive.class, "my.jar")
    .addPackages(true, "org.example");            ◁

System.out.println(jar.toString(true));
/*
package-jar.jar:
/org/
/org/example/
/org/example/shrinkwrap/
/org/example/shrinkwrap/util/
/org/example/shrinkwrap/util/StringUtils.class
/org/example/shrinkwrap/GoodbyeWorld.class
/org/example/shrinkwrap/ShrinkWrapUsage.class
/org/example/shrinkwrap/HelloWorld.class
*/
```

The most useful version of this method, where true denotes a recursive call that adds all child packages and classes

4.3.3 Adding resources

You'll invariably need to know how to add resources to an archive. These include things like the following:

- A beans.xml file for CDI
- A persistence.xml file for JPA
- Service implementations
- Tag-library descriptors
- Other common configuration files

Here's how to add these items to the archive:

Adds the test resource test-persistence.xml to the archive under META-INF/persistence.xml

```
Archive jar = ShrinkWrap.create(JavaArchive.class, "my.jar")
    .addPackages(true, "org.example")
    .addAsResource("test-persistence.xml", "META-INF/persistence.xml")  ◁
```

```
            .addAsWebInfResource(EmptyAsset.INSTANCE, "beans.xml");
```

Creates an empty file asset, and adds it to the archive as beans.xml

```
//Alternative methods...

URL persistenceXml = getClass().getClassLoader()
    .getResource("test-persistence.xml");
```

Alternative method of locating and adding a resource from the test classpath

```
jar.addAsResource(persistenceXml
    , new BasicPath("META-INF/persistence.xml"));
```

Adds the alternative resource to the archive using a BasicPath descriptor

Both methods produce the same output:

```
System.out.println(jar.toString(true));
/*
my.jar:
/META-INF/
/META-INF/beans.xml
/META-INF/persistence.xml
*/
```

As you can see, ShrinkWrap has many ways to achieve the same result. You don't have to know how to use all of these methods right now, but it's nice to know that there's nearly always a simple way to do whatever you want.

4.3.4   *Adding libraries and dependencies*

Your application is likely to require additional libraries and third-party dependencies, such as the Apache Commons Libraries (https://commons.apache.org). Adding a few items to your archive is reasonably concise:

Adds a single class. ShrinkWrap knows where to add this in a WAR file (/WEB-INF/classes/).

Creates a JAR file, in this case an SPI (more about SPIs in the next section)

```
Archive jar = ShrinkWrap.create(JavaArchive.class, "service-provider.jar")
.addClass(CdiExtension.class)
.addAsServiceProvider(Extension.class, CdiExtension.class);

WebArchive war = ShrinkWrap.create(WebArchive.class, "web-library.war")
.addClass(StringUtils.class)
.addAsWebResource(new File("src/main/webapp/images/1.gif")
    , "/images/1.gif")
.addAsLibrary(jar);
```

Adds a standard resource to a defined path

```
System.out.println(war.toString((true)));
/*
web-library.war:
/WEB-INF/
/WEB-INF/lib/
/WEB-INF/lib/service-provider.jar
/WEB-INF/classes/
/WEB-INF/classes/org/
```

Adds the JAR file to a WAR file. Again, ShrinkWrap automatically adds this to the correct path (/WEB-INF/lib/).

```
/WEB-INF/classes/org/example/
/WEB-INF/classes/org/example/shrinkwrap/
/WEB-INF/classes/org/example/shrinkwrap/util/
/WEB-INF/classes/org/example/shrinkwrap/util/StringUtils.class
/images/
/images/1.gif
*/
```

As you'd expect, ShrinkWrap provides simple methods to achieve something complex. But what if your application is far more than just a Hello World example? ShrinkWrap alone isn't going to be enough. That leads us into the next topic.

4.3.5 *Adding complex dependencies with the Maven resolver*

The *Maven resolver* is another powerful utility class that allows you to add heavyweight options to an archive. It's designed to complement what you've already learned about the ShrinkWrap utility class. We'll only touch on what's required for its basic use; you can gain deeper insight at the project's website, https://github.com/shrinkwrap/resolver.

Using the resolver is simple and is best described using an example:

Imports the Maven utility class

Defines the Maven coordinate you want to resolve using the groupId:artifactId:version (GAV) schema

```
import org.jboss.shrinkwrap.resolver.api.maven.Maven;
....
String hibernate = "org.hibernate:hibernate-core:5.2.3.Final";
```

Resolves the defined GAV coordinate

```
File[] files = Maven.resolver().resolve(hibernate)
    .withTransitivity()
    .asFile();
```

Additionally fetches all the transient (related) dependencies for the main artifact

Adds a complete list of dependencies as a File array

```
WebArchive war = ShrinkWrap.create(WebArchive.class, "my.war")
    .addAsLibraries(files);
```

Adds all the dependencies to a WAR archive

The resolver can return more than just a file, if you know the type of the resource. An addition to GAV, you can also specify the package type (P, for archives such as WAR or JAR) and the classifier (C, a user-defined name). Here's a complete list of explicit resource types at the time of writing:

```
Maven.resolver().resolve("G:A:V").withTransitivity()
    .as(File.class);

Maven.resolver().resolve("G:A:V").withTransitivity()
    .as(InputStream.class);

Maven.resolver().resolve("G:A:V").withTransitivity()
    .as(URL.class);

Maven.resolver().resolve("G:A:V").withTransitivity()
    .as(JavaArchive.class);
```

```
Maven.resolver().resolve("G:A:P:V").withoutTransitivity()
    .asSingle(WebArchive.class);

Maven.resolver().resolve("G:A:P:C:V").withTransitivity()
    .as(MavenCoordinate.class);
```

The `MavenCoordinate.class` provides detailed metainformation about the specified artifact. If you're unsure what resources the artifact provides, you can use this class to discover the details.

> **NOTE** You're responsible for closing a retrieved `InputStream` type. The stream is a direct connection to the repository artifact.

As powerful as the resolver is, you may have noticed that there's one small potential drawback: the artifact version number is hardcoded in the GAV coordinate string. For a small number of fixed dependencies, keeping them in sync maybe not be an issue; but if your application is forever evolving, this could be a problem. Not to worry: the API provides a solution. The resolver understands Maven *pom.xml* files (https://maven .apache.org/pom.html). You can import dependencies from any pom.xml file location, so it could be your project POM or one completely separate from your build:

```
Maven.resolver().loadPomFromFile("/path/to/pom.xml")       ◁─┐  Specifies a file path to
                                                              │  the pom.xml to load

.importRuntimeAndTestDependencies()              ◁─────┐

                                                        Defines the scopes you want to import
.resolve().withTransitivity().asFile();      ◁───┐     (there are multiple methods that cover
                                                  │     all the scopes)
                         Resolves the complete list of
                         dependencies as a File array
```

4.3.6 *Adding a service implementation*

Service provider implementations (SPIs, mng.bz/i7QX) are a way of enabling the extension of an application in a standard fashion. ShrinkWrap understands this mechanism and can remove most of the standard boilerplate code required to add a known SPI to your archive.

The various `addAsServiceProvider` methods are handy for getting ShrinkWrap to create the services file for the specified interface and classes. The following code will create the javax.enterprise.inject.spi.Extension file, add the class name of the service to it, and then place the file in the standard META-INF file structure:

```
Archive jar = ShrinkWrap.create(JavaArchive.class, "service-provider.jar")
.addAsServiceProviderAndClasses(Extension.class, CdiExtension.class);   ◁─┐

System.out.println(jar.toString(true));                    Adds the required
/*                                                         structure for an SPI
service-provider.jar:
/javax/
/javax/enterprise/
/javax/enterprise/inject/
```

```
/javax/enterprise/inject/spi/
/javax/enterprise/inject/spi/Extension.class
/org/
/org/example/
/org/example/shrinkwrap/
/org/example/shrinkwrap/CdiExtension.class
/META-INF/
/META-INF/services/
/META-INF/services/javax.enterprise.inject.spi.Extension
*/
```

Sometimes the added interface is provided by the container.

```
Archive jar2 = ShrinkWrap.create(JavaArchive.class, "service-provider-2.jar")
.addClass(CdiExtension.class)
.addAsServiceProvider(Extension.class, CdiExtension.class);
```

```
System.out.println(jar2.toString(true));
/*
service-provider-2.jar:
/org/
/org/example/
/org/example/shrinkwrap/
/org/example/shrinkwrap/CdiExtension.class
/META-INF/
/META-INF/services/
/META-INF/services/javax.enterprise.inject.spi.Extension
*/
```

It's often better to use the addAsServiceProvider method and add the class separately.

Providing both methods for adding an SPI gives you all the flexibility required to add any implementation.

4.4 *Write once and reuse your code*

Now that you understand how to create archives, you may wonder why you should go to all this trouble when your build tool can do it all for you. Aside from the obvious answer—"That's how it's done with Arquillian"—there are a number of good reasons. The most important reason is that Arquillian significantly lowers the barrier to performing integration and functional tests. Even if you chose not to use Arquillian, you'd still need to do the following:

- Create an archive that can be deployed.
- Deploy that archive to a running container/application server.
- Run the tests in the deployed archive.
- Retrieve the results of the tests from the container.
- Undeploy the archive.
- Shut down the container.

Arquillian handles this for you in a transparent fashion. It's trivial to create an abstract base class for all your tests to extend, override, and reuse:

```
public class MyTest extends MyAbstractTest {
    ....
    @Deployment
    public static WebArchive createDeployment() {
        WebArchive w = createMyBaseDeployment();    ◁─┐
        w.addClass(MyExtra.class);
        return w;
    }
    ....
}
```

Calls a static parent or utility method that delivers a ready-made WebArchive to add additional requirements to

This base class generalizes your application, and test classes just need to add the additional requirements. You can even create your own utility class for this purpose.

> **TIP** Most, if not all, applications share common foundations that can be extracted to abstract classes. This is no different when it comes to testing. Identify the code that's common to your testing strategy, and do exactly the same thing—create an abstract test class. This will save you time in the long run.

Your build may help with creating the archive, but you'll need to make sure you have all the testing dependencies added, which your regular build probably doesn't include without considerable extra configuration. Creating these smaller deployments, *microdeployments*, helps isolate the test from other parts of the application. It also helps you think in terms of the smallest testable unit of work.

Microdeployments also allow you to skip the full build, which is both a reason to use them and a side effect. If your full build takes one minute to create the testable archive, that's one additional minute you'll need to run a test! That time can quickly add up while you're testing, especially if you're running tests locally. The side effect is that not only do you skip the build, but, if you're using an incremental compiler, you also skip an implicit compile phase. That can lead to some serious time savings!

4.5   *Build-script modifications*

You now have a good grasp of the elements you add to a basic JUnit test to make an Arquillian test, but where do all these elements come from? You've got it: dependencies!

There are numerous build environments, so it would be almost impossible to cover them all. We use the two most popular systems throughout the example projects: Maven and Gradle. Detailing both of these systems will give you more than enough information to configure any other system, because they're closely linked to the Maven GAV coordinate system and also allow for specifying the packaging and a classifier if required:

```
groupId:artifactId:packaging:classifier:version
```

Arquillian, ShrinkWrap, and Resolver all provide a Maven *bill of materials* (BOM) pom.xml file.[1] A BOM defines all the required dependencies you'll need, including

---

[1] See "Introduction to the Dependency Mechanism," *Apache Maven Project*, (http://mng.bz/OR0F).

version numbers. This eliminates needing a lot of individual dependency declarations. The Arquillian BOM imports the ShrinkWrap and Resolver BOMs, so you only need to include the Arquillian BOM in the <dependencyManagement> section of the project pom.xml.

4.5.1 Defining Maven dependencies

If you're using Maven for your build, adding the dependencies for Arquillian is trivial. Declare the BOM using the import scope in the <dependencyManagement> section of your project pom.xml. You can see in the following listing that a WildFly (http://wildfly.org) BOM is provided. BOMs are useful!

Listing 4.2 code/game/pom.xml: <dependencyManagement>

```
<dependencyManagement>
    <dependencies>
        <dependency>
            <groupId>org.wildfly.swarm</groupId>
            <artifactId>bom</artifactId>
            <version>${version.wildfly.swarm}</version>
            <scope>import</scope>
            <type>pom</type>
        </dependency>
        <dependency>
            <groupId>org.jboss.arquillian</groupId>
            <artifactId>arquillian-bom</artifactId>
            <version>1.1.13.Final</version>
            <scope>import</scope>
            <type>pom</type>
        </dependency>
    </dependencies>
</dependencyManagement>
```

> **NOTE** A BOM is used to define the versions and transient dependencies of specific artifacts that are *likely* to be used in the project. In a multimodule build, <dependencyManagement> should be in the parent pom.xml and serve as a contract for all the child modules. The actual dependencies used are then defined in the <dependencies> section, where the <version> definition is omitted.

You also need to add the Arquillian container adapter and an implementation to the <dependencies> section of your project. This example uses the WildFly container adapter from Red Hat (www.redhat.com), but it can be any adapter implementation you like, such as the Apache TomEE adapter (http://mng.bz/O5fo).

Listing 4.3 code/game/pom.xml: <dependencies>

```
<dependency>
    <groupId>org.jboss.arquillian.junit</groupId>
    <artifactId>arquillian-junit-container</artifactId>
```

```
        <scope>test</scope>
</dependency>
<dependency>
        <groupId>org.wildfly.swarm</groupId>
        <artifactId>arquillian</artifactId>
        <scope>test</scope>
</dependency>
```

> **TIP** The mere fact that you now have an adapter implementation on the test classpath is enough for Arquillian to find and use it. It's possible to define multiple implementations using Maven build profiles—we'll discuss this further in chapter 5.

You'll always be able to find the adapter for your application server by searching the internet for "[container name]+arquillian." Note that the defined `<scope>` is `test`, because you should only be using Arquillian for testing.

> **NOTE** The `arquillian-junit-container` artifact pulls in ShrinkWrap and resolvers as transient dependencies. If you want to use ShrinkWrap or resolvers in your application, you need to define them individually, using the required scope.

4.5.2   *Defining Gradle dependencies*

Gradle doesn't understand the concept of a BOM out of the box. Fortunately, a few plugins enable this feature—otherwise, you'd have to add all the dependencies individually. You still have to add a few more dependency definitions, but the BOM declares all the versions and transient dependencies for you.

> **NOTE** We've formatted long coordinate lines for the book, so please replace `o.j.s` with `org.jboss.shrinkwrap`, `o.j.a` with `org.jboss.arquillian`, and `o.g` with `org.glassfish`. If in doubt, check the example code.

The following listing shows an example build.gradle file taken from the aggregator-service application (code/aggregator/build.gradle).

> **Listing 4.4   Example build.gradle file**

**Defines the dependency-management plugin
that allows you to use Maven BOM imports**

```
plugins {
    id "io.spring.dependency-management" version "0.6.1.RELEASE"
}
```

**Uses the plugin to import the Arquillian,
ShrinkWrap, and resolver dependencies**

```
dependencyManagement {
    imports {
        mavenBom 'o.j.a:arquillian-bom:1.1.13.Final'
        mavenBom 'o.j.s:shrinkwrap-bom:1.2.6'
        mavenBom 'o.j.s.resolver:shrinkwrap-resolver-bom:2.2.4'
    }
}
```

Adds the Arquillian dependency. Because the BOM defines all the required version numbers, you don't need to include them here (unless an override is desired).

```
apply plugin: 'war'

group = 'org.gamer'
version = '1.0-SNAPSHOT'
war.archiveName = "gameaggregatorservice.war"

sourceCompatibility = 1.8
targetCompatibility = 1.8

dependencies {

    testCompile 'junit:junit:4.12'

    testCompile group: 'o.j.a.junit',name: 'arquillian-junit-container'

    testCompile 'o.j.a.container:arquillian-tomcat-embedded-8:1.0.0'

    testCompile 'o.j.s:shrinkwrap-api'
    testCompile 'o.j.s:shrinkwrap-spi'
    testCompile 'o.j.s:shrinkwrap-impl-base'

    testCompile 'o.j.s.resolver:shrinkwrap-resolver-api'
    testCompile 'o.j.s.resolver:shrinkwrap-resolver-spi'
    testCompile 'o.j.s.resolver:shrinkwrap-resolver-api-maven'
    testCompile 'o.j.s.resolver:shrinkwrap-resolver-spi-maven'
    testCompile 'o.j.s.resolver:shrinkwrap-resolver-api-maven-archive'
    testCompile 'o.j.s.resolver:shrinkwrap-resolver-impl-maven'
    testCompile 'o.j.s.resolver:shrinkwrap-resolver-impl-maven-archive'

    compile 'o.g.jersey.containers:jersey-container-servlet:2.22.2'
    compile 'o.g.jersey.core:jersey-client:2.22.2'
    compile 'o.g:javax.json:1.0.4'
    compile 'o.g:jsonp-jaxrs:1.0'
}
```

Declares all the dependencies the application requires

Adds any container implementation. Here, you use an embedded Apache Tomcat container.

Adds the ShrinkWrap dependencies declared in the BOM

Adds the Resolver dependencies declared in the BOM

4.6 Overriding the default Arquillian configuration

We've now covered all the elements required to run a standard Arquillian unit test. These include using required annotations, packaging and deploying an application archive, and including all the required dependencies in the build scripts. As indicated at the beginning of the chapter, all of this relies on an as-yet-unexposed default configuration.

There may come a time when the default configuration requires customization. For example, you may need to start the container on a different port than the default one (to avoid port conflicts) or in HTTPS mode (to test security), or specify options like a key-store file.

Arquillian checks for configuration settings in a file named arquillian.xml in the root of your classpath. If this file exists, it's loaded; otherwise, default values are used. Until now, Arquillian has been using a default set of configuration options transparently in the background. These default options are supplied by the vendor-specific container-adapter implementation found on the classpath.

The usual location for this file in a typical Maven project is [project]/src/test/resources/arquillian.xml. Files in this test resources directory are only available on the test classpath during runtime, which is usually the required scenario. The following listing shows an example.

Listing 4.5   Example arquillian.xml file with two containers

```
<?xml version="1.0" encoding="UTF-8"?>
<arquillian>

    <!-- Configuration of container one -->
    <container qualifier="widlfly-remote">
        <configuration>
        <property name="javaVmArguments">
            -Dprop=val
        </property>
        </configuration>
    </container>

    <!-- Configuration of container two -->
    <container qualifier="widlfly-managed" default="true">
        <configuration>
        <property name="javaVmArguments">
            -Dprop=val
        </configuration>
    </container>
</arquillian>
```

Following the standard XML declaration comes <arquillian>, the body definition with schema references.

It's common to have only one <container qualifier="[name]">; we'll explain why there are two here in a moment.

The second container, flagged as the default

Container property definition—there can be multiple properties

This configuration is XML, so there are no surprises in the layout. Let's take a deeper look at the most important configuration options.

NOTE   Because each container is vendor specific, some of the contents of the arquillian.xml file will have vendor-specific options. Use the information in listing 4.5 as an example, but ensure that you use the correct options for your chosen container. We'll highlight the areas that require attention throughout this section.

4.6.1   *The container definition*

In section 4.5.1, you learned how to add a default container adapter to the test classpath using the Maven coordinates. <container qualifier="[name]"> is where you make a declaration for a specific runtime container that you'll test against. If Arquillian finds only one container definition, it will always be used as the default.

We'll discuss using multiple containers in depth in chapter 7. In brief, if multiple container definitions exist, Arquillian looks for two things:

- A container with a `default="true"` attribute. This container will be used as the default—that makes sense.
- The system property `arquillian.launch`, with the name of the container to use for the current runtime.

The `arquillian.launch` system property can be defined or overridden using Maven profiles.

4.6.2 Specifying container properties

A container property is straightforward: `<property name="[name]">[value]</property>`. You can add any number of container properties to the `<configuration>` element. As we warned earlier in the chapter, these properties are vendor specific.

The most common use for container properties is to define a server port to bind to, to prevent conflicts. Some providers allow a random port, which is a cool feature because it allows tests to run in parallel. The example in listing 4.5 set a system property `javaVmArguments` for both WildFly container definitions. You'll see the relevance of this later in this section. As you can imagine, listing all the available properties for all the available container implementations here would be impossible. Table 4.1 gives a few; please take the time to find the properties that are available for your container of choice.

Table 4.1   Common containers and properties

Container	Property	Value
Apache TomEE	`httpPort`	-1 (Random)
Apache TomEE	`stopPort`	-1 (Random)
WildFly	`serverConfig`	server.xml (File)
GlassFish	`bindHttpPort`	[port]

TIP When you're using an embedded container (remote container adapters are always named as such), you can also set system properties via `maven-surefire-plugin`. See http://mng.bz/cI7V.

4.7 Using Arquillian REST extensions

REST web services are now commonplace, and it's increasingly unlikely that a web-based or microservice application isn't using this technology today. That doesn't mean a microservice can't use a different protocol (far from it); but that would be an edge case and specific to a business scope. Here, we'll focus on REST over HTTP/S, and how Arquillian can lighten the load when you're building a test environment.

Two modules are available. The REST client extension is designed to be used in a black-box test environment: the client is completely isolated from the application and sees only the endpoints as a real remote client. The Warp REST module is for much more complex tests, where you want to intercept incoming and outgoing REST requests and responses. The next two sections cover these modules.

4.7.1   *The Arquillian REST client extension*

Sometimes you need to test a REST application in a black-box environment, the test acting as if it were a real client, to ensure that your endpoint is working as expected when called by an external source. When you know the interface (the contract) and you have well-defined input, and you also know what results you expect to get from a resource call, then the Arquillian REST client extension will be useful to you. Let's look at a concise example (code/comments/src/test/java/book/comments/boundary/CommentsResourceTest.java).

Listing 4.6   Using the Arquillian REST client extension

The now all-too-familiar
@RunWith(Arquillian.class) testing annotation

When you know that all the tests
in a class will act as black-box
clients, use the testable = false
option, rather than
@RunAsClient. The packaging
here adds the REST
CommentsResource.class and
required dependencies.

```
@RunWith(Arquillian.class)          <-
public class CommentsResourceTest {

    @Deployment(testable = false)                 <-
    public static WebArchive createDeployment() {

        final WebArchive webArchive = ShrinkWrap
            .create(WebArchive.class)
            .addPackage(CommentsResource.class.getPackage())
            .addClass(MongoClientProvider.class)
            .addAsWebInfResource("test-resources.xml","resources.xml")
            .addAsWebInfResource(EmptyAsset.INSTANCE, "beans.xml")
            .addAsLibraries(Maven.resolver()
                .resolve("org.mongodb:mongodb-driver:3.2.2")
                .withTransitivity().as(JavaArchive.class));

        System.out.println("webArchive = " +
        webArchive.toString(true));

        return webArchive;
    }

    @Test
    public void getCommentsOfGivenGame(
        @ArquillianResteasyResource final CommentsResource resource)   <-
            throws Exception {

        Assert.assertNotNull(resource);

        final Response game = resource.getCommentsOfGivenGame(1);     <-
        Assert.assertNotNull(game);
    }
}
```

Injects the CommentsResource.class
REST resource interface directly into
the test method using the
@ArquillianResteasyResource
annotation

Uses the CommentsResource.class REST
resource interface directly in the test method

If you've ever used the JAX-RS `ClientBuilder` in a REST-based test, then it should be obvious here how much boilerplate has been replaced by using the `@Arquillian-ResteasyResource` annotation. It's fair to say that this extension has removed a significant amount of code required to access the endpoint. Under the hood, real HTTP requests and responses are performed, but the interface now acts as a simplified proxy.

> **TIP** You'll find several tests in the book's code that use the JAX-RS `ClientBuilder` to test resources. For finer testing, it's more useful than `@ArquillianResteasyResource`. You can decide which path to follow—both have their merits.

If you want to use the REST extension in your tests, you need to add the following dependencies to your build script:

```
org.jboss.arquillian.extension:arquillian-rest-client-api:1.0.0.Alpha4
org.jboss.arquillian.extension:arquillian-rest-client-impl-3x:1.0.0.Alpha4
```

> **NOTE** At the time of writing, we used the latest available release. It was flagged as an alpha version, but it's very stable. Please check for and use the latest release where possible.

4.7.2 The Warp REST extension

The Arquillian Warp REST extension allows you to test your RESTful applications on the server side. This extension provides utilities for intercepting the state of the executing service, and provides the state in container tests that may be executed directly before or after the service is invoked. It supports JAX-RS major versions including 1.1 and 2.0 and the most popular implementations.

This topic is advanced and requires a good understanding of the underlying protocol to be useful. The following test adds an inspection that fires after the endpoint is invoked (code/comments/src/test/java/book/comments/boundary/CommentsWarpTest.java). Internally, a REST endpoint is invoked by a servlet that understands the client/server protocol. The Warp annotations `@AfterServlet` and `@BeforeServlet` can be used on methods to gain access to the current protocol states.

Listing 4.7 Adding an inspection after an endpoint

```
@WarpTest                              ◁──┐  Flags the test class as a
@RunWith(Arquillian.class)                 │  Warp-enabled test using the
public class CommentsWarpTest {            │  @WarpTest annotation

    @BeforeClass
    public static void beforeClass() {                          ◁──┐  Ensures that the
        RegisterBuiltin.register(ResteasyProviderFactory            │  REST environment
            .getInstance());                                        │  is available for the
    }                                                               │  test class
```

```
        @Deployment
        @OverProtocol("Servlet 3.0")
        public static WebArchive createDeployment() {
            final WebArchive webArchive = ShrinkWrap.create(WebArchive
                    .class).addPackage(CommentsResource.class
                    .getPackage()).addClass(MongoClientProvider.class)
                    .addAsWebInfResource("test-resources.xml",
                        "resources.xml").addAsWebInfResource
                        (EmptyAsset.INSTANCE, "beans.xml")
                    .addAsLibraries(Maven.resolver().resolve("org" +
                        ".mongodb:mongodb-driver:3.2.2")
                        .withTransitivity().as(JavaArchive.class));

            System.out.println("webArchive = " + webArchive.toString
                    (true));

            return webArchive;
        }

        private CommentsResource resource;

        @ArquillianResource
        private URL contextPath;

        @Before
        public void before() {
            final ResteasyClient client = new ResteasyClientBuilder()
                    .build();
            final ResteasyWebTarget target = client.target(contextPath
                    .toExternalForm());
            resource = target.proxy(CommentsResource.class);
        }

        @Test
        @RunAsClient
        public void getCommentsOfGivenGame() {

            Warp.initiate(() -> {

                final Response commentsOfGivenGame = resource
                        .getCommentsOfGivenGame(1);
                Assert.assertNotNull(commentsOfGivenGame);

            }).inspect(new Inspection() {

                private static final long serialVersionUID = 1L;

                @ArquillianResource
                private RestContext restContext;

                @AfterServlet
                public void testGetCommentsOfGivenGame() {
```

Defines the underlying protocol using the @OverProtocol annotation

Injects the REST context path that's used to access the server

Configures the REST client proxy to the server resource

Isolates the test method in a black-box environment using the @RunAsClient annotation

Initiates the REST call and adds an inspection

Indicates that the method should be called directly after the servlet call

Provides the REST call context to access protocol information

```
                    assertEquals(HttpMethod.GET, restContext
                        .getHttpRequest().getMethod());
                    assertEquals(200, restContext.getHttpResponse()
                        .getStatusCode());
                    assertEquals("application/json", restContext
                        .getHttpResponse().getContentType());
                    assertNotNull(restContext.getHttpResponse()
                        .getEntity());
                }
            });
        }
    }
```

> Access to protocol states allows testing.

If you want to use the REST Warp extension in your tests, you need to add the following dependencies to your build script:

```
org.jboss.arquillian.extension:arquillian-warp-api:[version]
org.jboss.arquillian.extension:arquillian-rest-warp-impl-jaxrs-[version]
```

> **NOTE** As noted earlier, at the time of writing, we used the latest available release in the code. Even though this was flagged as an alpha version, it's very stable for testing. Please check for and use the latest release where possible.

4.8 Testing Spring applications using Arquillian

One of the key benefits of the microservices architecture that we mentioned in chapter 1 is the ability to delegate service development to multiple teams, using multiple technologies. The only important aspect in a multitechnology environment is that the resource component is accessible using a defined protocol, in this case REST over HTTP. How the actual service is implemented is irrelevant from a team-to-team perspective. To demonstrate this principle, the video service in the book's demo application is a Spring Boot application. You still need to test this application just like any other.

Arquillian provides a Spring v4+ extension that can be used to aid testing.

4.8.1 The Arquillian Spring Framework extension

The Spring Framework extension works in a fashion similar to @SpringJUnit4Class-Runner, but it remains within the Arquillian test-environment context and has less boilerplate code to get started writing tests. If you're already familiar with Spring JUnit integration, we suggest taking a look at this approach and making an educated evaluation of its use before dismissing it. If you aren't, then this is likely to be the easiest approach for you to start with, because the setup is less verbose than the Spring runner. The extension supports the following implementations:

- Injecting Spring beans into test classes
- Configuring from both XML- and Java-based configs

- Injecting beans configured in web applications (for example, `DispatcherServ-let`) for tests annotated with `@SpringWebConfiguration`
- Support for both Spring (`@Autowired`, `@Qualifier`, `@Required`) and JSR 330 (`@Inject`, `@Named`) annotations
- Support for bean initialization (`@PostConstruct`)
- Autopackaging the `spring-context` and `spring-web` artifacts

To add the Spring extension to your project, you need to add the following artifacts to your build script (using the latest versions from http://arquillian.org/modules/spring-extension):

```
                                          ┌─  Required base artifact
<dependency>                          ◁──┘
    <groupId>org.jboss.arquillian.extension</groupId>
    <artifactId>arquillian-service-integration-spring-inject</artifactId>
    <version>${arquillian.spring.version}</version>
    <scope>test</scope>                        Optional artifact, required
</dependency>                                  when using annotation-
<dependency>                            ◁──┐   based configuration
    <groupId>org.jboss.arquillian.extension</groupId>  │ (recommended)
    <artifactId>arquillian-service-integration-spring-javaconfig</artifactId>
    <version>${arquillian.spring.version}</version>
    <scope>test</scope>
</dependency>
```

We're not going to look at the file-based configuration, because we're sure even the most hardcore Spring gurus are now using annotation-based configuration. Let's look at a basic test that contains all the relevant elements (code/video/i-tests/src/test/java/book/video/YoutubeVideosArquillianTest.java).

Listing 4.8   Using the Spring Framework extension

```
                                    Lists all the classes that produce @Bean implementations
                                    (the Spring equivalent of the Java EE @Produces annotation)
@RunWith(Arquillian.class)
@SpringAnnotationConfiguration(classes =
        {YoutubeVideosArquillianTest.class, ControllerConfiguration
                .class, ThreadExecutorConfiguration.class})
@Configuration
public class YoutubeVideosArquillianTest {       A typical @Bean producer—the perfect
                                                 place to create a mock, if required
    @Bean                               ◁──┘
    public JedisConnectionFactory jedisConnectionFactory() {
        final JedisConnectionFactory jcf = new
                JedisConnectionFactory();
        jcf.setHostName("localhost");
        return jcf;
    }

    @Primary
    @Bean
    public YouTubeVideos getYouTubeVideos() {
```

```
        return new YouTubeVideos();
    }
                                    ┌─── The usual Arquillian deployment archive
    @Deployment              ◁──┘
    public static JavaArchive createTestArchive() {
        return ShrinkWrap.create(JavaArchive.class, "spring-test" +
                ".jar").addClasses(YouTubeVideos.class);
    }
                                 ┌── Injects an implementation using
                                 │   the @Autowired annotation
    @Autowired              ◁──┘
    private YouTubeVideos youtubeVideos;
                                      ┌── Standard test that can use
                                      │   the injected resources
    @Test                        ◁──┘
    public void test() {
        Assert.assertNotNull(this.youtubeVideos);
    }

}
```

That covers all you need to know about testing a standard Spring application. There are a few more annotations covering more-advanced topics that are outside the scope of this book and border on requiring a Spring tutorial; visit the extension website at mng.bz/Y4J8 to get a better understanding of what's available. The following annotations are supported and will be familiar to Spring developers:

- `@SpringWebConfiguration`—For MVC testing
- `@EnableWebMvc`—Also for MVC testing
- `@ComponentScan`—Scanning for `@Component`-annotated beans, rather than `@Bean` producers
- `@OverProtocol`—For defining the underlying protocol

4.8.2 *Testing Spring Boot applications*

Spring Boot is a technology that's rapidly growing in popularity. At the time of writing, there's only experimental Arquillian integration with the Spring Framework extension for a Spring Boot–based application.

It would be possible to create a test that ignores or sidesteps the defining `@Spring-BootApplication` annotation, but that would be cheating. For now, it's helpful to see and understand how you can test a Spring Boot application that's intended to run as a microservice. The application consists of a `Main` class that's annotated with `@Spring-BootApplication`. This clearly denotes the beginning of a Spring Boot application, and it fires up classpath scanning and discovery. That's what we mean by sidestepping—you could create an Arquillian test that emulates the automatic configuration that's performed by `@SpringBootApplication`. We'll leave that as an exercise for experienced Spring developers.

Here's the `Main` class used in the book's video service project.

Listing 4.9   code/video/src/main/java/book/video/Main.java

```java
package book.video;

import org.springframework.boot.actuate.system
        .ApplicationPidFileWriter;
import org.springframework.boot.autoconfigure.SpringBootApplication;
import org.springframework.boot.builder.SpringApplicationBuilder;
import org.springframework.scheduling.annotation.EnableAsync;

import java.util.HashMap;
import java.util.Map;

@SpringBootApplication          ⟵   Denotes the Main class as a—
@EnableAsync                         you guessed it—Spring Boot
public class Main {                  application

    public static void main(final String[] args) {   ⟵   A standard static void main
                                                           method for a runnable Java
        final Map<String, Object> map = new HashMap<>();   application class
        map.put("endpoints.shutdown.enabled", true);
        map.put("endpoints.shutdown.sensitive", false);

        new SpringApplicationBuilder(Main.class).listeners(new
                ApplicationPidFileWriter("./video.pid"))
                .logStartupInfo(true).properties(map).run(args);
    }
}
```

The next step is to tell the test class where to find the Main class. This is done by adding the @SpringApplicationConfiguration that points to the class in hand (code/video/i-tests/src/test/java/book/video/YoutubeVideosTest.java).

Listing 4.10   Adding @SpringApplicationConfiguration

```java
@RunWith(SpringJUnit4ClassRunner.class)           ⟵   Initializes the unit test using
@SpringBootTest(classes = {Main.class})           ⟵       the Spring JUnit class, rather
public class YoutubeVideosTest {                          than Arquillian

    private static RedisServer redisServer;           Points to the Spring Boot
                                                       application class, Main.java
    @BeforeClass
    public static void beforeClass() throws Exception {
        redisServer = new RedisServer();
        redisServer.start();
    }

    @AfterClass
    public static void afterClass() {
        redisServer.stop();
    }

    @Rule
```

Injects a bean class

```
                  public RedisRule redisRule
                      = new RedisRule(newManagedRedisConfiguration().build());

               @Autowired
               YouTubeVideos youtubeVideos;

               @Test
               @UsingDataSet(loadStrategy = LoadStrategyEnum.DELETE_ALL)
               @ShouldMatchDataSet(location = "expected-videos.json")
               public void shouldCacheGamesInRedis() {
                   youtubeVideos.createYouTubeLinks("123", Collections
                           .singletonList("https://www.youtube.com/embed/7889"));
               }
           }
```

From this point on, the test will work exactly as you'd expect.

4.9 *More-complex Arquillian test examples*

The next few sections take a quick look at some example tests that build on everything we've just explained. If you see something that hasn't been discussed yet, don't worry: make note of it, and see if you can work out what it does by reading the code. Arquillian tries to be as easy to understand as possible, but having a wealth of plugins can sometimes increase the learning curve. The following chapters introduce these advanced plugin features along the way.

4.9.1 *Testing the remote component*

The remote component is where your microservice domain component touches anything that could be considered a remote resource. This wouldn't include something as complex as a remote database, because that dwells in the persistence scope and is masked by the ORM layer or some other conventional API. Think more along the lines of something for which you specifically have to write the client access code—your own remote API.

You're looking to test the interactions between your microservice domain component and the remote component; not the remote component to the actual remote resource—that would be considered a contract test, which is covered in chapter 6. In a component test, you're not allowed to make calls outside of the local machine.

The following listing is an example of code reuse (code/game/src/test/java/book/games/arquillian/ArquillianAbstractTest.java). You'll use it as a base class for some tests: creating the base deployment archive and mocking remote calls. Have a quick look, and then we'll explain.

Listing 4.11 Test for the remote component

```
...
import static com.github.tomakehurst.wiremock.client.WireMock.aResponse;
import static com.github.tomakehurst.wiremock.client.WireMock.equalTo;
import static com.github.tomakehurst.wiremock.client.WireMock.get;
import static com.github.tomakehurst.wiremock.client.WireMock.stubFor;
import static com.github.tomakehurst.wiremock.client.WireMock.urlPathEqualTo;
```

```
   ...
   public abstract class ArquillianAbstractTest {
                                          WireMock stubbing of the https://www.igdb.com/ API remote
       @Before                              calls that will be performed before each test (@Before)
       public void before() {
           stubFor(get(anyUrl()).withQueryParam("search", equalTo
                   ("The" + " Legend of Zelda: Breath of the Wild"))
                   .willReturn(aResponse().withStatus(200).withHeader
                       ("Content-Type", "application/json")
                       .withBody("[{\"id\":7346,\"name\":\"The " +
                           "Legend of Zelda: Breath of the " +
                           "Wild\"}]")));
       }

       @Rule
       public WireMockRule wireMockRule = new WireMockRule(8071);

       public static WebArchive createBaseDeployment(final String name) {
           return ShrinkWrap.create(WebArchive.class, name + ".war")
               .addClasses(GamesResource.class,
                       ExecutorServiceProducer.class, GamesService
                           .class, IgdbGateway.class,
                       SearchResult.class, Games.class, Game
                           .class, ReleaseDate.class)
           .addAsResource("test-persistence.xml",
                   "META-INF/persistence.xml")
           .addAsWebInfResource(EmptyAsset.INSTANCE, "beans" +
                   ".xml");
       }
   }
```

WireMockRule that defines which port to listen on. The rule can do a lot more than just define a port.

Utility method that creates the minimum archive to test against. You can use this archive in implementations and add more items to it using ShrinkWrap methods.

WireMock is basically a real HTTP proxy server that listens to a defined port (using `WireMockRule`). The IGDB API is well defined and version stable. It's a REST API, like the one the microservice resource component depicts. This means you can intercept remote calls on a defined port and simulate the runtime responses. You don't need to change a single line of code in any of your runtime classes!

In listing 4.11, `stubFor` is a comprehensive use case that intercepts a GET call to a known API path, /games/search, using a query parameter q with the value `"Zelda"` and with an HTTP `Authorization` header equal to `"Token . . ."`. If everything matches, it then returns a response with code 200 (OK) that contains JSON with a specific body content, as defined by the IGDB API (http://mng.bz/xVF4).

The power of WireMock

There's some pretty powerful magic going on in listing 4.11 with WireMock (http://wiremock.org). In the application, you'll find a class named `IgdbGateway.class`—this is the gateway component that the microservice remote-resource component `GamesService.class` wraps/uses to make real remote calls to the www.igdb.com API.

This is a concrete class with no interface that's injected into the application. If you wanted to mock this class, how would you do it? Without extracting an interface and separating the implementation, so that you could use a dummy implementation to test against, you'd have a difficult time. In the past, that's exactly what you would have done; or you would have had to think up another fancy solution like using CDI alternatives in tests, just to run a unit test.

Another approach could be to use something like Mockito's `when([method-call]).thenReturn([response]])`, which is great for mocking interfaces and *some* objects. We say *some* because mocking a concrete object can have many unknown side effects that require proper analysis and a good understanding of the class at hand. Even if you got that far, what would happen when this mocked object was packaged and deployed to a container? The simple answer is, try it and see. The long answer goes beyond the scope of this book.

To see the significance of the `stubFor` WireMock interceptor, let's look at a test that uses it: the `ArquillianRemoteTest` class (code/game/src/test/java/book/games/ arquillian/ArquillianRemoteTest.java).

Listing 4.12   Using a WireMock interceptor in a test

```
@RunWith(Arquillian.class)
public class ArquillianRemoteTest extends ArquillianAbstractTest {

    @Deployment
    public static WebArchive createDeployment() {
        return createBaseDeployment(ArquillianRemoteTest.class
            .getName()).addClass(ArquillianRemoteTest.class)
            .addClass(ArquillianAbstractTest.class)
            .addAsLibrary(Maven.resolver().resolve("com.github"
                + ".tomakehurst:wiremock-standalone:2.2.1")
            .withoutTransitivity().asSingleFile());
    }

    @Inject
    private IgdbGateway gateway;

    @Test
    public void testSearchGames() throws Exception {
        Assert.assertNotNull(this.gateway);

        final JsonArray json = gateway.searchGames("The Legend of "
            + "Zelda: Breath of the Wild");
        Assert.assertNotNull(json);

        final JsonObject game = json.getJsonObject(0);

        Assert.assertEquals("Unexpected id", 7346, game
            .getJsonNumber("id").intValue());
```

The test class extends the base class and is annotated in the usual fashion.

Creates the archive using the utility method, and adds the elements specific to this test—in particular, the WireMock standalone library

Injects the unchanged concrete IgdbGateway class

Directs testing of the concrete class method, which is intercepted by the WireMock proxy

```
        Assert.assertEquals("Unexpected name", "The Legend of " +
            "Zelda: Breath of the Wild", game.getString("name"));
    }
}
```

> **NOTE** You could at this point have injected and tested GamesService.class,
> which is the microservice remote-resource component in a real sense. The
> example instead injects IgdbGateway.class to demonstrate the WireMock
> stubbing for a concrete class.

You may be wondering how the IgdbGateway class knows to call the proxy. You may
remember that when discussing the arquillian.xml file, we mentioned the significance
of the javaVmArguments property. This property defines JVM system properties using
the standard Java command-line option -D. IgdbGateway defines the IGDB_API_KEY
property to set the API key and the IGDB_HOST property to set the host URL, to access
the real service:

```
...
<property name="javaVmArguments">
    -DIGDB_API_KEY=dummyKey -DIGDB_HOST="http://127.0.0.1:8071/"
</property>
...
```

When the test is run, Arquillian starts the container and provides the arguments via
the configuration. The IgdbGateway class reads the properties and uses the dummy
key and URL to make remote calls. These real remote calls are intercepted by the
local WireMock proxy, which returns the constructed response. How neat is that?
You'll see more from WireMock throughout the rest of the book.

4.9.2   Testing the resource component

The resource component is where you expose microservice features through a REST-
ful endpoint—like your own API. To test this component properly, you have to *think*
like a client application. How would a client call the endpoint resources in the wild?

Let's keep this test as simple as possible. Similar to the previous test, this test
extends ArquillianAbstractTest to reuse the archive and WireMock proxy. Let's
first look at the test, and then we'll explain what's going on (code/game/src/test/
java/book/games/arquillian/ArquillianResourceTest.java).

Listing 4.13   Test for the resource component

Reuses code by extending a base class that
provides a baseline testing environment

```
@RunWith(Arquillian.class)
public class ArquillianResourceTest extends ArquillianAbstractTest
{

    @Deployment(testable = false)                          New annotated option that creates
    public static WebArchive createDeployment() {          an archive for deployment
```

```
                    return createBaseDeployment(ArquillianResourceTest.class
                            .getName());
                }

                @Test
                @RunAsClient
              > public void testSearch(@ArquillianResource final URL url)
                        throws Exception {
                    final Client client = ClientBuilder.newBuilder().build();
                    final WebTarget target = client.target(url.toExternalForm()
                            + "?query=The Legend of Zelda: Breath of the Wild");

                    final Future<Response> futureResponse = target.request()
                            .async().get();
                    final Response response = futureResponse.get(5, TimeUnit
                            .SECONDS);

                    final List<SearchResult> results
                        = response.readEntity(new GenericType<List<SearchResult>>(){
                    });

                    Assert.assertEquals("Unexpected title", "The Legend of " +
                            "Zelda: Breath of the Wild", results.get(0).getName
                            ());
                }
            }
```

New annotated parameter @Arquillian-Resource that injects a URL

New @RunAsClient annotation for a test method

Uses the injected URL to build a JAX-RS target to call

Retrieves a strongly typed collection from the response to test

Obtains and waits for an asynchronous response from the server

There are several new elements to discuss here. First, we'll address the `@Deploy-ment(testable = false)` and `@RunAsClient` annotations, because they mean more or less the same thing. Defining an archive with `testable` as `false` means this archive will be completely isolated from the test class. It's a black-box test, where Arquillian has no knowledge of what the archive contains and deploys the archive as is. You can't inject or use anything from the archive in the test class, which makes this class a perfect example for the current use case. Using `@Deployment(testable = false)` effectively says *all* test methods in this class are to run as an isolated client.

Why do you need the `@RunAsClient` annotation on your test method? You don't! It's in this example to shorten the exercise. `@RunAsClient` basically says, "Run this specific test method isolated from the test." You'd *normally* use one or the other approach in a test class, but not both together. The advantage of `@RunAsClient` is then clear. You use it in a test class that has multiple mixed-mode test methods, with some running isolated and others using injected resources.

The next new annotation, `@ArquillianResource`, can be used either as a field annotation or, as you see here, as a method annotation. It's possible to write your own `ArquillianResource` provider so that virtually anything can be injected by this annotation. Describing that here would be out of scope; if you want to know more, search the internet for "arquillian-extension-producer."

Out of the box, you can inject a resource URL that's relevant to the scope of your test. You already know how to configure your server and change the listening port, for example. But how does your isolated client test know about this? You could try to scan for and read the configuration, but that would be error prone, and it would also be useless if the container was configured to use a random port. Now you know that you can use the @ArquillianResource annotation to inject your URL.

4.9.3   *Testing the domain component*

The domain component is tricky to describe from a testing point of view, not because it's hard to test, but because it's specific to your application. The main point to take away is that you need to test it no matter what. Arquillian may or may not be useful for this task.

You should always follow these basic rules:

- Use a solitary unit test.
- Never cross boundaries.
- The class under test should be the only concrete class in the test, if possible.

4.9.4   *Testing the persistence component*

Just about every application you'll ever write will contain some sort of persistence layer. It may be as trivial as a simple properties file to store application settings, or, at the opposite end of the scale, like the SAP Persistence Service. More often than not, you'll use a database. These days, especially with Java EE, you'll want to hide the native database implementations behind an object-relational mapping (ORM) system. We'll assume you're already familiar with topics like the Java Persistence API (JPA) and SQL. If you aren't, please take the time to read up on these important topics before moving on to chapter 5, where testing the persistence component in a fully integrated test is covered in depth.

You know you're not allowed to cross a remote boundary outside of your local machine, so how can you meet this challenge and use a database? You don't want to change the semantics of your persistence context, so you can either mock the Entity-Manager or test against an embedded database. Mocking the EntityManager isn't a great idea for a component test that needs to test persistence, because it sidesteps persistence. So, using an embedded database is our preferred option.

There are several embedded databases in the Java ecosystem, some in the SQL space and others in the NoSQL ecosystem. Some of these databases use disk storage, and others use volatile in-memory storage. Due to their high performance, we recommend that you use an in-memory database for testing, if possible. Table 4.2 lists several vendors from the Java ecosystem that provide embedded/in-memory databases.

Table 4.2   Database vendors

Type	Project	Site
SQL	HyperSQL	http://hsqldb.org
SQL	H2	www.h2database.com/html/main.html

Table 4.2 Database vendors *(continued)*

Type	Project	Site
SQL	Derby	http://db.apache.org/derby
NoSQL MongoDB	Fongo	https://github.com/fakemongo/fongo
NoSQL Neo4J	Neo4J	https://neo4j.com/
NoSQL Infinispan	Infinispan	http://infinispan.org/

Notice that currently, in the SQL sphere, you have several options to choose from out of the box. For the NoSQL ecosystem, you'll need to rely on vendor support for embedded-mode versions.

Based on our experience, the best SQL embedded in-memory database to use for testing purposes is H2. It provides good performance for both read and write operations, and it offers compatibility modes for major SQL vendors like IBM DB2, MS SQL Server, MySQL, Oracle, and PostgreSQL. All this and a small footprint of just 1 MB make it hard to beat.

The example Gamer application uses one SQL database and two NoSQL databases (Redis and MongoDB). Unfortunately, there's no support for embedded Redis; in cases where it wouldn't be possible to run component tests at the speed of light, we recommend that you skip them and write an integration test, instead. You'll learn more about this in chapter 5.

To use H2, you need to import the `com.h2database:h2:<version>` dependency in your project with the scope `test`, using the build tool you've chosen. The next step is to configure the JDBC driver using H2-specific parameters; for example:

```xml
<?xml version="1.0" encoding="UTF-8"?>
<persistence version="2.1" xmlns="http://xmlns.jcp.org/xml/ns/persistence"
   xmlns:xsi="http://www.w3.org/2001/XMLSchema-instance"
   xsi:schemaLocation="http://xmlns.jcp.org/xml/ns/persistence
   http://xmlns.jcp.org/xml/ns/persistence/persistence_2_1.xsd">
  <persistence-unit name="pu" transaction-type="RESOURCE_LOCAL">
    <properties>
      <property name="javax.persistence.jdbc.driver" value="org.h2.Driver"/>
      <property name="javax.persistence.jdbc.url" value="jdbc:h2:mem:test"/>  ◁
      <property name="javax.persistence.jdbc.user" value="sa"/>
      <property name="javax.persistence.jdbc.password" value=""/>
    </properties>
  </persistence-unit>
</persistence>
```

The last URL parameter (test) is used as the database identifier or name.

To use H2, you need to set the H2 JDBC driver to `org.h2.Driver` and the URL of the connection to `jdbc:h2:mem:test`. This URL defines the `mem` keyword, which tells the H2 driver to work using in-memory mode. The last parameter of the URL is the database identifier, which is used to avoid clashes when starting more than one in-memory database in the same JVM. Finally, you need to set the user and password (for testing, you can use sa as the username and a blank password). Following these steps reconfigures the persistence layer (boundary) to use the H2 database instead of the one configured for production.

All services in the application that use a SQL database should write component tests for the persistence boundary using H2, which will ensure that testing performance isn't compromised. Use the ShrinkWrap microdeployment feature to include the test-persistence configuration into the deployment file:

```
return ShrinkWrap.create(WebArchive.class, "test.war")
            .addAsResource(
                "test-persistence.xml",
                "META-INF/persistence.xml");
```

ShrinkWrap copies test-persistence.xml from src/test/resources and adds it to the microdeployment file at the location META-INF/persistence.xml.

The comments service uses a MongoDB database in the persistence layer. MongoDB also isn't available as an embedded solution, so every time you need to use it, you'll have to spin up a mongod process. To avoid this problem during testing, the Fongo project was established.

Fongo is an in-memory Java implementation of MongoDB. It intercepts calls to the standard mongo-java-driver for finds, updates, inserts, removes, and several other useful methods. Although it has some limitations, it supports most of the common operations required to use MongoDB. To use Fongo, you need to import the com.github.fakemongo:fongo:<version> dependency in your project with the scope test, using your build tool of choice.

The next step is to instantiate the com.github.fakemongo.Fongo class and get a com.mongodb.DB object reference, which in this case is a Fongo custom implementation:

```
Fongo fongo = new Fongo("test server");        ◁── Creates a Fongo instance

com.mongodb.DB db = fongo.getDB("mydb");           ◁──┐  Gets the MongoDB driver
com.mongodb.MongoClient mongo = fongo.getMongo();     │  overridden classes
```

The most important step is creating the Fongo instance. After that, you can get the overridden MongoDB classes from the Java driver, which can then be passed to the boundary instead of the real classes.

In chapter 5, we'll go deeper into this topic and highlight some problems you may encounter when writing persistence tests, and how to fix them. The only difference between what you've just learned and the discussion in chapter 5 is that this example used an in-memory embedded database, and later you'll use a *real* remote database. The concepts are the same.

When you read chapter 5, remember what you've learned here. Also, take a good look at the demo code and use it as a template for your own tests.

Exercises

Putting this chapter into practice may seem daunting right now, so start small and build up your confidence using the ShrinkWrap utility and the Arquillian testing framework. As a simple exercise, just to get started, find all the uses of `Shrink-Wrap.create` in the demo code; then, using the generated archive `toString` methods, print out the contents to the console. Doing so will help you understand how the archives are made up, and what's required to perform useful Arquillian tests.

For a more advanced task, look back at `ArquillianResourceTest` in the game service project. You'll see that it uses `ClientBuilder` to create a REST client. That's a lot of boilerplate for a test method, but you know Arquillian can make your life a little easier here. Try to convert this test to use the Arquillian REST client, and see how much of the boilerplate code you can remove.

Summary

- Use the Arquillian workflow to automate as much of your tests as possible.
- Annotate a standard test class with Arquillian-specific annotations to remove boilerplate code.
- Define repeated elements of deployment archives in base classes or utility classes—write once, and reuse.
- Inject testable elements into a test class to test against.
- Create flexible test environments against multiple containers using Maven profiles for plugins.
- Override the default container options in the arquillian.xml file.
- Use Arquillian extensions to provide a feature-rich testing environment.

Integration-testing microservices

This chapter covers

- Understanding integration tests in a microservices architecture context
- Differentiating between integration and component tests
- Writing integration tests for persistence layers and gateway layers
- Operating with multiple deployments in Arquillian

In the preceding chapters, you read about how to write *unit* and *component* tests for a microservices-based architecture. There are also *integration* tests, which in the microservices world have a meaning that's slightly different than in other architectures.

Integration tests check the interactions between different modules (or classes), usually belonging to the same subsystem, to verify that they collaborate as expected when providing a high-level feature. Integration tests also check that all communication paths performed through the subsystem are correct, and detect any incorrect premises that each module might have about how its peers are expected to act.

NOTE Usually a module is considered a *class* in an object-oriented language.

Generally speaking, integration tests aren't slow per se, but their speed depends on the logic and the interactions with modules in the subsystem under test that impact test performance. Because such subsystems usually require one or more container(s) in which to run (servlet container, CDI container, Spring container, and so forth), integration tests are slower than unit tests because they need to start and stop the container(s) they require.

Figure 5.1 illustrates what an integration test might look like. As you can see, a test involves calling at least one module (or class) and all the associated peers of that module. The purpose of such a test is to verify not the behavior of each module, but rather the communication between modules.

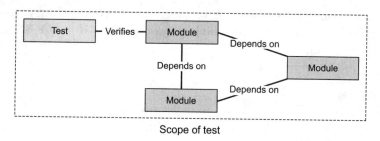

Figure 5.1 Integration tests involving different modules

Moving on from this brief introduction to the concept of integration tests, let's see how integration tests apply to the microservices architecture.

5.1 Integration testing in the microservices architecture

You know what integration testing is; in this section, you'll see how to apply integration test concepts to a microservices architecture. Integration tests can be written to test any subsystem. For microservices architectures, integration tests are typically focused on verifying the interaction between subsystems in charge of communicating with external components such as data stores and/or other (micro)services.

The goal of integration tests in microservices is to verify that the subsystem (or a concrete module) can communicate correctly, rather than testing the external element. For this reason, these tests should cover only basic success-and-error paths for integration between the subsystem and the external component at hand.

Figure 5.2 shows the schema of an integration test in a microservice scenario. You can see how a test verifies that one module (or class) can communicate with an external component, but without testing the external component.

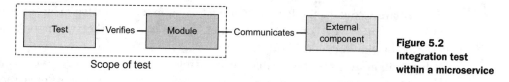

Figure 5.2 Integration test within a microservice

NOTE Because you're testing whether communication between a subsystem belonging to a microservice and the external service is possible, the *ideal* scenario would be to *not* use any test doubles for external components.

Keep the following important things in mind:

- Integration tests verify the connection between internal modules and *external* components, such as a database or other (micro)services, not other *internal* modules.
- Integration tests use real external components to validate whether communication with a real service is possible.
- Preparation of the environment for executing tests is likely to be difficult and/or tedious.

Before we look at a concrete example, the following sections review which parts of the microservice anatomy should be tested using integration tests. In figure 5.3, they're surrounded by broken lines.

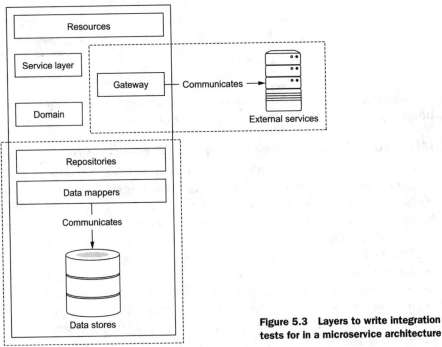

Figure 5.3   Layers to write integration tests for in a microservice architecture

5.1.1   Gateway component layer

Gateway layers contain the logic to connect to an external service, typically using an HTTP/S client. They connect to another microservice of the system or a service deployed outside your local infrastructure.

Integration tests are responsible for verifying connections to the service as well as for detecting any protocol issues, such as missing HTTP headers, incorrect SSL handling, or request/response body mismatches. All error-handling circumstances must be tested to ensure that the service and protocol client behave as expected when such conditions arise.

Sometimes it's difficult to verify abnormal behaviors such as timeouts or slow responses from external components. In chapter 9, you'll learn how to provoke these situations without having to use test doubles.

5.1.2 Data mappers and repositories

Repositories act as gateways to data sources by connecting to them, executing queries on them, and adapting the output to domain object models. Integration tests are responsible for verifying that the datasource schema is the one expected by the code. This assumption is especially important in the case of NoSQL databases. Because they don't have schema, they're considered *schemaless.* You need to be sure the code knows how to deal with this situation. When you're using an ORM such as JPA, these tests also give you confidence that any mapping configured on the entities is correct.

Now that you know how to apply unit testing techniques to a microservices architecture, let's see what tools you can use to write these tests.

> **NOTE** Many tools for writing integration tests are available, but the tools we'll examine in this chapter are currently the most widely adopted and accepted by the Java community. The following sections assume that you've already read chapter 4 and that you understand at least the basics of the Arquillian framework.

5.2 Persistence testing with the Arquillian Persistence Extension

Writing integration tests for a persistence layer is a bit more complicated than a simple unit test. Because results stored in the storage system are persistent, any execution of a test might influence the subsequent execution of another test by changing the data. This may be a cause for concern: tests are no longer completely *isolated* from each other. They're connected by data.

In all but a few edge cases, tests should be independent of external factors and also of each other, because any data change performed by one test could cause other tests to fail in often subtle ways that can be difficult to diagnosis. Let's look at an example of how this can happen in a simple persistence test. Suppose you have an object with two methods: one for creating a new movie and another for finding all movies. One possible test class might be the following:

```
@Test
public void shouldInsertAMovie() {
  Movie insertedMovie = movieRepository.insert(movie);
  assertThat(insertedMovie.getId(), notNullValue());
  //You can add more assertions here
}

@Test
public void shouldFindAllMovies() {
```

Depending on unique constraints, this test may fail the second time you execute it.

```
      movieRepository.insert(movie);
      List<Movie>; movies = movieRepository.findAllMovies();
      assertThat(movies, hasSize(1));                         ◁——
}
```
> **Depending on execution order, one or more movies may have been inserted.**

As you can see, this test isn't predictable. Although the repository code may be correctly written, tests may fail depending on test execution order. If the `shouldInsert-AMovie` test method is executed last (there's no guarantee of any execution order), then the `shouldFindAllMovies` test method will fail because no movies are stored in the database, and one is expected. This confirms how important it is that each test execution is isolated from another execution in terms of data. Figure 5.4 illustrates one test execution that causes the `shouldFindAllMovies` test to fail.

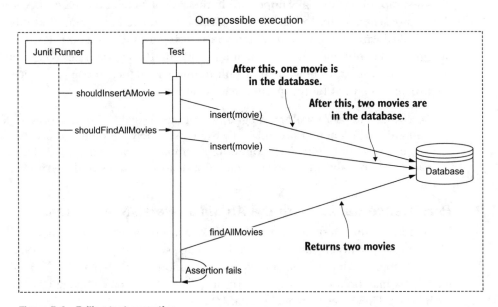

Figure 5.4   Failing test execution

Figure 5.5 shows a false-positive scenario, where all tests pass. A *false positive* can lull you into a false sense of security. You can see that this test has the potential to fail on any given run, but would you instantly spot the cause if it did?

It's easy to fix this problem with the right tools: you only need to revert the database data to a known and predictable state before each test method execution. This means that before each execution, the database must be modified by cleaning/reverting previous modifications; then you recreate the database in a known state by inserting some known/expected data for the test. Following this strategy, each test will always find a database with the same data, independent of the test execution order, as shown in figure 5.6.

Before each test execution, the database is purged of any data changes that were made previously. Then, all data that will be expected by the test is inserted; for example, a test may verify some expected query results. After this revert, you can

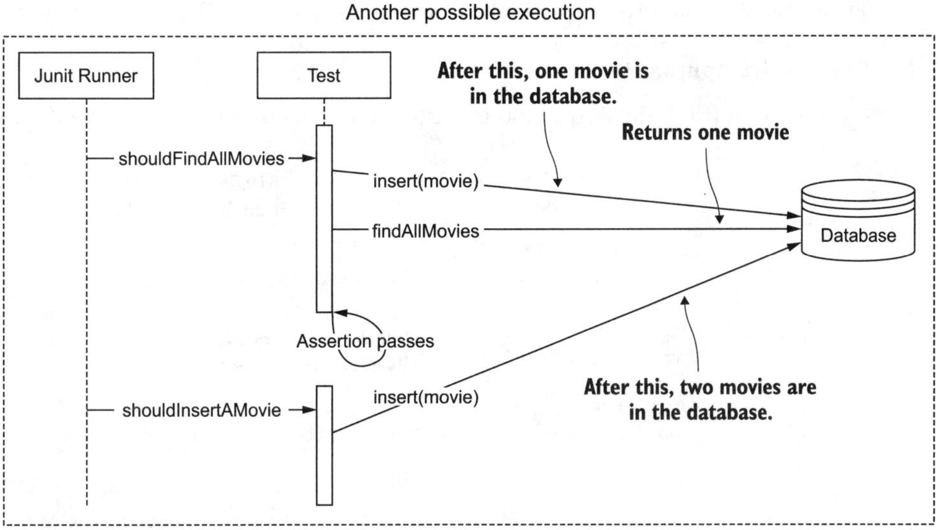

Another possible execution

Figure 5.5 Successful test execution

consider the database to be in a known state. It contains only the data you expect to be present, and each test can be executed in a consistent manner.

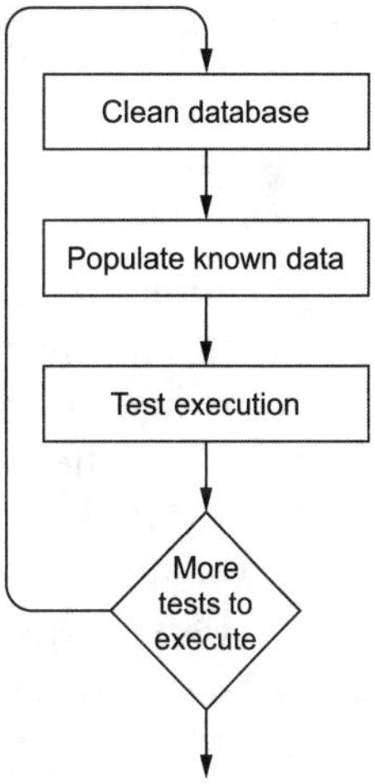

Even this solution has two aspects that make it imperfect and that could be improved:

- Maintaining the database in a known state involves a huge amount of boilerplate code that will be repeated before each persistence test.
- There's no standard mechanism to insert data, so you might have to write SQL statements over and over.

Fortunately, the *Arquillian Persistence Extension* drastically improves writing persistence tests using Arquillian. The Arquillian Persistence Extension can help you with the task of writing persistence tests correctly. It exposes the following features:

- Each test wrapped in an isolated transaction
- Database seeding at the class or method level using DbUnit
- Support for SQL, JPA, NoSQL, and more
- Support for XML, Excel (XLS), YAML, and JSON dataset formats
- Cleaning of the database before each test method execution
- Customizations using SQL files directly
- Comparison of database states at the end of each test using a known final dataset, which also supports column exclusions
- Unified programmatic (DSL) and declarative (annotations) ways of seeding data

Figure 5.6 Lifecycle of a safe persistence test

This extension can save you from having to write a lot of boilerplate code for each test.

5.2.1   *Declarative approach*

A test written using the Arquillian Persistence Extension might look like the following:

```
@RunWith(Arquillian.class)
public class GamesPersistenceTest {

    @Deployment
    public static WebArchive createDeploymentPackage() {}

    @EJB
    Games gamesService;

    @Resource
    javax.transaction.UserTransaction userTransaction;

    @Test
    @UsingDataSet("datasets/games.yml")
    public void shouldFindAllGames() {}

    @Test
    @ApplyScriptBefore("scripts/drop-referential-integrity.sql")
    @ShouldMatchDataSet("datasets/expected-games.yml")
    public void shouldInsertGames() {}
}
```

Defines the ShrinkWrap deployment file to be used

Defines the test as an Arquillian test

Injects any EJB or even the UserTransaction used

Applies a given SQL script before executing the test method

Populates the database with the specified data before executing the test method

Validates that the database content is as defined by the file after executing the test method

Notice that the Arquillian Persistence Extension relies heavily on annotations, which means you don't need to write any boilerplate code in your tests. Just let the extension maintain the database in a known state for you.

In the example, YAML format is used to populate and validate the database. For YAML datasets, an element found at far left in the document is a table name. This element can contain a list (or array) of elements. Each element's list in YAML is denoted with a hyphen (-) symbol. Each element is a row in the database. Finally, each element contains attributes that represent the column names and values:

```
table1:
  - column1: value1
    column2: value2
  - column1: value3
    column2: value4
table2:
```

This example defines two tables. Two rows are inserted in `table1`, adding values to `column1` and `column2`.

> **NOTE**   You can explicitly set a `null` value for a given column by using the `null` keyword. For example, `producedBy: "[null]"`.

In the sequence diagram in figure 5.7, you can see what happens internally when an Arquillian Persistence Extension test is executed. First, the application server of your choice is started, and the archive defined by the deployment method is packaged by ShrinkWrap and deployed. The test then starts its execution, and the following steps happen for each test method:

1 The database is cleaned so previous executions don't affect the current test method.
2 The entire test is executed within a transaction.
3 The database is seeded with a known dataset if the @UsingDataSet annotation is present.
4 The test body is executed.
5 The final state of the database is verified if a @ShouldMatchDataSet annotation is present.

After the execution of all tests, the deployment file is undeployed and the application server is terminated.

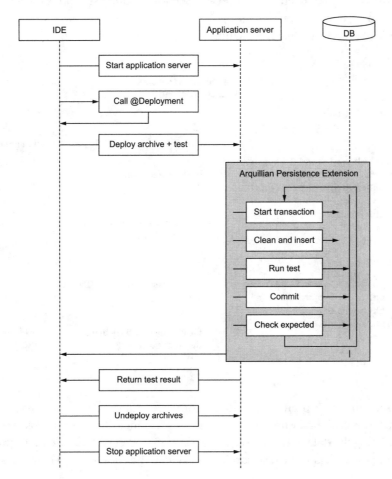

Figure 5.7
Arquillian Persistence
Extension lifecycle

You now know how to write persistence tests for SQL systems. Let's see how to do it for NoSQL databases.

5.2.2   *Programmatic approach*

You've seen how to populate your anemic environment with some data by using annotations. The Arquillian Persistence Extension also allows you to populate data using a programmatic approach. This approach is valid only when using Arquillian in client mode (or using the `standalone` dependency). One important aspect of the programmatic approach is that you can use an Arquillian runner (`@RunWith(Arquillian.class)`) or, alternatively, register a *JUnit rule* (`@Rule public ArquillianPersistenceRule arquillianPersistenceRule = new ArquillianPersistenceRule();`).

> **NOTE**   At the time of writing, the annotation approach can only be used with DbUnit.

STANDARD RDBMSS

Two different technologies are supported for populating data in relational databases. The first is DbUnit, introduced in the previous section, and the second is *Flyway*, a Java tool for describing database migrations.

Let's look at an example using DbUnit:

```
@RunWith(Arquillian.class)
public class DbUnitTest {            DbUnit annotation that sets
                                     DbUnit as the backend
    @DbUnit          <---
    @ArquillianResource
    RdbmsPopulator rdbmsPopulator;
                                                      Configures the JDBC connection
    @Test
    public void should_find_all_persons() {
      rdbmsPopulator.forUri(URI.create("jdbc:h2:mem:test;DB_CLOSE_DELAY=-1"))  <---
          .withDriver(Driver.class)
          .withUsername("sa")
          .withPassword("")
          .usingDataSet("test.json")    Updates the database using
          .execute();         <---     the provided dataset

      // Testing part

      rdbmsPopulator.forUri(URI.create("jdbc:h2:mem:test;DB_CLOSE_DELAY=-1"))
          .withDriver(Driver.class)
          .withUsername("sa")
          .withPassword("")
          .usingDataSet("test.json")   Cleans the database before
          .clean();           <---     the next execution
    }
}
```

As you can see, this test is pretty similar to any other Arquillian test, with one slight difference: the test is enriched with a `RdbmsPopulator` instance. This instance is responsible for populating the dataset for the required RDBMS backend. The DbUnit populator is injected into the test, and the test.json file, located at the root of the classpath, is used to seed the given SQL database instance. In a similar way, you can use Flyway by annotating a field with @Flyway, which points to a dataset migration directory.

NoSQL SYSTEMS

Next, let's see how to use same approach to populate datasets for NoSQL databases. The Arquillian Persistence Extension uses *NoSQLUnit* under the hood for the dataset format and populating data. (We'll cover this topic more deeply later in the chapter.) For now, the only thing you need to know is that NoSQLUnit is similar to DbUnit, but for NoSQL databases.

Currently, the Arquillian Persistence Extension supports the following NoSQL databases: Couchbase, MongoDB, Vault, and Redis. The following example uses MongoDB:

```
@RunWith(Arquillian.class)
public class MongoDbTest {

    @MongoDb                          ◁──────  MongoDB annotation that sets
    @ArquillianResource                        MongoDB as the backend
    NoSqlPopulator populator;

    @Test
    public void should_populate_mongodb() {
                                               Configures the
        populator.forServer("localhost", 27017)  ◁──  MongoDB connection
                .withStorage("test")
                .usingDataSet("books.json")
                .execute();             ◁────── Updates the database using
                                               the provided dataset
        // Testing part

        populator.forServer(hostIp, port)
            .withStorage("test")
            .clean();        ◁──────  Cleans the database before
    }                                 the next execution

}
```

This test is similar to the one for SQL databases. The test is enriched with a NoSqlPopulator instance, which is responsible for populating the dataset for the required NoSQL backend. The MongoDB populator is injected into the test, and the books.json file, located at the root of the classpath, is used to seed the specified NoSQL database instance.

In a similar way, you can configure your test to use any other of the supported NoSQL databases.

> **NOTE** Each supported populator has its own artifact. For example, to use the MongoDB populator, you'll need to register the org.arquillian .ape:arquillian-ape-nosql-mongodb artifact in the build script.

REST SERVICES

You've learned how to populate data into persistent storage before executing your test, and how to clean the environment after the execution. In a microservices architecture, it's common for a service A to call a service B to obtain data. In this kind of integration test, you can experience the same problems as for persistence backend tests. You need to populate some data to service B before testing the *gateway* of service A. This testing scenario is also supported in the Arquillian Persistence Extension using the same approach as in previous sections.

For REST services, Postman (www.getpostman.com) Collection Format v2 (https://schema.getpostman.com/json/collection/v2.0.0/docs/index.html) is the format used for setting the dataset of operations to execute against a service.

> ### About Postman
>
> Postman is a GUI program that allows you to develop and test (REST) APIs. It also supports importing REST definitions from different formats such as RAML and Swagger.
>
> In Postman, collections are the main place to store individual requests and responses so they can be organized to accurately mirror the API. From a user perspective, a *collection* is a group of requests that can be executed one by one or all at once. A collection can be exported into a JSON file following the JSON schema defined at https://schema.getpostman.com.

The Arquillian Persistence Extension for REST services reads JSON files following the Collection v2 format and replies using all defined requests against the specified service. To create this file, you can follow two possible approaches:

- Create a JSON file from scratch following the Collection v2 schema.
- Create a collection using Postman, and export it (see figure 5.8). We recommend using this approach because it's the easiest and fastest way to create the file.

Let's look at an example in which a Postman collection is used to populate a service with a Hello message.

Listing 5.1 `PostmanTest`

```
@RunWith(Arquillian.class)
public class PostmanTest {                   Sets Postman as the
                                             backend to populate data
  @Postman
  @ArquillianResource
  RestPopulator populator;

  @Test
  public void should_get_messages() {                    Configures the service
                                                         location to be updated
    populator.forServer("example.com", 8080)
       .usingDataSets("message.json")
       .execute();
                                        Sends REST calls to the
    // Testing part                     configured service

  }
}
```

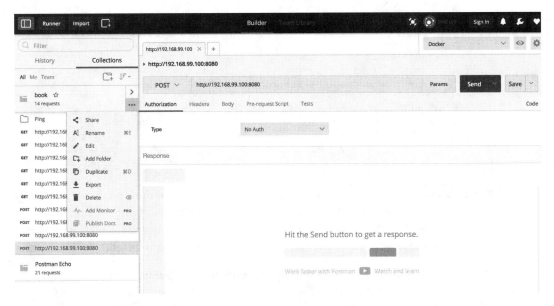

Figure 5.8 Example of exporting a collection

This test is similar to those for databases. It's enriched with a `RestPopulator` instance that's responsible for populating the dataset for the required service. The Postman populator is injected into the test, and the message.json Postman collection file, located at the root of the classpath, is used to replay all requests defined in the file against the configured service.

The message.json file is shown next.

Listing 5.2 message.json

```json
{
  "variables": [],
  "info": {
    "name": "Messenger",
    "_postman_id": "1803c743-318a-8751-b982-4f9475a00cea",
    "description": "",
    "schema": "https://schema.getpostman.com/json/collection/v2.0.0/collectio
    n.json"
  },
  "item": [
    {
      "name": "My message",
      "request": {
        "url": "http://localhost:8080/message",
        "method": "POST",
        "header": [
          {
            "key": "Content-Type",
            "value": "text/plain",
```

```
          "description": ""
        }
      ],
      "body": {
        "mode": "raw",
        "raw": "Message in a Bottle"
      },
      "description": ""
    }
  }
 ]
}
```

This collection contains only one request (but it can contain multiple lists), named `My message`. This creates a `POST` request against the specified `url` with a `Content-Type` header of `text/plain` and the body content `Message in a Bottle`, which is then executed when the `execute` method of the `RestPopulator` class is called.

> **NOTE** The URL field in this example points to `localhost`. Meanwhile, the test points to example.com. This is fine, because the Arquillian Persistence Extension adapts the `url` field for requests (host and port) to the one configured in the `RestPopulator`. So, in the message.json request, the URL http://localhost:8080/message is replaced at runtime with http://example .com:8080/message.

Now that you've seen how to use the Arquillian Persistence Extension, let's go a little deeper into how NoSQLUnit works.

5.2.3 *Persistence testing with NoSQLUnit*

In NoSQL databases, you face the same challenges you face with SQL databases, including the isolation problem. Because NoSQL databases are persistent from the point of view of the lifecycle of tests (although distributed caches usually aren't persistent), these tests still need to manage databases in order to revert them to a known state.

To write persistence tests for NoSQL databases, there's a project equivalent to DbUnit, called NoSQLUnit. NoSQLUnit is a JUnit extension that helps you write NoSQL persistence tests following the same approach taken by DbUnit, but adapted to common NoSQL databases. It comes with the following features:

- Manages the lifecycle of databases, including starting and stopping cycles.
- Seeds the database at the class or level method. Due to the heterogeneity of the NoSQL space, each implementation has its own format.
- Cleans the database before each test method is executed.
- Compares the database state at the end of each test using a known final dataset, and supports column exclusions.
- Supports Cassandra, Couchbase, CouchDB, Elasticsearch, HBase, Infinispan, MongoDB, Vault, Neo4J, and Redis.

Again, NoSQLUnit saves you from having to write a lot of boilerplate code for each test. The following listing shows a sample test written using NoSQLUnit.

Listing 5.3 CommentsPersistenceTest.java

```java
public class CommentsPersistenceTest {

    @ClassRule
    public static InMemoryMongoDb inMemoryMongoDb =
        newInMemoryMongoDbRule().build();

    @Rule
    public MongoDbRule embeddedMongoDbRule = newMongoDbRule()
        .defaultEmbeddedMongoDb("test");

    @Test
    @UsingDataSet(locations="initialData.json")
    @ShouldMatchDataSet(location="expectedData.json")
    public void shouldInsertComment() {}

}
```

Starts an in-memory instance of MongoDB (FongoDB project)

Configures a connection to the database to be used by the test

Populates a JSON document into the MongoDB instance before each test

Validates that the content of the database is as defined by the file after executing the test method

For MongoDB, NoSQLUnit expects a JSON file with the following schema for populating and validating data:

```json
{
    "collection1":{
        "indexes":[
            {
                "index":{
                    "code":1
                }
            }
        ],
        "data":[
            {
                "id":1,
                "code":"JSON dataset"
            },
            {
                "id":2,
                "code":"Another row"
            }
        ]
    }
}
```

Registers indexes for the collection

Specifies the collection in which documents are stored

Defines one index for the code field

Array of raw JSON documents to store

Any root element represents a collection where you can insert documents; in this case, the collection collection1 is defined. After that, you define an array with two kinds of documents: one that defines which indexes are created in the collection, and an array of raw JSON documents that are stored in the collection.

Notice that NoSQLUnit follows an approach similar to the Arquillian Persistence Extension by cleaning the database before executing each test method and then populating the database with the given data. It can also verify that the state of the database is as expected after each test method executes.

> **NOTE** Nothing is stopping you from using NoSQLUnit standalone outside of the Arquillian runner (using the NoSQLUnit JUnit runner). But we encourage you to use the Arquillian Persistence Extension together with NoSQLUnit.

Now you've seen how to use NoSQLUnit with MongoDB. But each NoSQL database is different, and it's easy to see that a graph database, such as Neo4J, models data completely differently than MongoDB: one deals with nodes and the relationships between them, and the other one stores data in "buckets."

Next, let's see how NoSQLUnit works with Redis. The first step is to configure a Redis connection. Instead of using an embedded connection, as in the previous example, you make a direct connection to an already running Redis instance.

Listing 5.4   RedisPersistenceTest.java

```
public class RedisPersistenceTest {          Rule defining the
                                             connection details
    @Rule                             ◄───
    public RedisRule redisRule = new RedisRule(
            RemoteRedisConfigurationBuilder.newRemoteRedisConfiguration()
            .host("192.168.1.1")
            .build());                 ◄───┐  Creates a connection to an
                                           │  already running Redis service
    @Test
    @UsingDataSet(locations="initialData.json")    ◄─── Populates the given data
    public void shouldGetData() {}

}
```

When using Redis, NoSQLUnit expects a JSON file with the following schema for populating and validating data:

```
{
"data":[
        {"simple": [                 ◄─── A simple key/value
            {
                "key":"key1",
                "value":"value1"
            }
            ]
        },
        {"list": [{                   ◄─── A key and a list of values
                "key":"key3",
                "values":[
                    {"value":"value3"},
                    {"value":"value4"}
```

```
                    ]
                }]
        },
        {"sortset": [{                          A key and a set of values
                "key":"key4",                   ordered by score
                "values":[
                        {"score":2, "value":"value5" },
                        {"score":3, "value":1 },
                        {"score":1, "value":"value6" }]
            }]
        },
        {"hash": [                              A key with a hash of
                                                key/values elements
                    {
                    "key":"user",
                    "values":[
                            {"field":"name", "value":"alex"},
                            {"field":"password", "value":"alex"}
                        ]
                    }
                ]
        },
        {"set":[{                               A key with a set of
                                                unduplicated values
                "key":"key3",
                "values":[
                        {"value":"value3"},
                        {"value":"value4"}
                    ]
                }]
            }
    ]
}
```

The root element must be called data. Depending on the kind of structured data you need to store, the root element should be followed by one or more child elements. The key field sets the key of the element, and the value field is used to set a value. You can store the following types of elements:

- simple—Contains an array of simple key/value entries.
- list—Contains a key field for the key name and a value field with an array of values.
- set—Stores a key in a set (no duplicates allowed). The structure is the same as for the list element.
- sortset—Stores a key in a sorted set of values. Each value also has a score field of type Number, to specify its order in the sorted set.
- hash—Stores a key in a map of fields/values. The field field sets the field name, and value sets the field's value.

Clearly, depending on the defined NoSQL database, the data-seeding file is likely to be very different.

Now that we've introduced two technologies for writing tests for data mappers and repositories, let's look at two more that will help you perform integration tests for gateways.

5.2.4 *Persistence testing with Arquillian multideployment*

Up to now, each test class in this book has had its own deployment method. But when you're writing integration tests for gateway components, you may need to deploy two archives: one that contains the gateway class and its related classes, and another that contains the service the gateway connects to.

Of course, you can only have multiple deployments if you're able to deploy the test on the other microservice. For example, if you're communicating with an external service that's outside the control of your project, such as YouTube or the IGDB site, you need to use the external service directly.

Also, sometimes a service can't be deployed using Arquillian; perhaps it isn't written in Java, or it was written by an external team and you don't have access and therefore can't deploy it. In these cases, you need to use a staging server with the service deployed, to test the gateway against the real service.

The examples thus far have used a single deployment for their tests. Arquillian allows more than one deployment per test class and also lets you operate on more than one deployment per test method. The @Deployment annotation has an attribute that's required for multiple deployment usage: name. Setting your own name for an archive overrides the default DEFAULT value. The order attribute may also come in handy when testing against multiple deployments; it defines the order in which the deployments are sent to the container, if the order matters. You also need to use the @OperateOnDeployment Arquillian annotation to specify which deployment context a test uses. This annotation takes a string, which must match the name specified in the @Deployment annotation.

Here's an example of multiple deployment:

```
                              ┌──── Deploys the first
@Deployment(name = "X", order = 1)  ⟵──┘    deployment file
public static WebArchive createDep1() {}

@Deployment(name = "Y", order = 2)
public static WebArchive createDep2() {}
                                        ┌──── URL of the first
@ArquillianResource @OperateOnDeployment("X")  ⟵──┘   deployment
private URL firstDeployment

@Test @OperateOnDeployment('X')
public void test(@ArquillianResource @OperateOnDeployment("Y")
        URL secondDeployment) {}                  ⟵──┐
                                                      │
            URL of the second deployment ────────────┘
```

Deploys the first deployment file

Deploys the second deployment file

URL of the first deployment

Test that operates on the X deployment context

URL of the second deployment

Here, two archives are deployed to the application server. Subsequently, you can refer to each one by using @OperateOnDeployment annotation to inject the URL where they're deployed or to choose the deployment context for the test.

WARNING Arquillian multideployment works only if you're using the same container for all deployment artifacts. You can't mix two or more different containers in the same test. This is a limitation if you're using different application services for each microservice; if you're using the same application service, then you can use this approach to write integration tests for gateway applications.

NOTE You can use Arquillian multideployment to test cluster capabilities or a cluster's configuration.

Arquillian multideployment is useful for writing integration tests that verify communication between two services. But another Arquillian feature may help you test gateway components to other services: an Arquillian sequence.

5.2.5 *Persistence testing with Arquillian sequence*

Sometimes, when you're writing tests for gateways that communicate with another service, you want to set the execution order for the integration tests. A typical example is authentication: before accessing an external service, you may need to authenticate against it. So, it seems logical that the test of logging in to the service should be executed before any other test. The test is dependent on the order of execution.

There are many different strategies to address this, but in Arquillian you can use the `InSequence` annotation. `InSequence` forces a method-execution order for JUnit tests. It receives one integer as a parameter, which indicates the execution order of each test method:

```
@Test
@InSequence(1)          <── Sets the execution order
public void login() {}

@Test
@InSequence(2)
public void logout() {}
```

This example uses `@InSequence` to first execute the `login` test and then execute the `logout` test.

NOTE You can run both `login` and `logout` tests individually from your IDE. The `InSequence` annotation is useful when the full test class is executed.

Now that you're familiar with integration test tools, let's see what you need to do to start using them.

5.2.6 *Build-script modifications*

To use the Arquillian Persistence Extension or NoSQLUnit, you need to define them as test dependencies in your build script. In the case of Gradle, this information goes in the `dependencies` block.

To use Arquillian multideployment or the @InSequence annotation, you don't need to add extra dependencies—just the Arquillian dependency, because this feature comes from the Arquillian core. As you saw in chapter 4, to use Arquillian, you need to register an Arquillian BOM file and an Arquillian JUnit dependency; and if you're using WildFly Swarm, you need to add the WildFly Swarm Arquillian extension. After adding Arquillian as a dependency, you can start writing Arquillian tests and using multideployment and sequence features.

If you need to write integration tests for the SQL persistence layer, you must add an Arquillian Persistence Extension dependency:

```
dependencies {
  testCompile group: 'org.jboss.arquillian.extension',
          name: 'arquillian-persistence-dbunit',
          version: '1.0.0.Alpha7'
}
```

Finally, to write integration tests for NoSQL databases, you need to add a NoSQLUnit dependency. Because NoSQL databases are by definition heterogeneous, each NoSQLUnit-supported database has its own dependency. This is the dependency for MongoDB:

```
dependencies {
  testCompile 'com.lordofthejars:nosqlunit-mongodb:1.0.0-rc.5'
}
```

And this is the dependency for Redis:

```
dependencies {
  testCompile 'com.lordofthejars:nosqlunit-redis:1.0.0-rc.5'
}
```

Once you've registered dependencies in the build script, you can begin to write integration tests for repositories and gateways.

5.3   *Writing integration tests for the Gamer application*

In this section, you'll write integration tests for the Gamer application. Usually, unit tests are created in the de facto test directory, src/test/java. For integration tests, you can follow three different strategies:

- Create a special package in src/test/java called, for example, `integrationtests`.
- Create another source folder in the project called, for example, src/integrationTests/java.
- Create a new module/subproject in the main project called, for example, `integration-tests`.

Each of these strategies has advantages and disadvantages and may require you to modify your build script. We don't have a strong opinion about which strategy is best; it depends on what your team is comfortable with. In this book, you'll use the first and third strategies, because they're the most common and the easiest to integrate with build tools.

5.3.1 Testing the Comments class

Let's look at how to write an integration test for the book.comments.boundary.Comments class. This simple class, shown in the next listing, implements logic for storing comments in MongoDB and getting comments with ratings from MongoDB (code/comments/src/main/java/book/comments/boundary/Comments.java). It also creates a MongoDB connection from the configuration provided in the resources.xml file.

Listing 5.5 Comments class

```java
@Dependent
public class Comments {

    private static final String COMMENTS_COLLECTION = "comments";
    private static final String MATCH = "{$match:{gameId: %s}}";
    private static final String GROUP = "{ $group : " + "             " +
            "   { _id : \"$gameId\", " + "                 comments: { " +
            "$push: \"$comment\" }, " + "              rate: { $avg: " +
            "\"$rate\"} " + "            count: { $sum: 1 } " + "     " +
            "            }" + "}";

    @Resource(name = "mongodb")
    private MongoClientProvider mongoDbProvider;

    private MongoCollection<Document>; commentsCollection;

    @PostConstruct
    public void initComentsCollection() {
        commentsCollection = mongoDbProvider.getMongoClient()
                .getDatabase(mongoDbProvider.getDatabase())
                .getCollection(COMMENTS_COLLECTION);
    }

    public String createComment(final Document comment) {
        commentsCollection.insertOne(comment);
        return comment.getObjectId("_id").toHexString();
    }

    public Optional<Document>; getCommentsAndRating(final int gameId) {
        final AggregateIterable<Document>; result =
                commentsCollection.aggregate
                        (createAggregationExpression(gameId));
        return Optional.ofNullable(result.first());
    }

    private java.util.List<Document>; createAggregationExpression
```

```
        (final int gameId) {
    return Arrays.asList(Document.parse(String.format(MATCH,
            gameId)), Document.parse(GROUP));
    }


}
```

Listing 5.6 shows a test for the `createComment` logic (code/comments/i-tests/src/test/java/book/comments/CommentsTest.java). In this persistence test, you need three elements:

- A running MongoDB instance. It can be started manually or using a build script. In chapter 8, you'll learn another way that uses Docker.
- An empty MongoDB `comments` collection into which to insert data. It's important to create a document in an empty collection, to avoid any possibility of a constraint violation.
- The expected dataset, to verify that the `comments` collection has the expected data.

Listing 5.6   Testing the `createComment` logic

```
@RunWith(Arquillian.class)              ⟵─┐  Sets the test as
public class CommentsTest {                │  an Arquillian test

    @Deployment
    public static WebArchive createDeployment() {
        final WebArchive webArchive = ShrinkWrap.create(WebArchive
                .class).addClasses(Comments.class,
                MongoClientProvider.class).addAsWebInfResource
                (EmptyAsset.INSTANCE, "beans.xml").addAsLibraries(
                Maven.resolver().resolve("org" +
                        ".mongodb:mongodb-driver:3.2.2", "com" +
                        ".lordofthejars:nosqlunit-mongodb:0.10.0")
                        .withTransitivity().as(JavaArchive.class))
                .addAsWebInfResource("resources-test.xml",
                        "resources.xml")
                .addAsWebInfResource("expected-insert-comments" +
                        ".json",
                        "classes/book/comments/expected-insert" +
                            "-comments.json");      ⟵─┐  Adds the expected
                                                       │  dataset to the package
        return webArchive;
    }
    @Rule                   ⟵───── Registers the NoSQLUnit
    public MongoDbRule remoteMongoDbRule = new MongoDbRule(mongoDb
            ().databaseName("test").host("localhost").build());

    @Inject            ⟵───── Injects the Comments
    private Comments comments;           boundary class into the test
```

Adds a NoSQLUnit libraries archive, because the test is executed on a container ──▷

Renames the MongoDB test configuration file resources-test.xml to the correct name and location ──▷

Registers the NoSQLUnit MongoDB rule

**Cleans the MongoDB database
before executing the test**

```
@Test
@UsingDataSet(loadStrategy = LoadStrategyEnum.DELETE_ALL)
@ShouldMatchDataSet(location = "expected-insert-comments.json")
public void shouldInsertAComment() {
    final Document document = new Document("comment", "This " +
            "Game is Awesome").append("rate", 5).append
            ("gameId", 1);

    comments.createComment(document);
}

}
```

**Sets the expected data in the
comments collection**

The following things are important to note about the persistence test:

- It's a normal Arquillian test that executes a NoSQLUnit JUnit rule.
- The test is executed on the container side, which means you must add everything you need in the classpath in the `WebArchive`.
- `UsingDataSet` and `ShouldMatchDataSet` simplify the management of the persistence state by asserting that the test is always in a known/desired state for execution.

The expected dataset is shown next (code/comments/i-tests/src/test/resources/expected-insert-comments.json).

Listing 5.7 Dataset

```
{
  "comments": [
     {
       "comment" : "This Game is Awesome",
       "rate": 5,
       "gameId": 1
     }
   ]
}
```

Here, you set the desired state of the MongoDB database after test execution. In this case, the database should contain a collection called `comments` that holds one document with these three attributes:

- `comment`, which has the value `"This Game is Awesome"`.
- `rate`, which has the value 5
- `gameId`, which has the value 1

After you execute the test, if the MongoDB database is in the given state, the test will succeed; if not, the test will fail.

5.3.2   Testing the CommentsGateway class

Now, let's look at how to write an integration test for the `book.aggr.CommentsGateway` class. This class, shown in listing 5.8, is a simple boundary class that acts as gateway between the aggregator service and the comments service (code/aggregator/src/main/java/book/aggr/CommentsGateway). It's responsible for communicating with the comments service to create new comments or get information about them.

NOTE   HK2 is a lightweight, dynamic DI framework that can be used with Jersey.

Listing 5.8   CommentsGateway class

```
@Service
public class CommentsGateway {              ⟵┐  Annotation placed on classes that are
                                            └─ to be automatically added to HK2

    public static final String COMMENTS_SERVICE_URL =
            "COMMENTS_SERVICE_URL";
    private Client client;
    private WebTarget comments;
                                      ┐ Builds a connection to
                                      │ the comments service
    public CommentsGateway() {   ⟵───┘

        String commentsHost = Optional.ofNullable(System.getenv
                (COMMENTS_SERVICE_URL))
                .orElse(Optional.ofNullable(System.getProperty
                    ("COMMENTS_SERVICE_URL")).orElse
                    ("http://localhost:8282/comments-service/"));
        initRestClient(commentsHost);
    }

    void initRestClient(final String host) {
        this.client = ClientBuilder.newClient().property("jersey" +
                ".config.client.connectTimeout", 2000).property
                ("jersey.config.client.readTimeout", 2000);
        this.comments = this.client.target(host);
    }

    public Future<Response>; createComment(final JsonObject comment)
    {
        return this.comments.path("comments").register
                (JsonStructureBodyWriter.class)
                .request(MediaType.APPLICATION_JSON).async()
                .post(Entity.entity(comment, MediaType
                    .APPLICATION_JSON_TYPE));
    }

    public Future<JsonObject>; getCommentsFromCommentsService(final
                                                        long gameId) {
        return this.comments.path("comments/{gameId}")
                .resolveTemplate("gameId", gameId).register
                    (JsonStructureBodyReader.class).request
                    (MediaType.APPLICATION_JSON).async().get
                    (JsonObject.class);
```

- **Gets URL to connect to Comments service** → `String commentsHost = Optional.ofNullable(...)`
- **Creates a comment** → `public Future<Response>; createComment(...)`
- **Registers a marshaller to convert a JsonObject to JSON** → `register(JsonStructureBodyWriter.class)`
- **Executes a POST**
- **Makes an asynchronous call that returns the java.util.concurrent.Future class**

```
    }

    @PreDestroy
    public void preDestroy() {
        if (null != client) {
            client.close();
        }
    }
}
// end:test[]
```

Let's write a test for the `createComment` method: see listing 5.9 (code/aggregator/i-tests/ src/test/java/book/aggr/CommentsGatewayTest.java). Notice that in this case, you need to do the following:

1. Deploy the comments service in Tomcat.
2. Start a MongoDB instance, because it's the storage server used in that service.
3. Execute the test from the aggregator service for the `CommentsGateway` class.

Ideally, this test should deploy two artifacts: the comments service is deployed in its application server (Apache Tomcat); and, from the aggregator, `CommentsGateway` should be deployed in its application server (Apache TomEE). This seems like a perfect match for Arquillian's multideployment feature.

The problem is that you can't use that feature in this case. The aggregator service runs on an Apache Tomcat server, and the comments service runs on an Apache TomEE server—and Arquillian multideployments only work when you're using the same server for all deployments. Despite this limitation, you can use Arquillian in client mode and deploy the entire comments service in its own server (Apache TomEE), and use `CommentsGateway` in client mode instead of deploying it, too.

This test has the following features:

- A `@Deployment` method with the `testable` attribute set to `false` so the test is run in client mode
- Deployment of an entire application, rather than a microdeployment
- The test, using the `CommentsGateway` class

Listing 5.9 Testing the `createComment` method

```
@RunWith(Arquillian.class)                              Builds an artifact by running
public class CommentsGatewayTest {                      the Gradle assemble task in
                                                        the comments service
    @Deployment(testable = false)
    public static WebArchive createCommentsDeployment() {
        return ShrinkWrap.create(EmbeddedGradleImporter.class,
            CommentsGatewayTest.class.getName() + ".war")
            .forProjectDirectory("../../comments")
            .importBuildOutput().as(WebArchive.class);
    }
}
```

Sets the test in
client mode

```
@ArquillianResource                              Injects the URL where
private URL url;                                  the comments service
                                                 is deployed
@Test
public void shouldInsertCommentsInCommentsService() throws
        ExecutionException, InterruptedException {

    final JsonObject commentObject = Json.createObjectBuilder()
            .add("comment", "This Game is Awesome").add("rate",
                5).add("gameId", 1234).build();

    final CommentsGateway commentsGateway = new CommentsGateway
            ();
    commentsGateway.initRestClient(url.toString());

    final Future<Response>; comment = commentsGateway      Instantiates a new
            .createComment(commentObject);                 CommentsGateway
                                                           class, and executes
    final Response response = comment.get();               the create method
    final URI location = response.getLocation();

    assertThat(location).isNotNull();
    final String id = extractId(location);

    assertThat(id).matches("[0-9a-f]+");          Asserts that the returned
                                                  ID is a MongoDB object ID

}

}
```

This test runs in client mode. This means Arquillian deploys the test archive "as is" to the container and runs the test in the same JVM as the test runner.

The test also demonstrates another way to use the ShrinkWrap project. In the previous chapter, you saw how to use ShrinkWrap to create a microdeployment (a deployment file containing only parts of the application). But in this example, you create the project dynamically by using EmbeddedGradleImporter. With EmbeddedGradleImporter, you set the root directory where the build.gradle file is located, and ShrinkWrap takes care of calling Gradle tasks to assemble the project and return it as a valid archive. It ignores the test steps by default, to avoid possible infinite recursion.

There's also a MavenImporter class you can use if the project will be managed by Maven.

> **TIP** You can use the *Maven resolver* to resolve an artifact from your artifact repository instead of building it every time. An example of such a call is Maven.resolver().resolve("org.gamer:game-aggregator:war:1.0.0") .withTransitivity().as(WebArchive.class);.

Integration tests should also cover unexpected behaviors such as timeouts, slow responses from external communications, and internal errors. Such cases can be difficult to reproduce, so the best approach is to use a stub version of the external component with WireMock, which we introduced in chapter 4. It's best to put these corner test cases in a class other than the one containing the tests that validate whether the gateway works in normal conditions. Dividing test classes between expected and abnormal behaviors provides several advantages:

- You can run these tests in parallel.
- For an external reader, it's easier to understand how the class works in normal circumstances.
- You don't mix infrastructure code. In one case, you're deploying the real service; and in the other, you're deploying a stub service.

The following integration test checks abnormal situations for the CommentsGateway class (code/aggregator/i-tests/src/test/java/book/aggr/CommentsNegativeTest.java).

Listing 5.10 Testing unexpected behavior

```
public class CommentsNegativeTest {                          Starts the WireMock server

    @Rule
    public WireMockRule wireMockRule = new WireMockRule(8089);      ◄──┘

    @Test
    public void
    shouldReturnAServerErrorInCaseOfStatus500WhenCreatingAComment()
            throws ExecutionException, InterruptedException {
        stubFor(                              ◄── Records stub execution
                post(urlEqualTo("/comments")).willReturn(aResponse
                        ().withStatus(500).withBody("Exception " +
                        "during creation of comment")));

        CommentsGateway commentsGateway = new CommentsGateway();
        commentsGateway.initRestClient("http://localhost:8089"); // ◄──┐

        final JsonObject commentObject = Json.createObjectBuilder()
                .add("comment", "This Game is Awesome").add("rate",
                        5).add("gameId", 1234).build();

        final Future<Response>; comment = commentsGateway
                .createComment(commentObject);
        final Response response = comment.get();          Configures
                                               CommentsGateway to
                                               use a WireMock stub
        assertThat(response.getStatus()).isEqualTo(500);
        assertThat(response.getStatusInfo().getReasonPhrase())
                .isEqualTo("Server Error");   ◄──┐
    }                                            Verifies that the error code
                                                 and message use an internal
                                                 server error type
    @Test
    public void shouldThrowAnExceptionInCaseOfTimeout() throws
            ExecutionException, InterruptedException {
        stubFor(post(urlEqualTo("/comments")).willReturn(aResponse
                ().withStatus(201).withHeader("Location",
```

```
                    "http://localhost:8089/comments/12345")
                    .withFixedDelay(1000)                    ┌──────────────────┐
        ));                                                  │ Sets the response│
                                                             │ time to 1 second │
        CommentsGateway commentsGateway = new CommentsGateway();
        commentsGateway.initRestClient("http://localhost:8089");

        final JsonObject commentObject = Json.createObjectBuilder()
                .add("comment", "This Game is Awesome").add("rate",
                        5).add("gameId", 1234).build();

        final Future<Response>; comment = commentsGateway
                .createComment(commentObject);

        try {
            comment.get();
        } catch (Exception e) {
            assertThat(e).isInstanceOf(ExecutionException.class);
            final Throwable processingException = e.getCause();
            assertThat(processingException).isInstanceOf
                    (ProcessingException.class);
            assertThat(processingException.getCause()).isInstanceOf
                    (SocketTimeoutException.class);
        }


        }
    }
```

Verifies that a timeout exception is thrown (annotation pointing to the catch block)

In this case, you're testing two scenarios: how the gateway behaves when the external service returns a server error, and how the gateway behaves when the external service takes more time than expected to return a response. For the latter case, you configure a fixed delay of 1 second: it's enough, because CommentsGateway is configured with a timeout of a half second.

You can test other abnormal situations in a similar way. This test demonstrates the most common use cases.

This is the last integration test we'll show you. As you've learned, you can write integration tests to verify communication with external elements of the service, such as other services or persistence servers.

5.4   *Exercises*

After reading this chapter, you're ready to write tests for book.games.boundary.Igdb-Gateway, which is located in the aggregator service. This gateway connects to an external public service: the IGDB site.

For this test, we suggest that you use what you learned in chapter 4 about Arquillian and WildFly Swarm: deploy the gateway class into WildFly Swarm, because the service to which the gateway connects is already deployed, and test the methods. To test abnormal behaviors, use WireMock, as you did to test the comments gateway earlier in this chapter.

Also try writing a test for `book.video.boundary.YouTubeVideos` from the video service. This is a persistence test using Redis as the backend. Use what you learned about the Spring Boot testing framework in chapter 4 and section 5.2.

Summary

- Integration tests are responsible for testing communication between a microservice and its data stores or external components.
- You can develop persistence tests for SQL and NoSQL databases that are isolated between executions.
- Tests for gateway classes may need to communicate with external services.
- You can resolve artifacts in tests from an artifact store or build them before executing the test.
- The main difficulty with integration tests is having external components and data stores deployed, up, and running. For example, you may need to install in your test environment the data store used in production, or deploy an external service the same way you do in production.
- Arquillian provides a multideployment feature, but it's limited because you need to run the deployments on the same application server. One possible workaround is to deploy the entire application using Arquillian and Shrink-Wrap resolvers, and use a gateway class from outside the container. This is a valid approach, but you're still constrained by the technology used in the gateway and the external component implementation.

Contract tests

This chapter covers

- Understanding and writing contract tests
- Using consumer-driven contracts
- Working with Pact JVM
- Integrating with Arquillian

So far in this book, you've learned about unit, component, and integration tests. One thing they have in common is that they don't test the entire application, but rather isolated parts of it. With unit tests, the unit under test consists of only one or a few classes; with integration tests, you test whether boundaries can connect to a real service. This is the first chapter in which you'll write tests to understand the application as a whole. In this chapter, you'll learn why it's important to use contract tests to verify the entire system, and how to write them.

6.1   Understanding contracts

The microservices architecture involves a lot of intercommunication between microservices. In this book's Gamer example, you saw interactions between the aggregator service, the video service, the comments service, and so on. These interactions effectively form a contract between the services: this contract consists of expectations of input and output data as well as pre- and post-conditions.

A contract is formed for each service that *consumes* data from another service, which provides (or *produces*) data based on the first service's requirements. If the service that produces data can change over time, it's important that the contracts with each service that consumes data from it continue to meet expectations. *Contract tests* provide a mechanism to explicitly verify that a component meets a contract.

6.1.1 *Contracts and monolithic applications*

In a monolithic application, services are developed in the same project, side by side. What makes them look different is that each service is developed in a separate module or subproject, running under the same runtime.

In this kind of application, you don't need to worry about breaking the contract (or compatibility) between services, because there's an invisible verifier called a *compiler*. If one service changes its contract, the compiler will reject that build due to a compilation error. Let's look at an example. Here's serviceA.jar:

```
public class ServiceA {
  void createMessage(String parameterA, String parameterB) {}
}
```

And this is serviceB.jar:

```
public class ServiceB {
  private ServiceA serviceA;

  public void callMessage() {
    String parameterA;
    String parameterB;
    // some logic for creating message
    serviceA.createMessage(parameterA, parameterB);
  }

}
```

The two services, service A and service B, are developed in two different JAR files. Service A calls service B by calling its method `createMessage`, which requires that you pass it two `String` parameters. And precisely this method is the contract between both services.

But what if service A changes its contract to something like the following?

```
public class ServiceA {
  void createMessage(String parameterA, Integer parameterB) {}
}
```

The method signature has been changed to receive one `String` and one `Integer`. This breaks compatibility with service B (one consumer of the service). This isn't an issue in a monolithic application, because you'll get a compilation error informing you that method `createMessage` requires (`String`, `Integer`) but (`String`, `String`) was found. Thus it's quick and easy to detect when a contract is broken.

From the point of view of testing, modules can be set in the test logic by instantiating them using the new keyword or, with container support like context dependency injection (CDI) or Spring inversion of control (IoC), by using Arquillian or the Spring Test Framework. But in with a microservices architecture, things become more complex and harder to detect. If a contract between two services is broken, it may not be detected for quite some time.

6.1.2 *Contracts and microservice applications*

Each microservice has its own lifecycle, is deployed in its own runtime, and lives remotely from other microservices. In this scenario, any change to the contract of one service can't be caught by the compiler. Figure 6.1 illustrates how each service runs in a different runtime.

Breaking the compatibility between services could happen and would be hard to detect. It's easier to break compatibility because you don't have direct feedback that something has been broken. It's harder to detect that you've broken compatibility because, depending on the kind of (or lack of) tests you run, you may find the problem in (pre)production environments.

Usually, each service is developed by a different team, making compatibility issues more complicated to detect if there isn't good communication between teams. In our

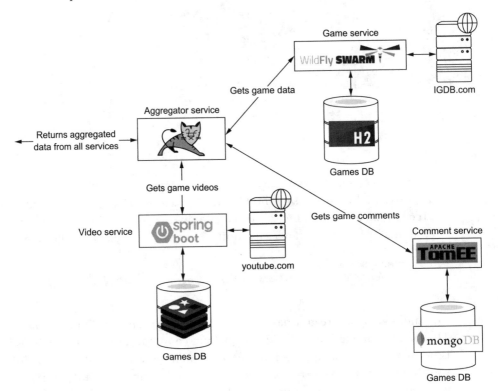

Figure 6.1 Big-picture overview of the example application

experience, the most common problems come from a change in the *provider* side so that the *consumer* can't interact with the provider.

The most common issues are these:

- A service renames its endpoint URL.
- A service adds a new mandatory parameter.
- A service changes/removes an existing parameter.
- A service changes the validation expression of input parameters.
- A service changes its response type or status code.

Consider an example where you have two services, producer and consumer A. The producer service exposes a blog-post resource in JSON format, which is consumed by consumer A.

A possible representation of this document might be thus:

```
{
  "id" : 1,
  "body" : "Hello World",
  "created" : "05/12/2012",
  "author" : "Ada"
}
```

The message contains four attributes: id, body, created, and author. Consumer A interacts only with the body and author fields, ignoring the others. This is summarized in figure 6.2.

After some time, a new consumer consumes the producer resource API. This new consumer, consumer B, requires both the author and body fields, as well a new field (author id) that's the identifier for the blog post's author.

At this point, the maintainers of the producer service can take two different approaches:

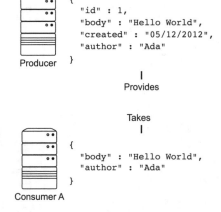

Figure 6.2   Data exchange between producer and consumer A

- Add a new field at the root level.
- Create a composite object with the author field.

The first approach adds a new field to the document called authorId at same level as author. A representation of this document might be as follows:

```
{
  "id" : 1,
  "body" : "Hello World",
  "created" : "05/12/2012",
  "author" : "Ada",
  "authorId" : "123"
}
```

With this change, consumer B's requirements are met. If consumer A follows *Postel's Law*, it will be able to continue consuming messages from the producer service.

> **The robustness principle**
>
> The *Robustness Principle*, also known as *Postel's Law*, comes from Jon Postel. He wrote an early specification of the TCP protocol and asserted the following:
>
> > *Be conservative in what you do, be liberal in what you accept from others.*
> > —Jon Postel
>
> This was an awful principle when applied to HTML, because it created the ridiculous browser battles that have now been largely resolved by a much stricter HTML5 specification. But for payload parsing, this principle still holds true. In other words, adapted to our case, producers and consumers should ignore any payload fields that aren't important to them.

Figure 6.3 shows that both consumers can still consume messages from the provider. But suppose the maintainers decide on the second approach and create a composite object from the authorInfo field:

```
{
  "id" : 1,
  "body" : "Hello World",
  "created" : "05/12/2012",
  "author" : {
      "name" : "Ada",
      "id" : "123"
  }
}
```

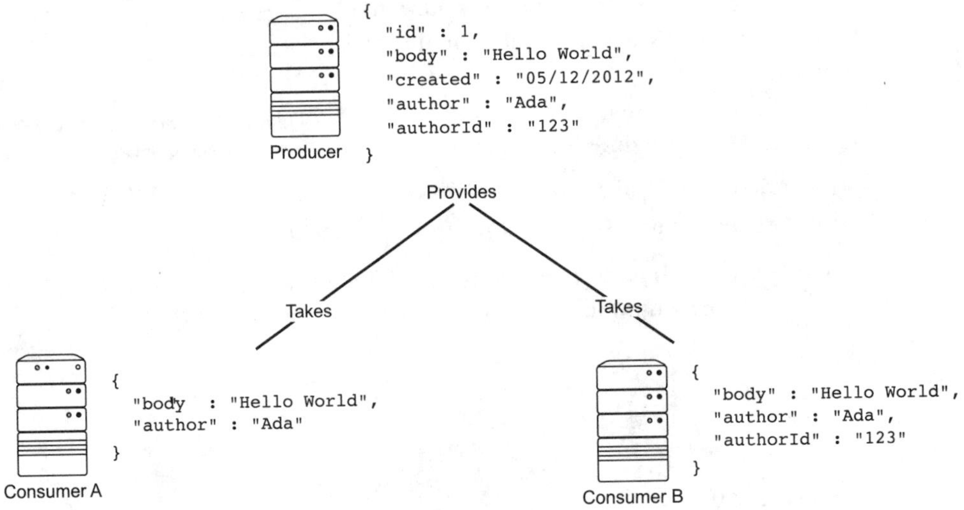

Figure 6.3   Data exchange between producer and consumers A and B

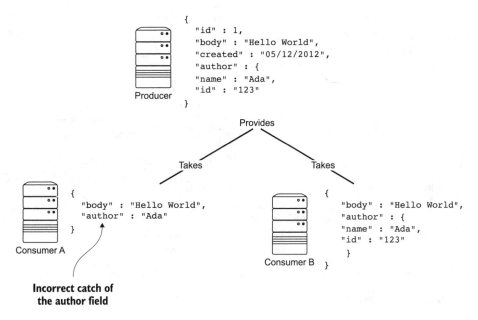

Figure 6.4 **Updated data-exchange scheme**

With this change, consumer B's requirements are met, but the change breaks compatibility with consumer A. In figure 6.4, you can see that although consumer B can process messages from the provider, consumer A can't, because it expects an `author` field of type `string`.

This change would be caught at compilation time if you were using the monolithic approach, but in this case, you don't know about it immediately. From the producer's point of view, even if all of its tests pass, you still don't know that the contract has been broken.

This problem will occur with consumer services, when the new producer service is deployed into a full environment with all services running and operating normally. At this point, consumers will begin operating incorrectly, because the contract has been broken. A new patch should be developed for all consumer services that have adapted the producer API and are now failing.

The later you catch a bug, the harder it is to fix it—and, depending on the phase in application deployment, the urgency can be severe. Suppose you found this bug in a production environment. At this phase, you'd need to roll back the new producer service to the old one, as well as all consumers that have been updated, to get the environment up and running again. Then you'd spend a substantial amount of time determining why the deployment failed and fixing it. The graph in figure 6.5 shows the cost of a bug found during different phases of a project.

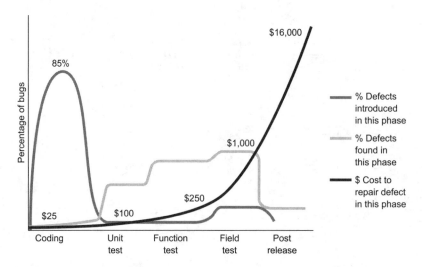

Source: Applied Software Measurement *by Capers Jones (McGraw-Hill, 1996)*

Figure 6.5   Costs of fixing bugs in specific development phases

Using a microservices architecture implies changing the way services are tested to detect such issues before a new producer service is deployed. Ideally, bugs should be detected in your CI/delivery run during the testing stage.

Deprecation method

You can also mix the two approaches to solving this problem, by deprecating the `author` field instead of removing it. The new document looks like this:

```
{
  "id" : 1,
  "body" : "Hello World",
  "created" : "05/12/2012",
  "author" : "Ada",
  "authorInfo" : {
      "name" : "Ada",
      "id" : "123"
  }
}
```

A new field called `authorInfo` has been created, and `author` is still valid but deprecated. This approach doesn't replace any tests, because you'll still have the same problem whenever you decide to remove the deprecated fields. But at least there's a transition, and there may be time for consumer maintainers to be notified about the change and adapt to it.

6.1.3 *Verifying with integration tests*

In chapter 5, you saw that you use integration tests to test whether it's possible for one system to communicate with another. Expressed in contract terms, you're testing that the *boundary* or *gateway* class of a given consumer can communicate correctly with a provider to get or post some data.

You may think that integration tests cover the use case where a contract is broken. But this approach has some issues that make running such tests for services difficult.

First, the consumer must know how to boot up the provider. Second, the consumer may depend on several providers. Each provider may have different requirements, such as a database or other services. So, starting a provider can imply starting several services and, without noticing it, converting integration tests into end-to-end tests.

The third and most important issue is that you need to create a direct relationship between the producer and all of its consumers. When any change is made to the producer, integration tests from all consumers related to this producer must be run to ensure that they can still communicate with the provider. This arrangement is difficult to maintain, because for each new consumer, you need to notify the producer team and provide a new set of running tests.

Although integration tests might be a solution for verifying that consumers of one producer can connect, such tests may not always be the best approach to follow.

6.1.4 *What are contract tests?*

As mentioned, a contract is a list of agreements between a service that acts as a client (or consumer) and another service that acts as a provider. The existence of a contract defining interactions between each consumer and its provider fixes all the problems described in section 6.1.3.

In figure 6.6, a contract between consumers and a provider is defined—let's say, by having a file describe it—and thus both provider and consumers have an agreement to follow. Now the relationship between consumers and the provider is indirect, because from the producer's point of view, you only need to verify that it meets the agreement described in the contract. The provider doesn't need to run the consumer's integration tests; it only needs to test that the consumer is able to consume requests and produce responses following the contract.

In this case, each provider has a/many contract(s) between it and all the consumers that are provisioning data. For every change made to a provider, all contracts are verified to detect any break, without having to run integration tests.

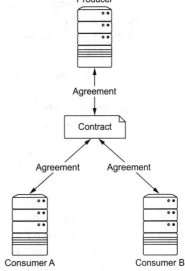

Figure 6.6 Provider and consumer interactions

The contract is also validated on the consumer side, verifying that its client classes (*gateways*) follow the contract. Notice that, again, you don't need to know how a producer is booted up or start any external dependency that may depend on it, because verifying the contract doesn't imply starting the producer; you're only verifying that the consumer also meets the contract.

Tests that verify contracts are known as *contract tests*. The next big question is, who's responsible for creating and maintaining contract files? We'll address this next.

6.1.5   *Who owns the contracts?*

As you just learned, the best way to validate that a consumer and a provider can communicate correctly and continuously is to define a contract between them. But we haven't addressed who has ownership of this contract: the consumer team or the provider team.

WHAT ARE PROVIDER CONTRACTS?

If the ownership of the contract lies with the team that's developing the provider, this implies that they not only know the business behavior of their own service (the provider) but also the requirements of all consumers their service supports. This kind of contract is called a *provider contract* because the contract belongs to the provider, and consumers are merely viewers of it (see figure 6.7). One example of where such a contract might be beneficial is an internal security authentication/authorization service, where consuming services must conform to the provider contract.

Provider contracts define what the provider will offer to consumers. Each consumer must adapt to what the provider offers. Naturally, this implies that the consumer is coupled to the provider. If the contract developed by the provider team no longer satisfies the requirements of a consumer, the consumer team must start a conversation with the maintainers of the provider service to address this deficiency.

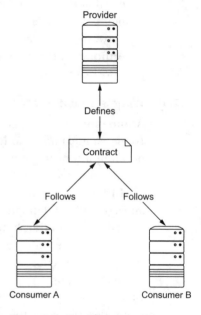

Figure 6.7   Provider contracts

WHAT ARE CONSUMER CONTRACTS?

On the other hand, to fix the problem of one-size-fits-all contracts without forcing the provider team to define a complete contract, you can change the ownership of the contract by making the developers of the consumer service define what they need and send that contract to the provider team to implement. Such a contract is called a *consumer contract* because it belongs to the consumer.

Consumer contracts define the consumer's needs from the consumer's point of view. Hence this contract applies only to that individual consumer and its particular use case.

Consumer contracts can be used to complete an existing provider contract (if there is one), or they can help develop a new one. Figure 6.8 shows that there's one consumer contract for each provider-consumer relationship instead of a single contract for all consumers.

As an example, consumer contracts might be beneficial for an internal checkout service in an organization, where the pace of the service's evolution will be controlled by the provider, but the data pulled from this service is used in different contexts. These contexts may evolve individually, but there's an internal locus of control and evolution.

WHAT ARE CONSUMER-DRIVEN CONTRACTS?

A *consumer-driven contract* represents an aggregation of all the contracts a provider has with all of its consumers (see figure 6.9). Obviously, a provider can evolve or extend consumers' contracts by creating a provider contract, as long as the provider's obligations to all consumers are satisfied.

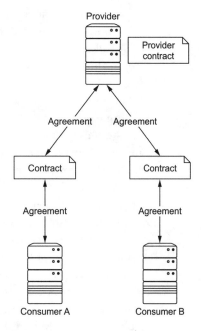

Figure 6.8   Consumer contracts

Consumer-driven contracts establish that a service provider is developed from its consumers' perspective. Each consumer communicates to its provider the specific

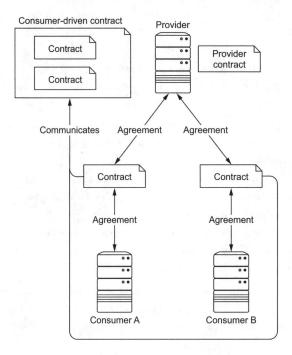

Figure 6.9   Consumer-driven contracts

requirements for meeting that consumer's use cases. These requirements create an obligation on the provider's side to meet all the expectations of the consumers.

Ideally, contract tests are developed, bundled by the consumer team, and sent to the producer team so they can develop the producing service. By assigning ownership of consumer contracts to consumer teams, you ensure that a provider's consumer-driven contract is what consumers need, rather than a provider's interpretation of consumer expectations. In addition, when the maintainers of the producing service change the provider-service code base, they know the impact of their changes on consumers, ensuring that there's no communication failure at runtime when the new version of the providing service is deployed.

There are also some obligations on the consumer side. Providers are obliged to follow a consumer-driven contract, and consumers must ensure that they follow their part of the contract—nothing more, nothing less. Consumers should consume only what they need from the provider side. This way, consumers protect themselves against evolution of the provider contract resulting from the provider adding to it.

One example of where consumer-driven contracts may be beneficial is an *external* (open to an outside organization) or *internal* user service that's used across the organization. Data is pulled from this service for multiple other contexts. These contexts all evolve individually, and there's an external locus of control/evolution.

So far in this chapter, we've discussed the problem of having services running in different runtimes, why integration tests aren't enough, and why consumer-driven contracts help you fix communication problems that may appear when updating the producer service. Let's see how to practice these principles, as well as which tools can help you use the consumer-driven-contracts pattern for the microservices architecture.

6.2   *Tools*

We've explained why it's important to write contract tests in the microservices architecture to avoid surprises when a service is deployed to production. Next, let's look at the tools you can use to write contract tests. These are the three most popular tools:

- *Spring Cloud Contract*—A test framework developed under the Spring ecosystem, in Groovy. Although it integrates well with Spring products, it can be used by any application developed with a JVM language.
- *Pact*—A family of test frameworks that provide support for consumer-driven contract testing. It has official implementations for Ruby, JVM languages, .NET, JavaScript, Go, Python, Objective-C, PHP, and Swift languages.
- *Pacto*—A test framework for developing consumer-driven contract tests and/or document-driven contracts. It's written in Ruby, although it can be used with several languages such as Python and Java by using the Pacto server.

In our opinion, Pact (https://docs.pact.io) is the most widely adopted and mature project on the contract-testing scene. One of its main advantages is its support for almost all major languages used today for writing microservices; the same concepts can be reused independently of the programming language, from frontend to back-end. For these reasons, we strongly believe that Pact is the most generic solution for writing consumer-driven contracts. It adapts well to microservices architectures developed in Java.

The next section explores in depth how Pact works and how to write contract tests with Pact.

6.2.1 Pact

The Pact framework lets you write contracts on the consumer side by providing a mock HTTP server and a fluent API to define the HTTP requests made from consumer to service provider and the HTTP responses expected in return. These HTTP requests and responses are used in the mock HTTP server to mock the service provider. The interactions are then used to generate the contract between service consumer and service provider.

Pact also provides the logic for validating the contract against the provider side. All interactions that occur on the consumer are played back in the "real" service provider to ensure that the provider produces the response the consumer expects for given requests. If the provider returns something unexpected, Pact marks the interaction as a failure, and the contract test fails.

Any contract test is composed of two parts: one for the consumer and another for the provider. In addition, a contract file is sent from consumer to provider. Let's look at the lifecycle of a contract test using Pact:

1 Consumer expectations are set up on a mock HTTP server using a fluent API. Consumer communication takes place with the mock HTTP server handling HTTP requests/responses but never interacting with the provider. This way, the consumer doesn't need to know how to deploy a provider (because it might not be trivial to do so, and will probably result in writing end-to-end tests instead of contract tests). The consumer verifies that its client/gateway code can communicate against the mock HTTP server with defined interactions.

   When consumer tests are run, all interactions are written into a pact contract file, which defines the contract that the consumer and provider must follow.

2 The pact contract file is sent to the provider project to be replayed against the provider service. The contract is played back against the real provider, and real responses from the provider are checked against the expected responses defined in the contract.

   If the consumer is able to produce a pact contract file, and the provider meets all the expectations, then the contract has been verified by both parties, and they will be able to communicate.

These steps are summarized in figure 6.10.

Step 1: Define consumer expectations.

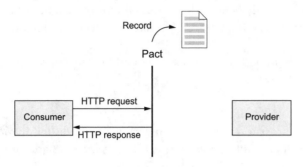

Step 2: Verify expectations on the provider.

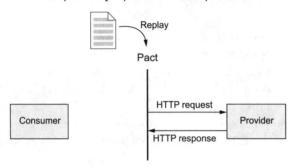

Figure 6.10   Pact lifecycle

In summary, Pact offers the following features:

- A mock HTTP server so you don't have to depend on the provider.
- An HTTP client to automatically replay expectations.
- States to communicate the expected state from the consumer side to the provider before replaying expectations. For example, an interaction might require that the provider database contains a user called *Alexandra* before replaying an expectation.
- *Pact Broker* is a repository for contracts, allowing you to share pacts between consumers and providers, versioning pact contract files so the provider can verify itself against a fixed version of a contract, and providing documentation for each pact as well as a visualization of the relationship between services.

Next, we'll explore Pact JVM: the implementation of Pact for the Java virtual machine.

6.2.2   *Pact in JVM languages*

Pact JVM is partially written in Scala, Groovy, and Java, but it can be used with any JVM language. It integrates perfectly with Java, Scala, Groovy, Grails (providing a Groovy DSL for defining contracts), and Clojure. In addition, it offers tight integration with test frameworks like JUnit, Spock, ScalaTest, and Specs2, as well as build tools such as

Maven, Gradle, Leiningen, and sbt. This book focuses on Java tools, but keep in mind that if you plan to use any other JVM language, you can still use Pact JVM for consumer-driven contract testing.

Let's see how to write consumer and provider tests using Pact JVM.

CONSUMER TESTING WITH PACT JVM

Pact JVM provides a mock HTTP server and a Java domain-specific language (DSL) for writing the expectations of the mock HTTP server. These expectations are materialized into pact contract files when the consumer test passes.

Pact JVM integrates with JUnit, providing a DSL and base classes for use with JUnit to build consumer tests. The first thing you do to write a consumer test using JUnit is register the `PactProviderRule` JUnit rule. This rule does the following:

- Starts and stops the mock HTTP server
- Configures the mock HTTP server with defined expectations
- Generates pact contract files from defined expectations if the test passes

Here's an example:

```
@Rule
public PactProviderRule mockProvider =
                       new PactProviderRule("test_provider",
                                            "localhost", 8080,
                                            this);
```

The first argument is the provider name that the current consumer contract is defining. This name is used to refer to the provider of a given contract. Next are two optional parameters: the host where the mock HTTP server is bound, and the listening port. If values aren't specified, *localhost* and *8080* are used, respectively. Finally, the `this` instance is the test itself.

Next, you define the expectations by annotating a method with `au.com.dius.pact` `.consumer.Pact`. This method must receive a class of type `PactDslWithProvider` and return a `PactFragment`. `PactDslWithProvider` is a Java class that's built around a DSL pattern to provide a description of the request that's expected to be received when a mock HTTP server is used. As its name suggests, the `PactFragment` object is a fragment of a contract. It's used as the expectation in the mock HTTP server and also to generate a pact contract file that's used to verify the provider. The fragment may be the complete contract or only part of it. If more than one fragment is defined in the same test class, the pact contract file consists of the aggregation of all fragments.

The `@Pact` method must have this signature:

```
@Pact(provider="test_provider", consumer="test_consumer")
public PactFragment createFragment(PactDslWithProvider builder) {
  //...
}
```

Notice that in the @Pact annotation, you set the name of the provider that should follow the contract and the name of the consumer that's defining the contract. This information is important for provider test execution, to be sure the provider-side test is executed against all consumers for which the provider provides data.

The next snippet defines a request/response expectation. PactDslWithProvider has several options you can define:

```
                       return builder
Reacts to the              .uponReceiving("a request for something")    ◄──┐ Defines a new
/hello path for                .path("/hello")                              request interaction
the HTTP POST  └──►             .method("POST")
                               .body("{\"name\": \"Ada\"}")   ◄──┐ The body of the request must
Defines the                                                      contain the given JSON document.
response to the └──► .willRespondWith()
previous request               .status(200)        ◄── Returns HTTP status code 200
                  ┌──►          .body("{\"hello\": \"Ada\"}")
The response body's        .uponReceiving("another request for something")
content is the given            .matchPath("/hello/[0-9]+")      ◄──┐
JSON document.                  .method("POST")                      Reacts to any path that
                                .body("{\"name\": \"Ada\"}")         starts with /hello/ and
                           .willRespondWith()                        any number
                               .status(200)
                               .body("{\"hello\": \"Ada\"}")
                           .toFragment();
```

This example defines two expectations. The first request happens when the consumer sends a request using the POST method at /hello. The body of the message must contain exactly the JSON document {"name": "Ada"}. If this happens, then the response is the JSON document {"hello": "Ada"}. The second request happens when the path starts with /hello followed by any valid number. The conditions are the same as for the first request.

Notice that you can define as many interactions as required. Each interaction starts with uponReceiving, followed by willRespondWith to record the response.

> **TIP** To keep your tests as readable and simple as possible, and to stay focused on the *one method, one task* approach, we recommend using several fragments for all interactions, instead of defining one big @Pact method that returns everything.

One important aspect of the previous definitions is that the body content is required to be the same as specified in the contract. For example, a request for something has a strong requirement that the response be provided only if the JSON document is {"name": "Ada"}. If the name is anything other than Ada, then the response isn't generated. The same is true for the returned body. Because the JSON document is static, the response is always the same.

This can be a restriction in cases where you can't set a static value, especially when it comes to running contracts against the provider. For this reason, the builder's body method can accept a `PactDslJsonBody` that can be used to construct a JSON body dynamically.

The PactDslJsonBody class

The `PactDslJsonBody` builder class implements a DSL pattern that you can use to construct a JSON body dynamically as well as define regular expressions for fields and type matchers. Let's look at some examples.

The following snippet generates a simple JSON document without an array:

```
                 Defines a field named name, of type
                 string, where value isn't important
DslPart body = new PactDslJsonBody()                Defines a field named happy, of
  .stringType("name")          ←                    type boolean, where value isn't
  .booleanType("happy")        ←                    important
  .id()
  .ipAddress("localAddress")          Defines a field named age, of type
  .numberValue("age", 100);    ←      number, with the specific value 100
```

Using the *xType* form, you can also set an optional value parameter that's used to generate example values when returning a mock response. If no example is provided, a random one is generated.

The previous `PactDslJsonBody` definition will match any body like this:

```
{
  "name" : "QWERTY",
  "happy": false,
  "id" : 1234,
  "localAddress" : "127.0.0.1",
  "age": 100,
}
```

Notice that any document containing all the required fields of the required type and having an `age` field with the value `100` is valid.

`PactDslJsonBody` also offers methods for defining array matchers. For example, you can validate that a list has a minimum or maximum size, or that each item in the list matches a given example:

```
                                                     Defines that the list
                                                     must contain at least
              DslPart body = new PactDslJsonBody()   one element
                .minArrayLike("products", 1)    ←
Specifies that each    ┌→   .id()
document in the             .stringType("name")
list must contain an        .stringMatcher("barcode", "a\\d+", "a1234")
ID, a name, and a           .closeObject()
barcode             └  .closeArray();
```

Here, the `products` array can't be empty, and every product should have an identifier and a name of type `string` as well as a barcode that matches the form `"a"` plus a list of numbers.

If the size of the elements isn't important, you can do this:

```
PactDslJsonArray.arrayEachLike()
    .date("expireDate", "mm/dd/yyyy", date)
    .stringType("name")
    .decimalType("amount", 100.0)
    .closeObject()
```

In this example, each array must contain three fields: `expireDate`, `name`, and `amount`. Moreover, in the mocked response, each element will contain a `date` variable value in the `expireDate` field, a random `string` in the `name` field, and the value `100.0` in `amount`.

As you can see, using `DslPart` to generate the body lets you define field types instead of concrete specific field/value pairs. This makes your contract more resilient during contract validation on the provider side. Suppose you set `.body("{'name': 'Ada'}")` in the provider-validation phase: you expect the provider to produce the same JSON document with the same values. This may be correct in most cases; but if the test dataset changes and, instead of returning `.body("{'name': 'Ada'}")`, it returns `.body("{'name': 'Alexandra'}")`, the test will fail—although from the point of view of the contract, both responses are valid.

Now that you've seen how to write consumer-driven contracts with Pact on the consumer side, let's look at how to write the provider part of the test.

PROVIDER TESTING WITH PACT JVM

After executing the consumer part of the test and generating and publishing the pact contract file, you need to play back the contract against a real provider. This part of the test is executed on the provider side, and Pact offers several tools to do so:

- *JUnit*—Validates contracts in JUnit tests
- *Gradle, Lein, Maven, sbt*—Plugins for verifying contracts against a running provider
- *ScalaTest*—Extension to validate contracts against a running provider
- *Specs2*—Extension to validate contracts against a running provider

In general, all of these integrations offer two ways to retrieve published contracts: by using Pact Broker and by specifying a concrete location (a file or a URL). The way to configure a retrieval method depends on how you choose to replay contracts. For example, JUnit uses an annotations approach, whereas in Maven, a plugin's configuration section is used for this purpose.

Let's examine how you can implement provider validation using Maven, Gradle, and JUnit.

USING MAVEN FOR VERIFYING CONTRACTS

Pact offers a Maven plugin for verifying contracts against providers. To use it, add the following to the `plugins` section of pom.xml.

Listing 6.1 Adding the Maven plugin

```
<plugin>
  <groupId>au.com.dius</groupId>
  <artifactId>pact-jvm-provider-maven_2.11</artifactId>
  <version>3.5.0</version>
</plugin>
```

Then you need to configure the plugin, defining all the providers you want to validate and the location of the consumer contract that you want to use to check them.

Listing 6.2 Configuring the Maven plugin

```
<plugin>
  <groupId>au.com.dius</groupId>
  <artifactId>pact-jvm-provider-maven_2.11</artifactId>
  <version>3.2.10</version>
  <configuration>
    <serviceProviders>                               Provider (or providers)
      <serviceProvider>              ◄──┘            to verify
        <name>provider1</name>
        <protocol>http</protocol>
        <host>localhost</host>                       Name of the provider (must be unique)
        <port>8080</port>                            and the location where it's deployed
        <path>/</path>               ◄──┘
        <pactFileDirectory>path/to/pacts</pactFileDirectory>    ◄──┐
      </serviceProvider>
    </serviceProviders>
  </configuration>                                   Directory where all Pact
</plugin>                                             contracts are stored
```

To verify contacts, execute `mvn pact:verify`. The Maven plugin will load all Pact contracts defined in the given directory and replay those that match the given provider name. If all the contracts validate against the provider, then the build will finish successfully; if not, the build will fail.

USING GRADLE FOR VERIFYING CONTRACTS

The Gradle plugin uses an approach similar to Maven's to verify contracts against providers. To use it, add the following to the `plugins` section of .build.gradle.

Listing 6.3 Adding the Gradle plugin

```
plugins {
  id "au.com.dius.pact" version "3.5.0"
}
```

Then configure the plugin, defining the providers you want to validate and the location of the consumer contract you want to use to check them.

Listing 6.4   Configuring the Maven plugin

```
pact {

  serviceProviders {                       Provider (or providers)
                                           to verify
    provider1 {
      protocol = 'http'
      host = 'localhost'
      port = 8080                          Name of the provider (must be unique)
      path = '/'                           and the location where it's deployed

      hasPactsWith('manyConsumers') {      Directory where all Pact
        pactFileLocation = file('path/to/pacts')   contracts are stored
      }
    }
  }
}
```

To verify contacts, execute `gradlew pactVerify`. The Gradle plugin will load all Pact contracts defined in the given directory and replay those that match the given provider name. If all the contracts validate against the provider, then the build will finish successfully; if not, the build will fail.

Finally, let's see how to validate providers by using JUnit instead of relying on a build tool.

USING JUNIT FOR VERIFYING CONTRACTS

Pact offers a JUnit runner for verifying contracts against providers. This runner provides an HTTP client that automatically replays all the contracts against the configured provider. It also offers convenient out-of-the-box ways to load pacts using annotations.

Using the JUnit approach, you need to register `PactRunner`, set the provider's name with the `@Provider` annotation, and set the contract's location. Then, you create a field of type `au.com.dius.pact.provider.junit.target.Target` that's annotated with `@TestTarget` and instantiates either `au.com.dius.pact.provider.junit.target.HttpTarget` to play pact contract files as HTTP requests and assert the response or `au.com.dius.pact.provider.junit.target.AmqpTarget` to play pact contract files as AMQP messages.

> **Note**
> *Advanced Message Queuing Protocol* (AMQP) is an application layer protocol for message-oriented middleware. The features it defines are message orientation, queuing, routing, reliability, and security.

Let's look at an example using `HttpTarget`, from PactTest.java.

Listing 6.5   Using the JUnit runner

```
                    @RunWith(PactRunner.class)          ◄──┐   Registers PactRunner
Sets the
provider's          @Provider("provider1")
name     └─▷        @PactFolder("pacts")                ◄──┐
                    public class ContractTest {            │  Sets where contract files are stored.
Sets the                                                   │  In this case, the location resolves to
target to                                                  │  src/test/resources(pacts).
use for tests └─▷     @TestTarget
                     public final Target target = new HttpTarget("localhost", 8332);  ◄─┐
                    }
                                                         Configures the provider location
```

Notice that there's no test method annotated with `@Test`. This isn't required, because rather than a single test, there are many tests: one for each interaction between a consumer and the provider.

When this test is executed, the JUnit runner gets all the contract files from the pacts directory and replays all the interactions defined in them against the provider location specified in the `HttpTarget` instance.

`PactRunner` automatically loads contracts based on annotations on the test class. Pact provides three annotations for this purpose:

- `PactFolder`—Retrieves contracts from a project folder or resource folder; for example, `@PactFolder("subfolder/in/resource/directory")`.
- `PactUrl`—Retrieves contracts from URLs; for example, `@PactUrl(urls = {"http://myserver/contract1.json"})`.
- `PactBroker`—Retrieves contracts from Pact Broker; for example, `@PactBroker (host="pactbroker", port = "80", tags = {"latest", "dev"})`.
- `Custom`—To implement a custom retriever, create a class that implements the `PactLoader` interface and has one default empty constructor or a constructor with one argument of type `Class` (which represents the test class). Annotate the test like this: `@PactSource(CustomPactLoader.class)`.

You can also easily implement your own method.

PACT STATES

When you're testing, each interaction should be verified in isolation, with no context from previous interactions. But with consumer-driven contracts, sometimes the consumer wants to set up something on the provider side before the interaction is run, so that the provider can send a response that matches what the consumer expects. A typical scenario is setting up a datasource with expected data. For example, when testing the contract for an authentication operation, the consumer may require the provider to insert into a database a concrete login and password beforehand, so that when the interaction occurs, the provider logic can react appropriately to the data. Figure 6.11 summarizes the interaction between consumer, states, and provider.

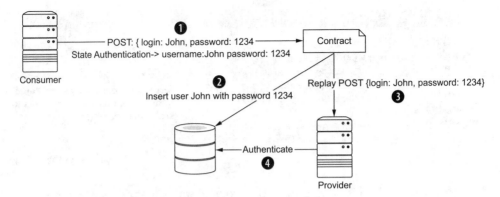

Figure 6.11 Interactions between consumer and provider

First, the consumer side defines that the authentication process should be done using a POST method containing a JSON body:

```
{
  "login": "John",
  "password": "1234"
}
```

Because this snippet will be used when replaying the contract against the provider, the consumer needs to warn the provider that it should prepare the database with the given information before executing this interaction. For this reason, the consumer creates a state called *state authentication* with all the required data. The state information is stored in the contract.

When the contract is replayed against the provider, before the interaction occurs, the state data is injected into the test so the test can prepare the environment for contract validation. Finally, contract validation is executed with the database containing the expected user information.

To define the state from the consumer side, you need to use the special method given when defining the contract:

```
@Override
protected PactFragment createFragment(PactDslWithProvider builder) {
    Map<String, Object> parameters = new HashMap<>();      ⊲   Defines the data
    parameters.put("login", "John");                           required in the state
    parameters.put("password", "1234")
    builder
      .given("State Authentication", parameters)          ⊲   Registers the state in
      .uponReceiving("")                                      the contract with a
      ....                                                     name and parameters
```

To react to a state on the provider side, you need to create a method annotated with
@State:

```
@State("State Authentication")                          Sets the name of the
                                                        state to react to
public void testStateMethod(Map<String, Object> params) {
  //Insert data                          The method receives as a Map the
}                                         parameters defined by the consumer.
```

Notice that with states, you can share information between consumer and provider, so you can configure the state of the test before interaction. Pact states are the preferred way to prepare the state of the provider from the consumer side.

Maven and Gradle integration also provide methods for setting states on the provider side. In these cases, for each provider, you specify a state-change URL to use for changing the state of the provider. This URL receives the providerState description from the pact contract file before each interaction, via a POST method.

6.2.3 *Integrating Pact JVM into the Arquillian ecosystem with Algeron*

Arquillian Algeron is an Arquillian extension that integrates Arquillian with contract testing. It provides common ground for integrating Arquillian with contract-testing frameworks.

Arquillian Algeron Pact is the integration of the Arquillian philosophy and extensions into the consumer-driven contracts approach using the Pact JVM core. By using Arquillian Algeron Pact, you get the best of both worlds: you can use the Pact-JVM approach to validate consumers and providers, and you can use Arquillian to run tests in an environment similar to production. Let's see how Arquillian Algeron Pact fits into the consumer and provider sides.

To implement a consumer gateway using a JAX-RS client, the code only uses the API interfaces (the implementation is usually provided by the application server). To run your tests, you'll need to define an implementation of JAX-RS; Apache CXF (http://cxf.apache.org) is a good choice. You can provide an implementation in your build tool, or you can write an Arquillian test. In Arquillian, the test and the business code are deployed and run on the application server you'll use in production with the same JAX-RS implementation and version.

On the provider side, you need to replay the contract against a running provider. You can rely on the build script to package and deploy the provider application, or you can use Arquillian to package and deploy the application in the test, avoiding dependence on a build tool.

> **TIP** When you're validating the provider side, you don't need to run providers with real databases or real external services; you can use in-memory databases or stubs. For this reason, using an Arquillian microdeployment can help you create deployment files that contain configuration files and classes that point to in-memory databases or stubbing implementations.

Arquillian Algeron offers other features in addition to integration between Pact and Arquillian:

- *Publishers*—On the consumer side, you can configure it to publish contracts into a specified repository if they're successfully generated. Currently supported publishers are *folder, URL, Git server,* and *Pact Broker,* but you can create your own as well.
- *Retrievers*—As with JUnit, you can configure contract loaders. In addition to those already supported in Pact JUnit (*folder, URL,* and *Pact Broker*), Arquillian Algeron supports *Git server* and *Maven artifact.*
- *Configuration*—Publishers and retrievers can be configured in an arquillian.xml file so everything is configured in a central place and not in every test class. Note that an annotation-based approach is also supported in retrievers.
- *TestNG*—Because Arquillian is test-framework-agnostic, you can use Pact and TestNG.

Later, we'll go deep into *publishers* and *retrievers* and how to use them.

> **TIP** It isn't mandatory to use Arquillian Algeron Pact on both the consumer and provider sides. You can use Pact JVM or any Pact implementation in any language on either the consumer or provider side, and use Arquillian Algeron Pact on the other side.

As with Pact JVM, Arquillian Algeron Pact is divided into consumer and provider parts.

> **WARNING** Because Arquillian Algeron uses Pact Core and not Pact JUnit, annotations are specific to Arquillian Algeron and aren't the same as in Pact JUnit.

WRITING THE CONSUMER SIDE WITH ARQUILLIAN ALGERON PACT

Following is an example of the consumer part of using Arquillian Algeron Pact, from ClientGatewayTest.java.

Listing 6.6 Arquillian Algeron Pact, consumer side

Arquillian runner ⊳

To define the contract, you annotate a method or class with org.arquillian.algeron.pact.consumer.spi.Pact and set the provider and consumer name.

Defines what you want to deploy to the defined container

```java
@RunWith(Arquillian.class)
@Pact(provider="provider", consumer="consumer")
public class ClientGatewayTest {

    @Deployment
    public static JavaArchive createDeployment() {
      return ShrinkWrap.create(JavaArchive.class)
        .addClasses(ClientGateway.class);
    }

    public PactFragment createFragment(PactDslWithProvider builder) {
```

```
                            return builder
                                ...
                                .toFragment();
Typical
Arquillian            }
enrichment
                    @EJB
                    ClientGateway clientGateway;

                    @Test
                    @PactVerification("provider")
                    public void should_return_message() throws IOException {
                        assertThat(clientGateway.getMessage(), is(....));
                    }
                }
```

Returns a fragment of the contract (may be the entire contract)

Defines which provider is validated when this test method is executed

Asserts that the gateway can read the kind of messages sent by the provider

Here, you're writing a consumer contract test that defines a contract between consumer and provider. The client gateway is implemented using a JAX-RS client; it's an EJB, so it knows to run that gateway under the same runtime it will find on production. For this reason, it's a good approach to use Arquillian Algeron instead of Pact JVM alone.

The @Pact annotation defines the interaction between consumer and provider. The annotation can be used at the class level, which means all contracts defined in this test are for the same provider; or, it can be used at the method level, which lets you specify that a concrete PactFragment defines only the interaction for the consumer-provider tuple defined in the annotation. Thus you could define contracts for different providers in the same consumer class. When the annotation is defined at the method level, it takes precedence over one defined at the class level.

TIP Defining contracts for several providers in the same test isn't something we recommend, because doing so breaks the pattern that one class should test one thing.

Finally, for each test case, you need to specify which provider is validated when that test is run. You do so by using @PactVerification and setting the provider name. Notice that setting the provider name isn't mandatory if you're using the @Pact annotation at the class level, because the provider name is resolved from there.

The steps executed when you use an Arquillian Algeron Pact consumer test are similar to a standard Arquillian test:

1 The chosen application server is started.
2 The (micro)deployment application file is deployed.
3 The Pact Stub HTTP server is started.
4 All interactions (PactFragments) are recorded.
5 Tests are executed.
6 For successful tests, contract files are generated.
7 The application is undeployed.
8 The application server is stopped.

If you're implementing more than one method that returns a `PactFragment` instance, you need to use the `fragment` attribute at `@PactVerification(.. fragment="create-Fragment")` to specify which fragment method is under test for that `@Test` method.

> **TIP** You can use Arquillian standalone with Arquillian Algeron if you want to skip the deployment step. This is useful if you're using a client gateway that doesn't depend on any features of your runtime.

WRITING THE PROVIDER SIDE WITH ARQUILLIAN ALGERON PACT

Now, let's see how to write the provider part using Arquillian Algeron Pact. Because Arquillian Algeron uses Pact JVM, the approach is exactly the same: it replays all requests defined in the contract against the real provider and validates that the response is the expected one.

Listing 6.7   Arquillian Algeron Pact, provider side

```
                        Arquillian runner     Sets the name of
                                              the provider used        Configures where
                                              in the test              to get the pact
@RunWith(Arquillian.class)     <—                                     contract files
@Provider("provider")          <—
@ContractsFolder("pacts")                           <—
public class MyServiceProviderTest {

  @Deployment(testable = false)                     <—  The test must be run as a
  public static WebArchive createDeployment() {          client; sets testable to false.
    return ShrinkWrap.create(WebArchive.class).addClass(MyService.class);
  }
                                    URL where the
  @ArquillianResource       <—      application is deployed
  URL webapp;

  @ArquillianResource      <—   A Target is a class that makes all the requests
  Target target;                to the provider. Arquillian Algeron Pact uses
                                an HTTP client target by default.
  @Test
  public void should_provide_valid_answers() {
    target.testInteraction(webapp);         <—   Executes the interaction against
  }                                              the deployed application, and
}                                              validates the response
}
```

This test validates that the provider meets the expectations defined by the consumer. Because you need to deploy a real provider, this is a good approach, because you can use Arquillian features to package, deploy, and start the application.

The first thing you do in a provider test is specify which provider you're validating. You do so by using `org.arquillian.algeron.pact.provider.spi.Provider` and setting the name of the provider given in the consumer test.

Arquillian Algeron supports two ways to retrieve contracts: by using annotations or by configuring the retriever in arquillian.xml. The latter option will be covered in the section "Registering publishers and retrievers," later in this chapter. In this test, contracts are retrieved from `pact` using the `org.arquillian.algeron.provider.core` `.retriever.ContractsFolder` annotation, but other annotations are also supported:

- `org.arquillian.algeron.provider.core.retriever.ContractsUrl`— Retrieves contracts from a URL
- `org.arquillian.algeron.pact.provider.loader.git.ContractsGit`— Retrieves contracts from a Git repository
- `org.arquillian.algeron.pact.provider.loader.maven.ContractsMaven-Dependency`—Retrieves contracts from Maven artifacts
- `org.arquillian.algeron.pact.provider.core.loader.pactbroker.Pact-Broker`—Retrieves contracts from a Pact Broker server

It's important to make this test run as a client, which means the test isn't executed in the application server. You can use Arquillian as the deployer; but replaying the interactions must be done from outside the container, as any other consumer would do.

Finally, you need to enrich the test with the URL where the application is deployed and an instance of `org.arquillian.algeron.pact.provider.core.httptarget.Target`, which you use to replay all interactions by calling the `testInteraction` method.

The steps executed in an Arquillian Algeron Pact provider test are similar to a standard Arquillian test:

1 The chosen application server is started.
2 The (micro)deployment application file is deployed.
3 Contracts are retrieved from the given location.
4 For each contract, Arquillian Algeron extracts each request/response pair, sends a request to the provider, and validates the response against the contract response.
5 The application is undeployed.
6 The application server is stopped.

Next, let's examine how you can use a feature provided by Arquillian Algeron that lets you publish contracts automatically and retrieve them in the provider.

REGISTERING PUBLISHERS AND RETRIEVERS

As mentioned earlier, Arquillian Algeron offers the possibility of publishing contracts to a repository and retrieving them for validation. Publishers are configured in an Arquillian configuration file called arquillian.xml. Retrievers can be configured using annotations, as you saw in the previous section, or in arquillian.xml.

At the time of writing, Arquillian Algeron defines four publishers out of the box:

- *Folders*—Copies contracts to a given folder
- *Url*—Makes a POST request to a given URL, with the contract as the body
- *Git*—Pushes contracts into a Git repository
- *pact-broker*—A specific publisher to store the contract in Pact Broker

Microdeployments

A provider can also be a consumer of other services, or it may have dependencies on datasources. This is inconvenient, because to validate the contract against the provider, you may have to boot up other providers and datasources, which is difficult and sometimes leaves you with flaky tests.

In the following figure, you can see that provider 1 is also a consumer of two services and requires a database.

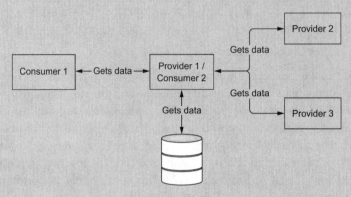

A provider that's also a consumer

The solution for avoiding dependency problems in tests depends on the kind of dependency. If you're dealing with another provider, you can use the service-virtualization approach using WireMock, as explained in chapter 4. If you're using a datasource, you can use your own stubs at database entry points with the required data, or use an in-memory database, as explained in chapter 5.

But in all cases, your deployment file will be different than the one you use in production. It contains test-configuration files that point to the service-virtualization instances and configure them to use an in-memory database or packaged alternative classes as stubs. In this context, as you learned in chapter 4, ShrinkWrap and microdeployment are helpful for generating deployment files dynamically in tests.

Arquillian Algeron also provides an SPI so you can implement your own publisher, but this topic is beyond the scope of this book. Refer to the Arquillian Algeron documentation for more information.

It's important to note that a Arquillian Algeron consumer won't publish contracts by default. This is a safety precaution to avoid publishing contracts every time consumer tests are run locally. To modify this behavior, you need to set the `publish-Contracts` configuration attribute to `true`. You should only do that if you're publishing a new version of a consumer, and this action should be performed by your continuous (CI/CD) environment.

TIP You can configure arquillian.xml attributes with system properties or environment variables by using a `${system_property}` placeholder or a `${env.environment_variable}` placeholder. You can add a default value by following the variable name with a colon (`:`) and the value.

Here's an example of how to configure a Git publisher in arquillian.xml:

Sets the publisher to Git

Retrieves the URL of the Git repository from the giturl environment variable

```
<extension qualifier="algeron-consumer">
  <property name="publishConfiguration">
    provider: git
    url: ${env.giturl}
    username: ${env.gitusername}
    password: ${env.gitpassword}
    comment: New Contract for Version ${env.artifactversion:1.0.0}
    contractsFolder: target/pacts
  </property>
  <property name="publishContracts">${env.publishcontracts:false}</property>
</extension>
```

The commit's comment field contains the version number, or 1.0.0 if the version isn't provided.

Sets the directory where contracts are generated

This snippet configures the publisher to push generated contracts to a Git repository. The publishing process is executed only when the environment variable `publishcontracts` is set to `true`; otherwise, contracts are generated in a local directory but not published.

Next, we'll look at how to configure retrievers in arquillian.xml. Registering a retriever in arquillian.xml uses the same approach as registering a publisher. The same retrievers mentioned in section 6.2.3, which can be used as annotations, are supported here.

Here's how to configure a retriever to get contracts from a Git repository:

```
<extension qualifier="algeron-provider">
  <property name="retrieverConfiguration">
    provider: git
    url: ${env.giturl}
    username: ${env.gitusername}
    password: ${env.gitpassword}
  </property>
</extension>
```

The format is similar to that for providers. Obviously, the property name and extension name are different, because retrievers are an important part of the provider side.

After this thorough introduction to contract testing, let's explore how to apply them to the book's example.

6.3 *Build-script modifications*

As you now know, contract tests are divided between the consumer side and the provider side. Each has its own dependencies. Let's look at each of these dependency cases, when using either Pact JVM or Arquillian Algeron.

6.3.1   *Using Pact JVM for contract testing*

If you're using Pact JVM for consumer-driven contracts, you need to add dependencies. For the consumer part, add the following dependencies:

```
dependencies {
   testCompile group: 'au.com.dius',
              name: 'pact-jvm-consumer-junit_2.11',
              version: '3.5.0'
}
```

And for the provider part, add these dependencies:

```
dependencies {
  testCompile group: 'au.com.dius',
              name: 'pact-jvm-provider-junit_2.11',
              version: '3.5.0'
}
```

6.3.2   *Using Arquillian Algeron for contract testing*

To use Arquillian Algeron with Pact JVM, you need to use at least two dependencies: Arquillian Algeron Pact, and Pact itself.

For the consumer part, add these dependencies:

```
dependencies {
   testCompile group: 'org.arquillian.algeron',
              name: 'arquillian-algeron-pact-consumer-core',
              version: '1.0.1'
   testCompile group: 'au.com.dius',
              name: 'pact-jvm-consumer_2.11',
              version: '3.5.0'
}
```

If you're using the Git publisher, you also need to add this dependency:

```
dependencies {
   testCompile group: 'org.arquillian.algeron',
              name: 'arquillian-algeron-consumer-git-publisher',
              version: '1.0.1'
}
```

For the provider part, add the following dependencies:

```
dependencies {
   testCompile group: 'org.arquillian.algeron',
              name: 'arquillian-algeron-pact-provider-core',
              version: '1.0.1'
   testCompile group: 'au.com.dius',
              name: 'pact-jvm-provider_2.11',
              version: '3.5.0'
}
```

Also add this, if you want to integrate with AssertJ:

```
dependencies {
   testCompile group: 'org.arquillian.algeron',
               name: 'arquillian-algeron-pact-provider-assertj',
               version: '1.0.1'
   testCompile group: 'org.assertj',
               name: 'assertj-core',
               version: '3.8.0'
}
```

If you're using the Git retriever, add this dependency:

```
dependencies {
   testCompile group: 'org.arquillian.algeron',
               name: 'arquillian-algeron-provider-git-retriever',
               version: '1.0.1'
}
```

If you're using the Maven retriever, add this dependency:

```
dependencies {
   testCompile group: 'org.arquillian.algeron',
               name: 'arquillian-algeron-provider-maven-retriever',
               version: '1.0.1'
}
```

And if you're using the Pact Broker retriever, you also need to add this dependency:

```
dependencies {
   testCompile group: 'org.arquillian.algeron',
               name: 'arquillian-algeron-pact-provider-pact-broker-loader',
               version: '1.0.1'
}
```

After you've registered the dependencies in the build script, you can start writing contract tests.

6.4 *Writing consumer-driven contracts for the Gamer application*

Let's write a contract test for the unique consumer that's provided in the current application: the aggregator service. We'll also show you the provider side, which validates the given contract. In this case, tests are created in a new module/subproject in the main project called, for example, c-tests.

6.4.1 *Consumer side of the comments service*

The aggregator service communicates with services such as game and comments, so it's effectively a consumer of all of them. Let's examine how to write the contract between the aggregator service and the comments service. The class responsible for communicating with the comments service is book.aggr.CommentsGateway. This is a simple boundary class that acts as a gateway between the aggregator service and the comments service. You'll use Arquillian Algeron, to take advantage of its publishing capabilities.

First, here's the contract for storing comments (code/aggregator/c-tests/src/test/java/book/aggr/CommentsContractTest.java).

Listing 6.8 Storing comments

Arquillian test runner

```
@RunWith(Arquillian.class)         ⟵──┘
@Pact(provider = "comments_service", consumer =
        "games_aggregator_service")     ⟵─────┘
public class CommentsContractTest {


    private static final String commentObject = "{" + "  'comment' " +
            ": 'This Game is Awesome'," + "  'rate' : 5," + "  " +
            "'gameId': 1234" + "}";


    private static final String commentResult = "{" + "    'rate': " +
            "5.0," + "   'total': 1," + "   'comments': ['This Game" +
            " is Awesome']" + "}";


    public PactFragment putCommentFragment(PactDslWithProvider
                                             builder) {
        final Map<String, String> headers = new HashMap<>();
        headers.put("Content-Type", "application/json");


        return builder.uponReceiving("User creates a new comment")
                .path("/comments").method("POST").headers(headers)
                .body(toJson(commentObject))
                .willRespondWith().status(201).matchHeader
                    ("Location", ".*/[0-9a-f]+",
                            "/comments/1234").toFragment();


    }

    @Test
    @PactVerification(fragment = "putCommentFragment") //     ⟵──
    public void shouldInsertCommentsInCommentsService() throws
            ExecutionException, InterruptedException {


        final CommentsGateway commentsGateway = new CommentsGateway();
        commentsGateway.initRestClient(url.toString()); //
        //


        JsonReader jsonReader = Json.createReader(new StringReader
                (toJson(commentObject)));
        JsonObject commentObject = jsonReader.readObject();
        jsonReader.close();


        final Future comment = commentsGateway
                .createComment(commentObject);
```

Sets the Pact annotation with the consumer and provider names

Creates the PactFragment that defines the contract for posting comments

Sets the body message

Configures the method as a contact validator of the fragment defined in putCommentFragment

Connects to the HTTP stub server

```
        final Response response = comment.get();
        final URI location = response.getLocation();

        assertThat(location).isNotNull();
        final String id = extractId(location);

        assertThat(id).matches("[0-9a-f]+");
        assertThat(response.getStatus()).isEqualTo(201);

    }
```

This test uses Arquillian standalone, because there's no @Deployment method. At this point, you don't need to deploy anything to the container. The contract for sending a comment to the comments service is defined in putCommentFragment, which defines the contract with the expected body and the canned response. Finally, there are the assertions for validating that the CommentsGateway class works as expected.

Now let's write the contract for getting comments for a given gameId (code/aggregator/c-tests/src/test/java/book/aggr/CommentsContractTest.java). In this case, you need to set a state for telling the provider which data you expect to be returned when the contract is validated against it.

Listing 6.9 Getting comments for a game

```
@StubServer
URL url;

public PactFragment getCommentsFragment(PactDslWithProvider
                                                    builder) {

    final Map<String, String> headers = new HashMap<>();
    headers.put("Content-Type", "application/json");

    return builder.given("A game with id 12 with rate 5 and " +
                    "message This Game is Awesome")
            .uponReceiving("User gets comments for given Game")
            .matchPath("/comments/12").method("GET")
            .willRespondWith().status(200).headers(headers)
            .body(toJson(commentResult)).toFragment();

}

@Test
@PactVerification(fragment = "getCommentsFragment")
public void shouldGetComentsFromCommentsService() throws
        ExecutionException, InterruptedException {
    final CommentsGateway commentsGateway = new CommentsGateway();
    commentsGateway.initRestClient(url.toString());

    final Future<JsonObject> comments = commentsGateway
            .getCommentsFromCommentsService(12);
    final JsonObject commentsResponse = comments.get();
```

Sets state information → (annotation pointing to `.given(...)` lines)

```
assertThat(commentsResponse.getJsonNumber("rate")          │ Asserts responses
        .doubleValue()).isEqualTo(5);              ◁──┘
assertThat(commentsResponse.getInt("total")).isEqualTo(1);
assertThat(commentsResponse.getJsonArray("comments"))
        .hasSize(1);

}
```

Notice that the definition of the contract is similar to the previous one. The biggest difference is the use of the `given` method to set a state. In this case, you're setting the data that will be required on the provider side.

Finally, you need to configure Arquillian Algeron to publish contracts in a shared place, so the provider can retrieve and validate them (code/aggregator/c-tests/src/test/resources/arquillian.xml). For the sake of simplicity, the folder approach is used here, but in the real world you'd probably use a Git repository.

Listing 6.10   Publishing contracts in a shared location

```
<?xml version="1.0"?>
<arquillian
xsi:schemaLocation="http://jboss.org/schema/arquillian
http://jboss.org/schema/arquillian/arquillian_1_0.xsd"
xmlns="http://jboss.org/schema/arquillian"
xmlns:xsi="http://www.w3.org/2001/XMLSchema-instance">
    <extension qualifier="algeron-consumer">
        <property name="publishConfiguration"> provider: folder
          outputFolder: /tmp/mypacts
          contractsFolder: target/pacts
        </property>
        <property name="publishContracts">
          ${env.publishcontracts:true}
        </property>
    </extension>
</arquillian>
```

Now that you've written the contract for the consumer side, let's see what you need to do to validate it against the provider.

6.4.2   *Provider side of the comments service*

To validate contracts generated on the consumer side, you need to create a test on the provider project that downloads contracts and replays them against a running instance of the provider (code/comments/c-tests/src/test/java/book/comments/boundary/CommentsProviderTest.java). You need to deploy the real comments service, so using Arquillian Algeron is a good choice: it takes care of creating the deployment file and deploying it to the application server. Contracts are stored in the same folder defined in the `publishConfiguration` property, as discussed in the previous section.

Listing 6.11   Testing the comments service on the provider side

```
                                      Sets the contract
                                         location
@RunWith(Arquillian.class)
@ContractsFolder(value = "/tmp/mypacts")      ◄─────  Configures
@Provider("comments_service")         ◄────────────   the provider
public class CommentsProviderTest {

    static {                          ◄────────── Sets the MongoDB
        System.setProperty("MONGO_HOME",         home directory
                "/mongodb-osx-x86_64-3.2.7");
    }
                                            Uses NoSQLUnit
                                            managed MongoDB
    @ClassRule                    ◄─────────────
    public static ManagedMongoDb managedMongoDb =
            newManagedMongoDbRule().build();
                                        Configures a MongoDB
                                        remote connection
    @Rule                      ◄────────────
    public MongoDbRule remoteMongoDbRule = new MongoDbRule(mongoDb
            ().databaseName("test").host("localhost").build());

   @Deployment(testable = false)
   public static WebArchive createDeployment() {
        final WebArchive webArchive = ShrinkWrap.create(WebArchive
                .class).addPackage(CommentsResource.class
Ensures that the test       .getPackage()).addClass(MongoClientProvider.class)
runs in client mode      .addAsWebInfResource("test-resources.xml",
                    "resources.xml").addAsWebInfResource
                    (EmptyAsset.INSTANCE, "beans.xml")
                .addAsLibraries(Maven.resolver().resolve("org" +
                    ".mongodb:mongodb-driver:3.2.2")
                    .withTransitivity().as(JavaArchive.class));

        return webArchive;
    }

    private static final String commentObject = "{" + "  'comment' " +
            ": '%s'," + "  'rate' : %d," + "  'gameId': %d" + "}";

    @State("A game with id (\\d+) with rate (\\d+) and message (.+)")
    public void insertGame(int gameId, int rate, String message)
            throws MalformedURLException {          ◄───────
                                            Populates the required
        RestAssured.given().body(toJson(String.format   data to the provider from
                (commentObject, message, rate, gameId))   the contract definition
                .contentType(ContentType.JSON).post(new URL
                (commentsService, "comments")).then().statusCode(201);

    }

    @ArquillianResource
    URL commentsService;
                                   Injects the Target class for
                                   replaying the contract
    @ArquillianResource     ◄──────┘
    Target target;
```

```
@Test
@UsingDataSet(loadStrategy = LoadStrategyEnum.DELETE_ALL)    ◁──┐   Cleans the
public void should_provide_valid_answers() {                    │   database after
    PactProviderAssertions.assertThat(target).withUrl           │   each run
            (commentsService).satisfiesContract();
}
```

WARNING   Be sure to adapt the contract location and MongoDB home to your environment before running the test.

This test prepares the environment by starting the MongoDB database and Apache TomEE. Then it deploys the application and replays the contract against the configured environment. Note the following three important things:

- You use NoSQLUnit to prepare the MongoDB environment. NoSQLUnit can be used in integration tests, as you saw in chapter 5, and also in any other kind of test.
- The state method insertGame is only used by the part of the contract that defined the state on the consumer side. This is the part of the contract that validates receiving comments from the service.
- In the state method, the test uses the POST method to populate the data, so you're effectively using the comments service endpoint to insert data into the database. You use the RestAssured test framework for this purpose.

Figure 6.12 summarizes the lifecycle when you run this test. First, the Arquillian test uses NoSQLUnit to start an instance of MongoDB installed on the system property/ environment variable MONGO_HOME. Then, it starts an instance of Apache TomEE and deploys the comments service inside it. If a contract defines a state following the form A game with id (\d+) with rate (\d+) and message (.+), some data is populated in MongoDB using the comments service. Finally, the test replays each of the contracts, cleaning the database before each execution.

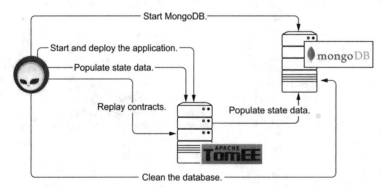

Figure 6.12   The test lifecycle

6.5 Contract type summary

The following table summarizes the types of contracts we've discussed.

Table 6.1 Consumer, provider, and consumer-driven contracts

Contract	Complete	Number	Bounded
Provider	Yes	Single	Space/Time
Consumer	No	Multiple	Space/Time
Consumer-driven	Yes	Single	Consumers

The provider- and consumer-driven approaches are *complete*: they provide a complete set of functionalities. With the consumer approach, contracts are incomplete from the point of view of the functionalities available to the system. In addition, the provider- and consumer-driven approaches are *singular* in their expression of business functionality; but with the consumer approach, each consumer has its own contract.

Exercise

You should now be able to write any pair of consumer/provider tests. We recommend that you try to define the consumer side of the game service, and then the provider side.

> **TIP** Take a look at chapter 4, which introduced writing tests for WildFly Swarm using Arquillian.

Summary

- Using consumer-driven contracts provides faster execution of tests.
- You won't end up with flaky tests, because with HTTP stub servers, you always receive reliable responses.
- Tests are split between consumer and provider, so it's easier to identify the cause of a failure.
- Incorporating consumer-driven contracts is a design process.
- Consumer-driven contracts doesn't mean *dictator*-consumer-driven contracts. The contract is the starting point of a collaborative effort that begins on the consumer side, but both sides must work on it.
- With contract tests, you avoid having to know from the consumer side how to package and deploy the provider side. The consumer side only needs to know how to deploy its part. When you validate the contract on the provider, the provider knows how to deploy itself and how to mock/stub its own dependencies. This is a huge difference from end-to-end tests, where you must start a full environment to be able to run the tests.
- A consumer-driven contract may not always be the best approach to follow. Normally it is, but in some situations (like those described in section 6.1.5), you may want to use provider-driven contracts or consumer contracts.

End-to-end testing

End-to-end tests build on integration tests, which in turn build on all the other forms of testing you've learned about. As the name indicates, end-to-end tests are designed to test your application from start to finish (or top to bottom, if you prefer). They should in theory simulate a real-world user of your application, or at least perform the actions of a real user. In practice, these tests are usually the most difficult to write and consume the most development time. End-to-end tests are nearly always slow in comparison to other types of tests, so they're often isolated from the usual development process—on a Jenkins build server, for example (https://jenkins.io).

> **NOTE** Learning everything about continuous integration and delivery would be beyond the scope of this book, so we're thinking there may be another mini book in the pipeline. (For those familiar with the topic, excuse the pun.) That said, to get you started, chapter 10 provides a reasonably detailed discussion of how to set up a deployment pipeline using Jenkins.

An end-to-end test should ideally provide an environment that's as close to your production environment as possible, yet is isolated, so it can't damage the actual system. This could mean providing something as simple as a copied directory of images for a gallery application, or something as complex as a snapshot of your enterprise database for a data-warehouse application. Sometimes this isn't possible—for example, having a real SAP endpoint to test against might be an exorbitant overhead that you'd like to avoid; so, using a dummy, a mock, or WireMock would be a legitimate solution.

7.1 End-to-end tests in the overall testing picture

End-to-end testing is required to verify that input is received correctly from the front-end entry all the way down to the backend. The real challenge is how to sew together all the standalone microservices on a single machine. The book's example has four microservices, one of which is a Spring Boot application, and a UI application that calls the services. To test the UI, the microservices must be available before the UI starts. After that, you need to perform the required tests, record and collect the results, and then shut down and clean up the environment. In a sense, you're putting your monolithic application back together to test it.

The individual microservices may also require that all dependent services, such as databases, be up and running and seeded with data. As you can imagine, this list of requirements can go on and on.

It may also be necessary to recycle the process for further tests, but we recommend that you try to keep everything up and running until all tests are complete. Try to batch tests together as much as possible, because restarting the environment is expensive in terms of time.

7.2 End-to-end testing techniques

In principle, there are two types of end-to-end tests: *horizontal* and *vertical*. We'll describe them both in a moment. Both types can be performed in either a white-box or black-box environment, or combined. A *white-box environment* is one where the visible or outwardly facing elements of the application are tested, whereas a *black-box environment* tests the actual functionality (in the background).

To put this in a practical context: suppose you have a UI that the end user must interact with. The user can visualize and perform actions on the exposed application. These actions result in user expectations about the outcome. Logically, to simulate user interaction with the UI, you must provide the UI for the test. This is a white-box environment, because the user can see actions occurring.

In the same scope as the white-box scenario where the user interacts with the UI, actions may invoke processes on the underlying server. These backend processes aren't visible to the user but may produce a result that the user will eventually encounter. This is a black-box environment, because actions are performed in the dark, so to speak.

End-to-end tests invariably combine both white- and black-box environments, especially in browser-based applications. The white box is the browser: you can see, and possibly influence, the test. The black box is the server: your actions send a request, which is invisibly processed, and a response is returned.

7.2.1   *Vertical tests*

Vertical end-to-end tests are designed to test the depth of a feature presented by the application. For a UI, this means testing that the correct validation is performed before one view transitions to another when the user performs an action. This validation might require specific user rights in LDAP and the retrieval of the correct settings from a database, for example.

You're basically looking up and down at what you see, and making sure everything is in order. All the elements should be present, based on the environment you've specified, as shown in figure 7.1.

The figure may seem simplistic, but it's important to perform these tests. Users of your application have associated user rights; how would users react if the Search button wasn't rendered or the input text box was disabled due to a misinterpreted user right in your code?

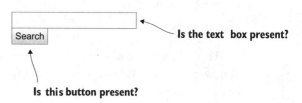

Figure 7.1   A simple white-box vertical test

7.2.2   *Horizontal tests*

Horizontal end-to-end tests are designed to test across the entire scope of an application. For a UI, this means testing that one view transitions to another when the user performs an action. The vertical test ensures that you're ready to make the transition through validation; the horizontal test checks that the action occurs and that the result is what you expect.

Here, you're looking from left to right for the correct transition from one view to the next. Has your action resulted in the correct expectation? Or, alternatively, has an invalid action been handled (negative testing)? Figure 7.2 shows an example.

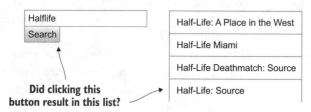

Figure 7.2   A black- and white-box horizontal test

The white-box action sends a request to the black-box server, which in turn delivers a response that's rendered as a list. You need to test the transition and ensure that the list is displayed and that the contents are correct.

7.3 *Introduction to end-to-end testing tools*

End-to-end tests are notoriously difficult and complicated to write in monolithic applications. In a microservices architecture, writing such tests is even more complex, so anything that will help you is a bonus. Fortunately, a range of great tools and (you've guessed it) Arquillian extensions are available to aid you in this endeavor. Let's take a look at some of them.

7.3.1 *Arquillian Cube*

Arquillian Cube (http://arquillian.org/arquillian-cube/) is an extension to the Arquillian testing framework that enables the management of containers hosted in a Docker environment. You can use this extension to deploy a designed Docker image and test against it or in it. The environment hosted on the image can be as simple or elaborate as you wish. So, rather than the developer having to know about and try to provide access to all the collaborators (such as databases or other services) required for the test in the test code, you ship your developer's test to an image that has everything in place already—only DevOps needs to worry about the evolving environment provided by the image.

The Docker image should typically host an application server. Arquillian packages your application in the usual manner and publishes the WAR or EAR file to the hosted server. This is the same lifecycle described in section 4.1; the only difference here is that rather than deploying to a local application server, you deploy to the server in your hosted environment.

This is a hefty subject, and you'll find everything you need to know in chapter 8, where we discuss Docker. For now, we'll focus on *basic* end-to-end unit testing—which may seem like a contradiction in terms, because there's still a lot to pull together. We're presenting things in this order so you'll understand the challenges involved in building up the environment and can see where things may go wrong. It's better to know what's going on under the hood before you step on the gas.

7.3.2 *Arquillian Drone*

Arquillian Drone (http://arquillian.org/arquillian-extension-drone/) is an extension to the Arquillian testing framework that enables access to the well-known Selenium WebDriver (https://seleniumhq.github.io/docs), which, in turn, is used for browser automation. Browser automation is a critical requirement when you're testing web-based UIs. It enables the test to mimic the actions of a real user browsing through your application and entering or manipulating data.

Why should you use this extension if it's just a wrapper for WebDriver? Well, anyone who has written tests using the naked WebDriver API will be quick to tell you that an incredible amount of boilerplate code is required, even for relatively simple tests. Drone hides much of this boilerplate code, enabling you to get on with writing the meat of your tests. There's still some setup to perform, but we'll walk through this in the example later in this chapter.

7.3.3   Arquillian Graphene 2

Arquillian Graphene 2 (https://github.com/arquillian/arquillian-graphene) is (as the name indicates) a second-generation rapid-development extension, designed to complement Selenium WebDriver. Although it can be used to create standalone AJAX-enabled tests, Graphene works best together with the Arquillian Drone extension.

7.3.4   JMeter

JMeter (http://jmeter.apache.org) is an Apache Software Foundation project that can be used to load-test just about any kind of endpoint. It's an entirely Java-based solution, so it can be used across all supported platforms. It's capable of simulating heavy network traffic and is primarily used to test the resilience of application endpoints. You'll use it to create a few simple stress tests to ensure that your services can stand up to some load.

7.3.5   Cukes in Space

Cukes in Space (https://github.com/cukespace/cukespace) is an Arquillian extension that allows you to run tests against a Cucumber JVM (https://cucumber.io/docs/reference) using the common Given-When-Then convention.

7.4   Example end-to-end test

Now that you have your tools, it's time for an example end-to-end test. As we've mentioned, such tests are complicated, and this one is no different. You're using a variety of technologies for the demo microservice applications, so you'll have to deal with this extra complexity in the end-to-end test. The bonus is that you get to see a range of solutions, which should help you develop your own tests in the future. There are no hard-and-fast rules here—you use the tools you have, to get the results you need. The gloves are off.

We're using a simple application for the frontend UI, to highlight the end-to-end processes; there are no surprises in store. Open a command line at the source code root directory, and run the following commands:

```
cd web
mvn clean install -DskipTests
```

This will build the web application and ensure that all required dependencies are available and cached. We're skipping the test here, because we want to explain it in detail first.

7.4.1 Building the microservices

The first thing you need to do is ensure that all the sample microservice code you've seen so far is built and ready for you to use. You'll use the real WAR and JAR files that these projects generate, to create a more realistic end-to-end test.

Open a command line at the source code root directory, and run the following commands:

```
cd comments
./gradlew war -x test

cd ../aggregator
./gradlew war -x test

cd ../game
mvn install -DskipTests

cd ../video
./gradlew build -x test
```

> **NOTE** You thoroughly tested all the microservice applications in previous chapters, so you'll cheat here by skipping the tests for brevity. Also, some of the tests in these projects are designed to fail, to highlight a point or to provide a user exercise.

7.4.2 Adding the build dependencies and configuration

Next, you need to add the relevant bill of materials (BOM) imports to the build script `dependencyManagement` section of your web UI application (in code/web/pom.xml). There's only one new import item: the `arquillian-drone-bom` artifact. This new BOM ensures that all the dependencies required for Drone are available.

Listing 7.1 Adding the `arquillian-drone-bom` artifact

```xml
<dependencyManagement>
    <dependencies>
        <dependency>
            <groupId>org.jboss.arquillian</groupId>
            <artifactId>arquillian-bom</artifactId>
            <version>${version.arquillian-bom}</version>
            <scope>import</scope>
            <type>pom</type>
        </dependency>
        <dependency>
            <groupId>org.jboss.arquillian.extension</groupId>
            <artifactId>arquillian-drone-bom</artifactId>
            <version>2.0.0.Final</version>
            <type>pom</type>
            <scope>import</scope>
        </dependency>
    </dependencies>
</dependencyManagement>
```

The `graphene-webdriver` artifact is required in the UI app for injecting the Selenium WebDriver. This WebDriver is what communicates with the browser to perform actions.

Listing 7.2   Adding the `graphene-webdriver` artifact

```
<dependency>
    <groupId>org.jboss.arquillian.graphene</groupId>
    <artifactId>graphene-webdriver</artifactId>
    <version>2.1.0.Final</version>
    <type>pom</type>
    <scope>test</scope>
</dependency>
```

INSTALLING BROWSER DRIVERS FOR AUTOMATION

You need to make sure the appropriate browser driver is installed for the testing browsers. We're using the Chrome browser as the default testing browser, so be sure the ChromeDriver binary (http://mng.bz/VZig) is downloaded and accessible to Arquillian in the test configuration. This is defined in the `webdriver` extension element, using the `chromeDriverBinary` property in the project arquillian.xml file. At the time of writing, you should be able to locate the current drivers for the extensive list of supported browsers from www.seleniumhq.org/download.

Listing 7.3   Adding the browser driver

```
                                         The browser property, with
                                         a default value of chrome
<extension qualifier="webdriver">
    <property name="browser">${browser:chrome}</property>      ◁
    <!--https://sites.google.com/a/chromium.org/chromedriver/-->
    <property name="chromeDriverBinary">/home/andy/dev/chromedriver
    ➥ </property>      ◁       The chromeDriverBinary property,
</extension>                           pointing to the driver binary
```

> **TIP**   As always, there's plenty of information on the internet regarding the use of different testing browsers. The ideal solution is to define a different build profile for each browser you wish to test against, overriding the `browser` property at runtime.

USING AND DEFINING NoSQL DATABASES

Some useful dependencies are the `de.flapdoodle.embed.mongo` and `embedded-redis` artifacts (code/web/pom.xml)

Listing 7.4   Adding dependencies

```
<dependency>
    <groupId>de.flapdoodle.embed</groupId>
    <artifactId>de.flapdoodle.embed.mongo</artifactId>
    <version>2.0.0</version>
```

```
            <scope>test</scope>
    </dependency>
    <dependency>
            <groupId>com.github.kstyrc</groupId>
            <artifactId>embedded-redis</artifactId>
            <version>0.6</version>
    </dependency>
```

WARNING It's possible to add all sorts of undefined magical plugins to the build scripts to ensure that these runtime dependencies are started. This is *not* recommended, because the test would no longer be self-contained and couldn't be run by IDEs out of the box.

The neat libraries in listing 7.4 enable your test to fire up a MongoDB instance and a Redis instance directly in the test with relatively little overhead. Due to the lifecycle management of the JUnit test as a whole, @BeforeClass usually isn't early enough to bootstrap these requirements. Implementing JUnit rules allows you to include them deeper in the test lifecycle. Variables in the rules are used to keep a reference to the process, so that you can clean up after the test is complete. The libraries used in the rules you'll define in a moment will download and initialize the MongoDB and Redis instances for you. You don't have to manually prepare anything, and your tests remain self-contained.

The simple Mongod rule shown in the following listing (code/web/src/test/java/book/web/rule/MongodRule.java) fires up a Mongod instance that's bound to the provided host and port. For your test, you don't need any more than this, but the library API allows for a complete configuration. It would be easy to modify the rule to accept more parameters if you needed them.

Listing 7.5   Mongod rule

```
package book.web.rule;

import de.flapdoodle.embed.mongo.MongodExecutable;
import de.flapdoodle.embed.mongo.MongodProcess;
import de.flapdoodle.embed.mongo.MongodStarter;
import de.flapdoodle.embed.mongo.config.MongodConfigBuilder;
import de.flapdoodle.embed.mongo.config.Net;
import de.flapdoodle.embed.mongo.distribution.Version;
import de.flapdoodle.embed.process.runtime.Network;
import org.junit.rules.ExternalResource;

import java.io.IOException;

public class MongodRule extends ExternalResource {

    private final MongodStarter starter
            = MongodStarter.getDefaultInstance();
    private MongodExecutable mongodExe;
    private MongodProcess mongodProcess;
```

```
    private String host;
    private int port;

    public MongodRule(String host, int port) {
        this.host = host;
        this.port = port;
    }

    @Override
    protected void before() throws Throwable {
        try {
            mongodExe = starter.prepare(new MongodConfigBuilder()
                    .version(Version.Main.PRODUCTION)
                    .net(new Net(this
                    .host, this.port, Network.localhostIsIPv6()))).build());
            mongodProcess = mongodExe.start();
        } catch (final IOException e) {
            e.printStackTrace();
        }
    }

    @Override
    protected void after() {
        //Stop MongoDB
        if (null != mongodProcess) {
            mongodProcess.stop();
        }
        if (null != mongodExe) {
            mongodExe.stop();
        }
    }
}
```

The before phase creates and executes the Mongod process.

The after phase ensures that the process is terminated and cleaned up.

The Redis rule is basically the same (code/web/src/test/java/book/web/rule/Redis-Rule.java), but it uses the RedisServer provided by the library.

Listing 7.6   Redis rule

```
package book.web.rule;

import org.junit.rules.ExternalResource;
import redis.embedded.RedisServer;

public class RedisRule extends ExternalResource {

    private RedisServer redisServer;
    private int port;

    public RedisRule(int port) {
        this.port = port;
    }

    @Override
    protected void before() throws Throwable {
```

```
        try {
            redisServer = new RedisServer(this.port);
            redisServer.start();
        } catch (final Throwable e) {
            e.printStackTrace();
        }
    }

    @Override
    protected void after() {
        //Stop Redis
        if (null != redisServer) {
            redisServer.stop();
        }
    }
}
```

NOTE Hats off to Krzysztof Styrc (https://github.com/kstyrc) and Michael Mosmann (https://github.com/michaelmosmann) and their teams for providing these great OSS projects!

We hope you can see that it's pretty easy to wrap all kinds of test resources using the JUnit rule mechanism. As we mentioned, you'll put these rules to use in the example test later.

PROVIDING THE MICROSERVICE RUNTIME ENVIRONMENTS

The principal runtime environment we're providing for this example test is Apache TomEE (http://tomee.apache.org). You could choose any Java EE environment to deploy your WAR files to, as long as it's EE compatible. You also have a Spring Boot application and a WildFly fat JAR, but you'll deal with those later.

Apache TomEE provides a Maven plugin that allows you to automatically create a ready-to-run server directory gamerwebapp in your target directory. This is a complete TomEE server distribution that's downloaded and extracted by the plugin. This process is attached to the Maven *validate* phase every time a build is run. Add the following code to code/web/pom.xml.

Listing 7.7 Adding the Apache TomEE runtime environment

```
<plugin>
    <groupId>org.apache.tomee.maven</groupId>
    <artifactId>tomee-maven-plugin</artifactId>
    <version>${version.tomee}</version>
    <configuration>
        <catalinaBase>target/gamerwebapp</catalinaBase>
        <tomeeClassifier>plus</tomeeClassifier>
        <deployOpenEjbApplication>true</deployOpenEjbApplication>
        <removeDefaultWebapps>true</removeDefaultWebapps>
        <removeTomeeWebapp>true</removeTomeeWebapp>
    </configuration>
    <executions>
```

```
        <execution>
            <id>gamerwebapp</id>
            <phase>validate</phase>
            <configuration>
                <attach>false</attach>
                <zip>false</zip>
            </configuration>
            <goals>
                <goal>build</goal>
            </goals>
        </execution>
    </executions>
</plugin>
```

There is one caveat: the plugin downloads the TomEE server in the Maven build phase to a local directory in the project. This would be fine if you were to just run the build script. But if you want to debug a test in your IDE, you need to have run the build script at least once:

```
cd web
mvn clean validate -DskipTests
```

The first time you run this, it will take a while, because TomEE needs to be downloaded and extracted to a project local directory. Subsequent builds will be much faster.

You then do a little Maven magic, using `<artifactId>maven-resources-plugin</artifactId>` to create multiple copies of the previously created gamerwebapp directory. The following code is repeated for each microservice WAR file that you want to deploy as a standalone microservice WAR. Again, open pom.xml in your IDE to get the full picture.

Listing 7.8   Copying target/gamerwebapp to target/commentsservice

```
<execution>
    <id>create-commentsservice</id>
    <phase>validate</phase>
    <goals>
        <goal>copy-resources</goal>
    </goals>
    <configuration>
        <outputDirectory>target/commentsservice</outputDirectory>
        <includeEmptyDirs>true</includeEmptyDirs>
        <resources>
            <resource>
                <directory>target/gamerwebapp</directory>
                <filtering>false</filtering>
            </resource>
        </resources>
    </configuration>
</execution>
```

ADDING A GROUP TO ARQUILLIAN.XML

You already know that you can define multiple containers in the arquillian.xml configuration file. This is perfect for what you need when it comes to providing multiple microservice environments supported by the Arquillian framework.

Listing 7.9   Defining a group

```
                                    Group definition, flagged
                                    here as the default
                                                      Defines a container
<group qualifier="tomee-cluster" default="true">  ⬅  with a unique qualifier
<container qualifier="gamerweb" default="true">  ⬅
    <configuration>
        <property name="httpPort">8080</property>        ⬅
        <property name="stopPort">-1</property>
        <property name="ajpPort">-1</property>               Container-
        <property name="classifier">plus</property>          specific
        <property name="appWorkingDir">target/gamerweb_work  properties to
    </property>                                              define the HTTP
        <property name="dir">target/gamerwebservice          port and
    </property>                                              protocol ports.
        </configuration>                                     TomEE uses -1 to
    </container>                                             indicate that a
    <container qualifier="commentsservice" default="false">  random port
        <configuration>                                      should be used.
Path to the actual  <property name="httpPort">8282</property>
server directory    <property name="stopPort">-1</property>
(as previously      <property name="ajpPort">-1</property>
defined/created in  <property name="classifier">plus</property>
pom.xml)            <property name="appWorkingDir">target/
    commentsservice_work</property>
        <property name="dir">target/commentsservice
    </property>
        </configuration>
    </container>
    <container qualifier="gameaggregatorservice" default="false">
        <configuration>
            <property name="httpPort">8383</property>
            <property name="stopPort">-1</property>
            <property name="ajpPort">-1</property>
            <property name="classifier">plus</property>
            <property name="appWorkingDir">target/
    gameaggregatorservice_work</property>
            <property name="dir">target/gameaggregatorservice
    </property>
            <property name="properties">
                com.sun.jersey.server.impl.cdi.
    lookupExtensionInBeanManager=true
            </property>
        </configuration>
    </container>
</group>
```

If you're still wondering about the Spring Boot and WildFly microservices, don't worry. You're nearly there; just one more section.

7.4.3   *Adding @Deployment and @TargetsContainer to the test*

The test class is getting large—it has a lot to accomplish. We'll focus on each core element. You can open the test in your IDE of choice to get the full picture, but you've already seen much of this in previous chapters. Outside the scope of an example, we suggest placing most of the initialization and deployment code in an abstract class for reuse in other tests.

> **TIP**   If possible, build a deployment starting with a ShrinkWrap of the WAR file for the microservice. Then add the `provided` scoped artifacts to the mix of dependencies that the microservice requires. This means the test is as close as possible to a real production deployment.

The next thing you need to do is to ensure that *all* of your microservices are made available to the test class. You'll begin with the easy deployments (code/web/src/test/java/book/web/EndToEndTest.java). Later sections will cover more elaborate deployments using JUnit rules.

Listing 7.10   Adding @Deployment and @TargetsContainer

```
@Deployment(name = "commentsservice", testable = false)
@TargetsContainer("commentsservice")
public static Archive commentsservice() throws Exception {

        return ShrinkWrap.create(ZipImporter.class, "commentsservice.war")
          .importFrom(getFile
          ("comments/build/libs/commentsservice.war"))
          .as(WebArchive.class).addAsLibraries(Maven.resolver()
          .resolve("org.mongodb:mongodb-driver:3.2.2")
          .withTransitivity().as(JavaArchive.class)).addClass
          (MongoClientProvider.class)
          .addAsWebInfResource("test-web.xml", "web.xml")
          .addAsWebInfResource("test-resources.xml"
          , "resources.xml");
    }

    @Deployment(name = "gameaggregatorservice", testable = false)
    @TargetsContainer("gameaggregatorservice")
    public static Archive gameaggregatorservice() throws Exception {
        return ShrinkWrap
          .create(ZipImporter.class, "gameaggregatorservice.war")
          .importFrom(
          getFile("aggregator/build/libs/gameaggregatorservice.war"))
          .as(WebArchive.class).addAsLibraries(
          Maven.resolver().resolve("org.mongodb:mongodb-driver:3.2.2")
          .withTransitivity().as(JavaArchive.class))
                .addClass(MongoClientProvider.class)
                .addAsWebInfResource("test-web.xml", "web.xml")
```

```
                .addAsWebInfResource("test-resources.xml", "resources.xml");
    }

    @Deployment(name = "gamerweb", testable = false)          ◁─┐    Defines a unique
    @TargetsContainer("gamerweb")                               │    deployment name,
    public static Archive gamerWebService() throws Exception {  │    which is important
        return ShrinkWrap.create(MavenImporter.class)           │    when testing against
            .loadPomFromFile("pom.xml")                         │    multiple containers
            .importBuildOutput().as(WebArchive
            .class).addAsWebInfResource("test-web.xml", "web.xml");
    }
```

**@TargetsContainer("[name]") ensures the application is deployed
to the specified container, as defined in arquillian.xml.**

You can in theory specify an endless number of containers in the arquillian.xml file, which can then be bound to an endless number of deployments in your test.

NOTE The TomEE plugin includes options to add provided scoped artifacts directly to the server runtime lib directory (which is what provided means, after all). For more information, check out the plugin documentation (http://tomee.apache.org/maven/index.html).

7.4.4 *Cross-origin resource sharing*

You may have noticed that, to allow access to RESTful endpoints from different hosts, you've enabled cross-origin resource sharing (CORS) on several of your microservices. You should only do this in your own environments once you fully understand the implications. But it's often necessary in test environments—especially where multiple services are bound to multiple ports on the same local machine.

CORS is required only for scenarios where a service receives requests from a different host than the serving host: for example, a standalone microservice. The configuration is required on the serving host to allow specified hosts to consume the available services.

The CORS configuration varies for different application servers, so you'll need to check the relevant documentation for your server of choice. The following example depicts a liberal configuration for Apache TomEE (code/web/src/test/resources/test-web.xml).

Listing 7.11 Enabling CORS for TomEE or Tomcat

```xml
<web-app xmlns="http://java.sun.com/xml/ns/javaee"
         xmlns:xsi="http://www.w3.org/2001/XMLSchema-instance"
         xsi:schemaLocation="http://java.sun.com/xml/ns/javaee
   http://java.sun.com/xml/ns/javaee/web-app_3_0.xsd" version="3.0">

    <filter>
        <filter-name>CorsFilter</filter-name>
        <filter-class>org.apache.catalina.filters.CorsFilter
            </filter-class>
```

```
        <async-supported>true</async-supported>
        <init-param>
            <param-name>cors.allowed.origins</param-name>
            <param-value>*</param-value>
        </init-param>
        <init-param>
            <param-name>cors.allowed.methods</param-name>
            <param-value>GET,POST,HEAD,OPTIONS,PUT</param-value>
        </init-param>
        <init-param>
            <param-name>cors.allowed.headers</param-name>
            <param-value>
                Content-Type,X-Requested-With,accept,Origin,
                Access-Control-Request-Method,Access-Control-Request-Headers
            </param-value>
        </init-param>
        <init-param>
            <param-name>cors.exposed.headers</param-name>
            <param-value>Access-Control-Allow-Origin,
            Access-Control-Allow-Credentials</param-value>
        </init-param>
        <init-param>
            <param-name>cors.support.credentials</param-name>
            <param-value>false</param-value>
        </init-param>
        <init-param>
            <param-name>cors.preflight.maxage</param-name>
            <param-value>10</param-value>
        </init-param>
    </filter>
    <filter-mapping>
        <filter-name>CorsFilter</filter-name>
        <url-pattern>/*</url-pattern>
    </filter-mapping>

</web-app>
```

Most of your services are likely to be hosted in the same domain in production and won't require such a liberal configuration.

7.4.5 *Coping with a mixed environment using @ClassRule*

At the time of writing, Arquillian isn't able to mix different container environments in the same runtime out of the box. This will be problematic when you require that in your tests, because you've used multiple environments. You can create your own container implementation that wraps multiple environments, but that goes beyond the scope of this book.

The solution we chose is simple, though a little verbose. You know that the Spring Boot and WildFly Swarm projects produce fat JARs, and that these JAR files are executable. You've also seen how to define JUnit rules to wrap external processes (Mongod and Redis). Armed with this knowledge, it's relatively straightforward to use the JVM

ProcessBuilder to execute these services and manage the process lifecycle in a rule, as shown in listing 7.12 (code/web/src/test/java/book/web/rule/MicroserviceRule.java).

The caveat is that even though the process may have started, you can't use the service until the endpoint is accessible. To solve this issue, you can use a simple connect method in the test sequence that waits for a valid connection to a specified endpoint.

Listing 7.12   code/web/src/test/java/book/web/rule/MicroserviceRule.java

```java
package book.web.rule;

import okhttp3.OkHttpClient;
import okhttp3.Request;
import org.junit.Assert;
import org.junit.rules.ExternalResource;

import java.io.File;
import java.net.MalformedURLException;
import java.net.URL;
import java.util.ArrayList;
import java.util.Arrays;
import java.util.concurrent.CountDownLatch;
import java.util.concurrent.TimeUnit;
import java.util.concurrent.atomic.AtomicBoolean;
import java.util.concurrent.atomic.AtomicReference;
import java.util.concurrent.locks.ReentrantLock;
import java.util.logging.Logger;

public class MicroserviceRule extends ExternalResource {

    private final Logger log =
        Logger.getLogger(MicroserviceRule.class.getName());

    private final ReentrantLock lock = new ReentrantLock();
    private final CountDownLatch latch = new CountDownLatch(1);
    private final AtomicBoolean poll = new AtomicBoolean(true);
    private final AtomicReference<URL> url =
        new AtomicReference<>();
    private File file;
    private String[] args;
    private ResolutionStrategy strategy =
        new DefaultJavaResolutionStrategy();
    private long time = 30;
    private TimeUnit unit = TimeUnit.SECONDS;

    public MicroserviceRule(URL url) {
        this.url.set(url);
    }

    public MicroserviceRule(String url) {
        try {
            this.url.set(new URL(url));
        } catch (MalformedURLException e) {
            throw new RuntimeException("Invalid URL: " + url, e);
```

```
        }
    }
```

Using a builder pattern for parameters makes it easy to use the rule inline.

```
public MicroserviceRule withExecutableJar(File file,
    String... args) {

    Assert.assertTrue("The file must exist and be readable: " + file,
        file.exists() && file.canRead());

    this.file = file;
    this.args = args;
    return this;
}

public MicroserviceRule withJavaResolutionStrategy(ResolutionStrategy
    strategy) {
    this.strategy = (null != strategy ? strategy : this.strategy);
    return this;
}

public MicroserviceRule withTimeout(int time, TimeUnit unit) {
    this.time = time;
    this.unit = unit;
    return this;
}

private Process process;

@Override
protected void before() throws Throwable {

    Assert.assertNotNull("The MicroserviceRule requires a
➥ valid jar file", this.file);
    Assert.assertNotNull("The MicroserviceRule requires a
➥ valid url", this.url.get());

    this.lock.lock();
```

Uses the default ResolutionStrategy to find the Java executable (Overridable)

```
    try {
        ArrayList<String> args = new ArrayList<>();
        args.add(this.strategy.getJavaExecutable().toString());
        args.add("-jar");
        args.add(this.file.toString());

        if (null != this.args) {
            args.addAll(Arrays.asList(this.args));
        }

        ProcessBuilder pb =
            new ProcessBuilder(args.toArray(new String[args.size()]));
        pb.directory(file.getParentFile());
        pb.inheritIO();
        process = pb.start();
```

Starts the microservice fat JAR executable process

```
        log.info("Started " + this.file);
```

```
            final Thread t = new Thread(() -> {
                if (MicroserviceRule.this.connect(
                    MicroserviceRule.this.url.get())) {
                    MicroserviceRule.this.latch.countDown();
                }
            }, "Connect thread :: " + this.url.get());

            t.start();

            if (!latch.await(this.time, this.unit)) {
                throw new RuntimeException("Failed to connect
    to server within timeout: "
                        + this.url.get());
            }

        } finally {
            this.poll.set(false);
            this.lock.unlock();
        }
    }

    @Override
    protected void after() {

        this.lock.lock();

        try {
            if (null != process) {
                process.destroy();
                process = null;
            }
        } finally {
            this.lock.unlock();
        }
    }

    private boolean connect(final URL url) {

        do {
            try {
                Request request = new Request.Builder().url(url).build();

                if (new OkHttpClient().newCall(request)
                    .execute().isSuccessful()) {
                    return true;
                } else {
                    throw new Exception("Unexpected family");
                }
            } catch (Exception ignore) {

                if (poll.get()) {
                    try {
                        Thread.sleep(2000);
                    } catch (InterruptedException e) {
```

Polls the specified endpoint URL for a successful connection

Waits for a connection or a timeout after the specified period

Uses a lock to synchronize the startup and shutdown process

You're only interested in a valid connection to the endpoint, not the response.

```
                        return false;
                    }
                }
            }
        } while (poll.get());

        return false;
    }


}
```

Just as `before` is used to initialize resources, you use `after` to clean them up.

> **NOTE** You aren't actually testing the endpoints; you're using them to confirm
> that your end-to-end tests are ready to be performed. Feel free to write your
> own connection-checking routine to suit your needs.

Now the rules have been implemented, and all you need to do is use them in the test.

> **WARNING** Avoid using the non-static JUnit `@Rule` annotation, because it
> would stop and start *all* the rule processes for *each* individual test!

Listing 7.13   code/web/src/test/java/book/web/EndToEndTest.java - @ClassRule

Uses a static JUnit RuleChain to ensure
that the rules are executed in the
defined order, as early as possible

```
@ClassRule
public static RuleChain chain = RuleChain          ◁────────────  Begins with the
        .outerRule(new MongodRule("localhost", 27017))  ◁──────     MongodRule
        .around(new RedisRule(6379))
        .around(new MicroserviceRule("http://localhost:8899/?videoId=5123
 &gameName=Zelda").withExecutableJar
            (getFile("video/build/libs/video-service-0.1.0.jar"),
            "--server.port=8899")
            .withJavaResolutionStrategy
                (new DefaultJavaResolutionStrategy()).withTimeout
                (1, TimeUnit.MINUTES))

        .around(new MicroserviceRule("http://localhost:8181?query=")
            .withExecutableJar(getFile
            ("game/target/gameservice-swarm.jar"), "-Dswarm" +
            ".http.port=8181").withJavaResolutionStrategy
            (new DefaultJavaResolutionStrategy()).withTimeout(1,
            TimeUnit.MINUTES));
```

Uses the RedisRule → (points to `.around(new RedisRule(6379))`)

The RedisRule is followed by the MicroserviceRule, which can be specified in any order if they aren't dependent on each other.

If any of your services are dependent on each other, this is where you can define the
startup order.

> **TIP** Defining timeouts is hardly deterministic in all cases. For end-to-end
> tests, you have to break this rule for obvious reasons—the connection polling
> might never be successful. Try to tune the parameters to be as deterministic
> as possible for your environment.

7.4.6 Operating on the deployments with @OperateOnDeployment

You've seen several times how to define and use multiple deployments. In listing 7.13, the @OperateOnDeployment annotation refers to the deployment that a particular test should use. You're also injecting the resource URL using the @ArquillianResource annotation. You're using the @InSequence annotation to provide the order of tests, which, strictly speaking, is a big no-no for normal unit tests. For end-to-end tests, you already know that you have to logically coordinate the environment, so it's virtually impossible to allow tests to run arbitrarily. There will always be an order of action, but the tests should still be performing a unit of work.

Listing 7.14   Defining multiple deployments

```
private static final AtomicReference<URL>
    commentsservice = new AtomicReference<>();
private static final AtomicReference<URL>
    gameaggregatorservice = new AtomicReference<>();
private static final AtomicReference<URL>
    gamerweb = new AtomicReference<>();

@Test
@InSequence(1)
@OperateOnDeployment("commentsservice")
public void testRunningInCommentsService(@ArquillianResource final URL url)
    throws Exception {
    commentsservice.set(url);
    Assert.assertNotNull(commentsservice.get());
    assertThat(commentsservice.get().toExternalForm(),
        containsString("commentsservice"));
}

@Test
@InSequence(2)
@OperateOnDeployment("gameaggregatorservice")
public void testRunningInGameAggregatorService(@ArquillianResource
    final URL url) throws Exception {
    gameaggregatorservice.set(url);
    Assert.assertNotNull(gameaggregatorservice.get());
    assertThat(gameaggregatorservice.get().toExternalForm(),
        containsString("gameaggregatorservice"));
}

@Test
@InSequence(4)
@OperateOnDeployment("gamerweb")
public void testRunningInGamerWeb(@ArquillianResource final URL url)
    throws Exception {
    gamerweb.set(url);
    Assert.assertNotNull(gamerweb.get());
    assertThat(gamerweb.get().toExternalForm(), containsString("gamerweb"));
}
```

7.4.7   *Introducing @Drone, page objects, @Location, and the WebDriver*

The WebDriver could be injected directly into your test using the @Drone annotation. A better way is to create *page objects* for all browser-related tests. Page objects are nothing more than virtual wrappers designed to represent a single viewable page or element of your UI application. They should only encapsulate logic specific to the page or element at hand.

The following listing shows an example of the Index page object (code/web/src/test/java/book/web/page/Index.java).

Listing 7.15   A sample page object

```
package book.web.page;

import org.jboss.arquillian.drone.api.annotation.Drone;
import org.jboss.arquillian.graphene.Graphene;
import org.jboss.arquillian.graphene.page.Location;
import org.openqa.selenium.WebDriver;
import org.openqa.selenium.WebElement;
import org.openqa.selenium.support.FindBy;

@Location("/")                      ◁——  The optional @Location
public class Index {                      annotation defines where the
                                          page is found on the server.

    @Drone
    private WebDriver browser;

    @FindBy(id = "tms-search")      ◁——  An element, located by its physical
    private WebElement search;            DOM identifier using the Selenium
                                          @FindBy annotation
    @FindBy(id = "tms-button")
    private WebElement button;

    @FindBy(className = "col-sm-3")
    private List list;
                                          Manages the browser
    public void navigateTo(String url) {  ◁——  environment
        browser.manage().window().maximize();    programmatically
        browser.get(url);
    }

    public List searchFor(String text) {
        search.sendKeys(text);                Uses Graphene to
                                              wait (block) for the
        Graphene.guardAjax(button).click();  ◁——  list response

        return list;        ◁——  Returns the page
    }                             fragment for further use

    public String getSearchText() {
        return search.getAttribute("value");
    }
}
```

- Uses the WebDriver to access browser features → `@Drone private WebDriver browser;`
- Provides an embedded page fragment (more on that in a moment) → `@FindBy(className = "col-sm-3") private List list;`
- Sends keypresses to the selected HTML element (the text box, in this case) → `search.sendKeys(text);`

Another cool feature is being used here: *page fragments*, which are objects that represent dynamic elements of the UI page. The next listing shows an example (code/web/src/test/java/book/web/page/List.java). You can use page fragments to provide a logical model for the test to operate on. They can be nested, which makes them useful for defining UI transitions. Using Graphene allows the test to automatically block while the UI performs the transition.

Listing 7.16   A sample page fragment

```java
package book.web.page;

import org.jboss.arquillian.graphene.Graphene;
import org.openqa.selenium.By;
import org.openqa.selenium.WebElement;
import org.openqa.selenium.support.FindBy;

import java.util.ArrayList;
import java.util.Collection;

public class List {

    @FindBy(className = "list-group")
    private WebElement list;

    @FindBy(id = "detail-view")
    private Detail detail;                          ◁─── Provides another nested page fragment

    public Collection<String> getResults() {        ◁─── Gathers results to use for validation in the test

        ArrayList<String> results = new ArrayList<>();

        if (null != list) {
            java.util.List<WebElement> elements = list.findElements
                (By.cssSelector("a > p"));

            for (WebElement element : elements) {
                results.add(element.getText());
            }
        }

        return results;
    }

    public Detail getDetail(int index) {
        java.util.List<WebElement> elements = list.findElements(By
            .cssSelector("a > p"));

        if (!elements.isEmpty()) {                                              Uses Graphene to wait (block)
            Graphene.guardAjax(elements.get(index)).click();    ◁───           for the detail response
        }

        return detail;          ◁─── Returns the Detail fragment for further use
    }
}
```

> **NOTE** This simple example opens the door to the big, wild world of Selenium browser automation. This subject would easily fill another book; take some time to visit the documentation at www.seleniumhq.org/docs.

7.4.8   *Working with page objects in a test*

Once you've defined a page object, you inject it into your test using the @Page annotation as shown next (code/web/src/test/java/book/web/EndToEndTest.java). This can then be used to operate on the testing browser to perform tests.

Listing 7.17   Injecting a page object

```
@Page
@OperateOnDeployment("gamerweb")
private Index page;                          ◁——   The page object is injected using @Page, and it
                                                    will @OperateOnDeployment("gamerweb").

@Test
@InSequence(7)
public void testTheUI() throws Exception {

    System.out.println("gameaggregatorservice = " +
        gameaggregatorservice.get().toExternalForm());      ◁   Uses the page
                                                                object methods

    page.navigateTo(gamerweb.get().toExternalForm());   ◁
    List list = page.searchFor("Zelda");

    Assert.assertEquals("", "Zelda", page.getSearchText());

    Assert.assertThat(list.getResults(),
        hasItems("The Legend of Zelda: Breath of the Wild"));

    Detail detail = list.getDetail(0);

    Assert.assertTrue(detail.getImageURL().startsWith("http"));

    if (null != System.getProperty("dev.hack")) {   ◁——   Simple developer trick to
        new ServerSocket(9999).accept();                   halt the test (more in the
    }                                                       "Development hack" sidebar)
}
```

Notice that you provide the URL in the navigateTo method. This is a programmatic alternative to using the @Location annotation, which can sometimes be too inflexible.

Development hack

Using a ServerSocket to halt the runtime is a simple development trick that you may find useful. In effect, by "running" the test class in either the IDE or Maven, you'll have fired up all your microservices at this point. This technique is useful for developing the UI, because you know where all the service endpoints are. Providing the -Ddev.hack=true system property to the test runtime will ensure that it waits indefinitely for a connection on port 9999.

You can deploy the web application to a debuggable container in your IDE and continue to develop against the running services. To stop the test runtime, make a simple `curl localhost:9999` call.

Obviously this approach won't be useful for everyone, and microservices are often developed and deployed by individual teams, but it may be food for thought.

The last things that may be of interest are the configuration options available to Graphene. The various guard methods block for a configurable period. The default configuration can be overridden via the command line

```
-Darq.extension.graphene.waitAjaxInterval=3
```

or in arquillian.xml, as shown in the following listing.

Listing 7.18 Overriding the default configuration

```
<extension qualifier="graphene">
    <property name="waitAjaxInterval">3</property>
</extension>
```

There are many more ways to use Graphene than we've laid out here, but again, this subject goes out of scope for this book. If you want more insight about what's available, you can find the project documentation at https://docs.jboss.org/author/display/ARQGRA2/Home.

7.4.9 Running the test

After all that, it's going to be a real nightmare to get this test up and running, right? Wrong! Running the test should be as intuitive as any other unit test—that's the idea, after all.

> **NOTE** If you haven't obtained the required API keys and defined the corresponding environment entries, as described in chapter 2, then please do so before running the test. Because it's an end-to-end test, this test makes real calls to the REST APIs using these keys; the test also requires an internet connection.

Here are the commands:

```
cd web
mvn clean install
```

That's it. If everything is in place, the following things occur:

1 The MongoDB and Redis servers are deployed and started by the test class rules.

2 The independent microservices are started by the test class rules.

3 All the Arquillian-managed containers are started, and the corresponding applications are deployed.

4 A test browser is started by Arquillian Drone, and the UI is displayed.

5 Each test runs in sequence to provide access to the microservices and web application.

6 The environment is terminated cleanly—all servers are shut down.

Figure 7.3 shows an example.

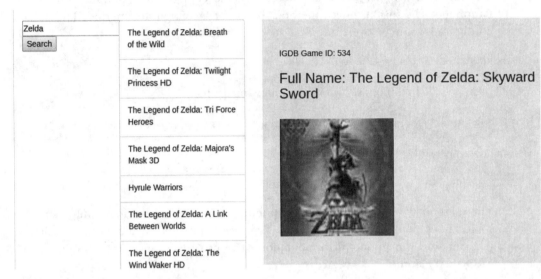

Figure 7.3   The UI automation during testing

> **WARNING**   If you encounter the error message "Target exists and we haven't been flagged to overwrite it," perform a `maven clean` cycle. This error usually means the last test run wasn't completed properly and failed to perform a cleanup on termination.

You'll notice that this test is extremely slow. This can rarely be avoided in end-to-end tests, due to the amount of wiring that needs to be performed. The only real solution is to perform end-to-end testing on a dedicated machine other than the developer machines. We suggest creating all end-to-end tests in a dedicated build module. This module can then be activated in a build profile that's only enabled on the external machine, such as Jenkins or Bamboo. See http://mng.bz/JDcT for more information on Maven build profiles.

7.5   *Exercise*

You now have a basic test template in place that contains all the features you need to perform an effective end-to-end test using several microservices. We know it's not pretty, but this is mostly because you're not using a thoroughbred environment. Your only real task here is to assess the information and environment provided for the test.

The `@InSequence(7)` test starts with a vertical test assertion that checks whether the input was correct. It then performs a horizontal action by triggering the search and retrieving the result `List`. The test is obviously breaking the rule of performing a unit of work, but it does so for demonstration purposes. Continue by extracting the assertions into further `@InSequence(x)` test methods.

Also, although you've started the Mongod and Redis instances, you haven't actually seeded the databases with any test data. Try skipping back to chapter 5 and adding a populator to the test. The world is your oyster!

Summary

- End-to-end testing is as important as all other forms of testing, if not more so, and should be performed on all applications that require any kind of user interaction. The overhead will reap rewards later: that's a promise!
- Always use abstractions and reuse code wherever possible to build your own test suite.
- Plan end-to-end testing early in the design of your UI application, to reduce the impact later.
- Adding logical, well-defined UI attributes such as `name` and `id` to featured tags in your application will ensure that it's ready to accept the automated actions promoted through the Selenium driver. Try to define and stick to your own naming conventions.

Docker and testing

This chapter covers

- Handling difficulties with high-level tests
- Understanding how Docker can help you with testing
- Creating reproducible testing environments
- Working with Arquillian Cube

A recurring message delivered by this book, and a message most developers would agree with, is that a high-level test implies a slower test—and that a huge amount of effort is usually required to prepare the test environment in which to run it. You encountered this in chapter 5, where you learned that to write an integration test against a database, you need an environment with the database you're going to use in production. The same thing happened in chapter 7, where you saw that you might need one or more microservices deployed along with their databases. And in the case of a web frontend, you might also need specific browsers installed.

When you want to test the application's big picture, you need more pieces in your environment to make it run. Here are a few:

- Databases
- Other microservices
- Multiple browsers
- Distributed caches

The problem is that first, you need to define your test environment; and second, you must provide a runtime under which to run this configuration. This probably won't be your development machine, a disadvantage for a developer because you'll lose the possibility of reproducing or debugging any given problem locally. Remote debugging, although not impossible, is much more complex.

Using Docker can mitigate some of these issues. Docker lets developers run test environments on their local machine.

8.1 Tools in the Docker ecosystem

The Docker ecosystem includes several tools such as Docker Compose, Docker Machine, and libraries that integrate with the ecosystem, such as Arquillian Cube. This section presents an overview of some of them.

8.1.1 Docker

Docker is an open source platform that simplifies the creation, deployment, and running of applications in *containers*. Imagine a container as being like a box where you deploy an application along with all the dependencies it needs, neatly packaged. In packaging the application this way, you can ensure that the application will run in a well-defined environment (one provided by the container), regardless of the underlying operating system. This enables you to move containers from one machine to another—for example, from a developer machine to a production machine—without worrying about the external configuration.

You can think of Docker as a virtual machine, but without the need to install and set up the entire OS yourself. Docker reuses the same Linux kernel regardless of where the container is actually running. This approach gives your startup time a significant performance boost and reduces the size of the application.

Figure 8.1 shows a comparison between a VM and a Docker container. The primary difference is that instead of having a guest OS for each application, a container runs atop a machine OS.

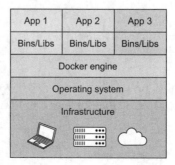

Figure 8.1 Virtual machine vs. container

To run Docker containers, you need at least three components:

- *Docker client*—A command-line interface (CLI) program that sends commands from the user to a host where the Docker daemon is installed/running.
- *Docker daemon*—A program that runs on the host OS and performs all major operations such as building, shipping, and running Docker containers. During the development and testing phases, the Docker daemon and the Docker client are probably running in the same machine.
- *Docker registry*—An artifact repository for sharing Docker images. There's a public Docker registry at http://hub.docker.com.

> **NOTE** The difference between an image and a container is that an *image* is all the bits and bobs, such as the application and configuration parameters. It doesn't have state and never changes. On the other hand, a *container* is a running instance of an image on the Docker daemon.

Figure 8.2 shows the schema of the Docker architecture. The Docker client communicates with the Docker daemon/host to execute commands. If a required Docker image isn't present on the host, it's downloaded from the Docker registry. Finally, the Docker host instantiates a new container from a given image.

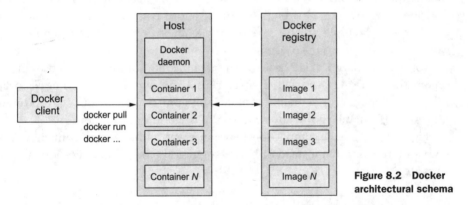

Figure 8.2 Docker architectural schema

Using the Docker client to retrieve an image from the Docker registry and running it on the Docker host might look like this:

```
docker pull jboss/wildfly
docker run -ti -p 8080:8080 jboss/wildfly
```

Pulls (downloads) the image from the Docker registry to the Docker host

Starts the JBoss/WildFly container on the Docker host

After executing the preceding commands, you can navigate in your browser to http://<dockerHostIp>;:8080, where you should see the WildFly server Welcome page shown in figure 8.3.

Figure 8.3 Welcome to WildFly

Now that you understand the Docker essentials, let's look at a Docker tool called *Docker Machine*.

8.1.2 Docker Machine

Docker Machine helps you to create Docker hosts on virtualization platforms like VirtualBox and VMware. It also supports most popular infrastructure as a service (IaaS) platforms, such as Amazon Web Services (AWS), Azure, DigitalOcean, OpenStack, and Google Compute Engine. In addition to installing Docker on given hosts, it also configures a Docker client to communicate with them.

Usually, the virtualization approach with VirtualBox is the best way to go on development machines. Note that in this case you need to have VirtualBox installed, because Docker Machine doesn't perform this installation step.

To create a VirtualBox image with Docker installed, run the following command:

```
docker-machine create --driver virtualbox dev
```

After some time, everything will be installed and ready to be used on your local machine. The final steps are to begin creating the VirtualBox image and configure the client to point to the instance:

```
docker-machine start dev          ⟵── Starts the host named dev
eval $(docker-machine env dev)    ⟵┐
                                    Configures the Docker client
                                    environment variables
```

> **Docker on a local machine**
>
> If you want to use Docker Machine on a local machine, the best way to get started is to use Docker Toolbox. It's available for both Windows and macOS.
>
> Docker Machine has an installer that installs the following tools:
>
> - Docker client
> - Docker Machine
> - Docker Compose
> - Oracle VirtualBox
> - Kitematic (Docker GUI) and a preconfigured shell

8.1.3   *Docker Compose*

Docker Compose is a multi-container-management tool composed of two elements:

- A format in YAML describing one or more containers that work together to form the application. It also specifies how containers interact with each other, as well as some other information such as networks, volumes, and ports.
- A CLI tool to read a Docker Compose file and create the application defined by the file.

By default, any Docker Compose file is appropriately named docker-compose.yml. A simple docker-compose.yml file might look like the following.

Listing 8.1   docker-compose.yml

```
                                          ┌── Defines a container name
Sets the image    tomcat:              ◄──┘
to be used    └─►  image: tutum/tomcat:7.0
                   ports:                  ┌── Defines a binding/exposed
                     - "8081:8080"      ◄──┤   ports pair
Defines a link between ┌─► links:
containers of the form │    - pingpong:pingpong
[service-name:alias]   │
                   pingpong:
                     image: jonmorehouse/ping-pong
```

When you run `docker-compose` up from the terminal on the file in listing 8.1, two containers are started: *tomcat* and *pingpong*. They're connected with a `link` named *pingpong*. And port 8081 for the Tomcat service is exposed to clients of the Docker host, forwarding all traffic to the internal container port 8080. The containers are reachable at a hostname identical to the alias or service name, if no alias is specified.

One of the best testing-related aspects of Docker Compose is the extension feature. It enables you to share common configuration snippets between different files.

Let's look at an example of a Docker Compose file using the `extend` keyword. You should first define the common or abstract container definition that other containers may extend in a Docker Compose file, which, by default, should *not* be named docker-compose.yml. You should strive to follow the naming convention that the file called docker-compose.yml is the *only* file that will be used by the running system, so to that end let's name this file common.yml.

Listing 8.2   common.yml

```
webapp:
  image: myorganization/myservice
  ports:
    - "8080:8080"
  volumes:
    - "/data"
```

There's nothing new here beyond the previous definition, other than defining a new service called webapp. Now, let's define the docker-compose.yml file to use common.yml, and set new parameters for the service.

Listing 8.3   docker-compose.yml

```
web:
  extends:              ◁── Starts an extension section
    file: common.yml
    service: webapp     ◁── Sets the element to extend
  environment: #
    - DEBUG=1
```

Sets the location of the extendible file →

Sets/Overrides a property →

You can run `docker-compose` in a terminal:

```
docker-compose -f docker-compose.test.yml up
```

As you can see, using Docker and Docker Compose, you can readily define testing environments that can be used on any machine where tests need to run. The two main advantages of using these tools together are as follows:

- Every environment that runs tests contains exactly the same versions of the required libraries, dependencies, and/or servers. It doesn't matter which physical machines are run: it could be the development, testing, or preproduction machine. All of them contain the same running bits and bobs.
- You don't need to install anything on testing machines other than Docker. Everything else is resolved at runtime.

NOTE   This chapter provides a very basic introduction to Docker Compose, and we encourage you to learn more at https://docs.docker.com/compose.

8.2   *Arquillian Cube*

So far, you've read that Docker and Docker Compose make a perfect pair for testing. They should help you define reliable and reproducible testing environments, so that each time you execute tests, you know the same environment is set up correctly.

The problem is that you need to manually run `docker-compose up` or add a step to the build tool in order to fire it up before executing the tests. You also need to deal with the Docker host IP address, which may be `localhost`—but not necessarily, because it may be a Docker machine or a remote Docker host.

Although starting Docker Compose manually could be a good approach, our opinion is that tests should be self-executing as much as possible and not require manual intervention or complicated runtimes. You've guessed it: there's a cool Arquillian extension that will help you achieve your goals. *Arquillian Cube* is an extension that can be used to manage Docker containers from within an Arquillian test. It uses an approach similar to what Arquillian Core does for application servers, but modified for Docker containers. Arquillian Cube can be used in the following scenarios:

- Preparing testing environments for high-level tests
- Testing Dockerfile compositions
- Validating Docker Compose compositions
- White box and black box testing

As you can see in figure 8.4, before executing tests, Arquillian Cube reads a Docker Compose file and starts all the containers in the correct order. Arquillian then waits until all the services are up and running so they're able to receive incoming connections. After that, tests are executed with the test environment running. Following execution, all running containers are stopped and removed from the Docker host.

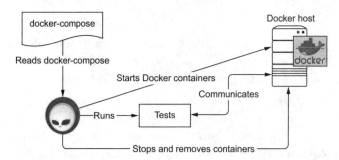

Figure 8.4   Arquillian Cube lifecycle

With Arquillian Cube, your Docker-based tests are fully automated. You can define your testing environment in the Docker Compose format, and the Arquillian runner takes care of everything for you. This again leaves you, the developer, free to write the actual tests.

> **NOTE** It isn't necessary to use Docker for production. You can also just take advantage of Docker to prepare a valid testing environment.

When using Docker in production, you can use Arquillian Cube to write tests that validate that your container image is created correctly or, for example, that the container is bootable and is accessible from outside of the Docker host. Obviously, in production, you can use a Docker Compose file that's almost, if not the same as, the one used to create the testing environment, and validate that all containers defined can communicate between each other and that environment variables are correctly set.

The potential use is unbounded, as there are an endless number of ways to use Arquillian Cube and Docker together for testing. We'll cover the most common use cases in the following sections.

8.2.1 Setting up Arquillian Cube

Arquillian Cube requires that you set up several parameters. It uses some default parameters that *may* work in most situations and others that are intelligently deduced from the environment. Sometimes you may need to modify these automatically defined parameters. Table 8.1 describes the most important configuration attributes that can be set in an arquillian.xml file.

Table 8.1 Arquillian Cube parameters

Attribute	Description	Default behavior
serverUri	URI of the Docker host where containers will be instantiated.	Gets the value from the environment variable `DOCKER_HOST` if set; otherwise, for Linux it's set to `unix:///var/run/docker.sock`, and on Windows and macOS it's set to `https://<docker_host_ip>;:2376`. `docker_host_ip` is resolved automatically by Arquillian Cube by obtaining the boot2docker or docker machine IP.
dockerRegistry	Sets the location of the Docker registry from which to download images.	By default, this is the public Docker registry at https://registry.hub.docker.com.
username	Sets the username to connect to the Docker registry. (You'll need an account.)	
password	Sets the password to connect to the Docker registry. (You'll need an account.)	
dockerContainers	Embeds the Docker Compose content as an Arquillian property, instead of as a Docker Compose file.	
dockerContainersFile	Sets the location of the Docker Compose file. The location is relative to the root of the project; but it can also be a URI that's converted to a URL, so you can effectively have Docker Compose definitions on remote sites.	

Table 8.1   Arquillian Cube parameters *(continued)*

Attribute	Description	Default behavior
`dockerContainersFiles`	Sets a comma-separated list of Docker Compose file locations. Internally, all of these locations are appended into one.	
`tlsVerify`	Boolean to set if Arquillian Cube should connect to the Docker server with Transport Layer Security (TLS).	Gets the value from the `TLS_VERIFY` environment variable if set; otherwise, it's automatically sets to `false` if the `serverUri` scheme is `http` or `true` if it's `https`. You can force a value by setting this property.
`certPath`	Path where certificates are stored if you're using HTTPS.	Gets the value from the `DOCKER_CERT_PATH` environment variable if set; otherwise, the location is resolved from boot2docker or docker-machine. You can force a value by setting this property.
`machineName`	Sets the machine name if you're using Docker Machine to manage your Docker host.	Gets the value from the `DOCKER_MACHINE_NAME` environment variable if set; otherwise, the machine name is resolved automatically if in the current Docker machine instance only one machine is running. You can force a value by setting this property.

TIP Remember that the arquillian.xml configuration attributes can be configured using system properties or environment variables by using `${system_property}` placeholders or `${env.environment_variable}` placeholders.

Arquillian Cube connection modes

The test environment is started and stopped for each test suite. This means that, depending on the elements' boot-up time, testing time may be affected, especially with small test suites.

With Arquillian Cube, you have the option to bypass the creation/start of Docker containers that are already running on a Docker host with the same container name. This allows you to prestart the containers (for example, in the continuous integration [CI] build script, or before starting work) and connect to them to avoid the extra cost during test execution.

Here's an example of how to configure the `connectionMode` property:

```
<extension qualifier="cube">;
  <property name="connectionMode">;STARTORCONNECT</property>;
</extension>;
```

You can set the following modes for this property:

- STARTANDSTOP—The default, if not specified. Creates and stops all Docker containers.
- STARTORCONNECT—Bypasses the creation/start steps if a container with the same container name is already running and this named container isn't to be terminated after the tests complete. If the container configured for Cube is not already running, then Arquillian will start it *and stop it* at the end of the execution, behaving much like the STARTANDSTOP mode.
- STARTORCONNECTANDLEAVE—Exactly the same as STARTORCONNECT mode; but if a container is started by Arquillian Cube, then it *won't be stopped* at the end of the execution, so it can be reused in the next cycle.

Now that you're familiar with the common configuration parameters in Arquillian Cube, let's explore how to write tests using it.

8.2.2 *Writing container tests*

The first use case we'll cover for Arquillian Cube is validating that the Dockerfile defined in the service to containerize the application is correct. Although you can perform several checks, the most common ones are as follows:

- Docker is able to build the image without any errors.
- The service exposes the correct ports.
- The service is started correctly and can correctly serve incoming requests.

Let's start by configuring Docker in arquillian.xml, and then create a minimal script to build and run the image under test.

Listing 8.4 Configuring Docker

```xml
<?xml version="1.0"?>;
<arquillian xmlns:xsi="http://www.w3.org/2001/XMLSchema-instance"
  xmlns="http://jboss.org/schema/arquillian"
  xsi:schemaLocation="http://jboss.org/schema/arquillian
  http://jboss.org/schema/arquillian/arquillian_1_0.xsd">;

  <extension qualifier="docker">;
    <property name="machineName">;dev</property>;        ⟵── This line is required
    <property name="dockerContainers">;  ⟵───┐              only if you're using
      myservice:                              │              Docker Machine.
        build: ./docker                       │
        ports:                                │
          - "8080:8080"                       └── Defines in Docker Compose format
    </property>;                                  how to build and run the image
  </extension>;

</arquillian>;
```

When you're using Docker Machine with more than one machine running, the machine named `dev` is used for building and running the Docker container under test. Then, with the `dockerContainers` property, you embed a Docker Compose container definition to build an image from an expected Dockerfile located in the docker directory and exposing port 8080. As mentioned earlier, Dockerfile is the default filename for a Docker definition. The Dockerfile may look like the following:

```
FROM tomee:8-jdk-7.0.2-webprofile

ADD build/libs/myservice.war /usr/local/tomee/webapps/myservice.war
EXPOSE 8080
```

The image defined here is based on the Apache TomEE `tomee:8-jdk-7.0.1-webprofile` Docker image. The `ADD` command adds your project-deployment WAR file to the specified image path—the TomEE hot deployment path in this image is /usr/local/tomee/webapps/, so adding a WAR file here will automatically deploy the application. Finally, the `EXPOSE` command exposes the TomEE HTTP port 8080 to the outside world.

Using this information, you can write a test to validate that the image is correctly built, exposes the correct port, and runs correctly.

Listing 8.5   Validating the image

```
@RunWith(Arquillian.class)                   ⟵  Arquillian runner
public class DockerImageCreationTest {
                                             The test is enriched with a Docker
  @ArquillianResource                    ⟵  client to access the Docker host.
  private DockerClient docker;
                                   The test is enriched with
  @HostIp                     ⟵   the Docker host IP.
  private String dockerHost;
                                                               Gets the binding port
  @HostPort(containerName = "myservice", value = 8080)   ⟵   for exposed port 8080
  private int myservicePort;                                   of the container
                                                               myservice
  @Test
  public void should_expose_correct_port() throws Exception {
    assertThat(docker)
      .container("myservice")              Asserts that the built image
      .hasExposedPorts("8080/tcp");  ⟵    is exposing port 8080
  }

  @Test
  public void should_be_able_to_connect_to_my_service() throws Exception {
    assertThat(docker)
      .container("myservice")         Asserts that the
      .isRunning();            ⟵     container is running

    final URL healthCheckURL = new URL("http", dockerHost,
➥ myservicePort, "health");
```

```
    String healthCheck = getHealthCheckResult(healthCheckURL);
    assertThat(healthCheck).isEqualTo("OK");
  }

}
```

Asserts that the healthCheck endpoint returns that the service is up and running

There are several things to note about this test. First, you apply the Arquillian runner, but without a @Deployment method. This is because these tests don't need to deploy anything in an application server: the container image receives the deployment file required to run the test, and the server is already running. You're effectively using all the elements provided by Arquillian but without deploying anything.

> **NOTE** Any test without a @Deployment annotated method must be used with either the arquillian-junit-standalone or arquillian-testng-standalone dependency, instead of the container dependency. All tests are run in the as-client mode, because they can't be deployed into an application server.

The second thing to note is that Arquillian Cube offers some enrichers for tests. In this test, the DockerClient object is injected. This object offers you some powerful operations to communicate with the Docker host and get information about running containers. Moreover, the test is enriched with the Docker host IP or hostname in the dockerHost variable. The binding port for the container's exposed port 8080 is also injected as the myservicePort variable. These variables provide information that allows the test to communicate with the TomEE server and the hosted application.

Last but not least are the test methods to verify that the Dockerfile is correctly configured, the build is correct, and the service it's exposing is correctly deployed. Arquillian Cube provides custom AssertJ assertions. So, for example, you can write assertions to assert that a specific Docker image is instantiated in the Docker host, or a port is exposed, or a specific process is running as expected.

If the construction defined by the Dockerfile fails, Arquillian Cube throws an exception, causing the test to fail. A health check of the endpoint for the deployed service is used to verify that the microservice deployed in the Docker container is operating correctly.

After test execution, Arquillian Cube removes the built image from the Docker host. This ensures that disk space doesn't increase every time you run a test, and also makes sure each test is run in isolation from the next.

Next, let's examine how you can use Arquillian Cube to test more-complex scenarios like integration tests.

8.2.3 *Writing integration tests*

You learned in chapter 5 that it's possible to validate the connection between two systems, such as the communication between a microservice and a database (such as SQL or NoSQL), or between two microservices. In such cases, it's normal to test your gateway code against any real system that you're going to use in production. This is a big difference when compared to *component tests*, where stubs or fakes are usually used.

The single biggest challenge for integration tests is how to consistently set up the environment to run these tests. For example, you'll probably need the same databases you're using in production on both the developer and CI machines. You may also need a way to deploy all dependent microservices for the actual microservice under test. In addition, ensuring that versions are maintained across all environments and machines isn't a trivial task. Prior to Docker, this kind of setup wasn't easy to realize without having everything in place on all machines.

You've seen that Docker and Docker Compose can help you prepare a consistent environment for testing, and how Arquillian Cube can help automate the process. In this section, we'll look at an example.

> ### Arquillian deployment and Docker
>
> As we said in chapter 4, Arquillian has three ways to manage an application server:
>
> - *Embedded*—The application server shares the same JVM and classpath with the test runtime (IDE, build tool, and so on).
> - *Managed*—The application server is booted up independently of the test runtime. It effectively creates a new JVM, independent of the actual test JVM.
> - *Remote*—Arquillian doesn't manage the lifecycle of the application server. It expects to reuse an instance that's already up and running.
>
> With this in mind, you can use Arquillian to deploy your (micro)deployment file in an application server that it's running in a Docker container. From an Arquillian point of view, this application server instance is a remote instance where the lifecycle is managed by another party (in this case, Docker).
>
> Think back to the fact that the runtime adapter in the classpath is how Arquillian knows how to manage the application-server lifecycle. For example, in the case of Apache Tomcat, for remote mode you need to define the `org.jboss.arquillian.container:arquillian-tomcat-remote-7:1.0.0.CR7` dependency.
>
> As you can see, it's possible to take advantage of (micro)deployment and use Docker to set up (part of) the environment.

Let's create an integration test using Arquillian Cube, to test the integration between a service and its database. You'll use a microdeployment approach to package the classes related to the persistence layer. In order to add to the previous Docker Compose file format, make sure to use Docker compose format version 2 rather than version 1.

The following listing shows what a test looks like.

Listing 8.6   Integration test

```
@RunWith(Arquillian.class)
public class UserRepositoryTest {

  @Deployment
  public static WebArchive create() {
    return ShrinkWrap.create(WebArchive.class)
```

Creates a microdeployment using only the required persistence-layer classes and files

```
                 .addClasses(User.class, UserRepository.class,
                                          UserRepositoryTest.class)
                 .addAsWebInfResource(EmptyAsset.INSTANCE, "beans.xml")
                 .addAsResource("test-persistence.xml", "META-INF/persistence.xml")
                 .addAsManifestResource(new StringAsset(
                                          "Dependencies: com.h2database.h2\n"),
                                "MANIFEST.MF");
      }

      @Inject
      private UserRepository repository;

      @Test
      public void shouldStoreUser() throws IOException {
         repository.store(new User("test"));
         User user = repository.findUserByName("test");

         assertThat(user.getName()).isEqualTo("test");
      }
   }
```

This is no different than running any other Arquillian test, so the test won't be aware of whether it's running against a local or a remote instance.

TIP You can also benefit from using the Arquillian Persistence Extension in these tests if you need to.

The next step is defining a docker-compose.yml file that starts the server and the database.

Listing 8.7 Starting the server and database

```
version: '2'
services:                          Sets environment variables
  tomcat:                          from a file named envs
    env_file: envs       ◄
    build: src/test/resources/tomcat   ◄──┐  The Tomcat image is
    ports:                                │  built from a Dockerfile.
      - "8089:8089"
      - "8088:8088"
      - "8081:8080"
  db:
    image: zhilvis/h2-db      ◄── Uses the H2 server Docker image
    ports:
      - "1521:1521"
      - "8181:81"
```

TIP Always pay close attention to the indentation in YAML files. It's vital!

In this file, a default network is created and shared between both containers. The container name is the hostname alias used by each container to look up other instances. For example, a tomcat container configuration for reaching db might be jdbc:h2:tcp://**db**:1521/opt/h2-data/test.

The Dockerfile should add a tomcat-users.xml file, ready with a user that has the roles to be able to deploy remotely. You need to define environment variables in order to configure Tomcat to accept deploying external applications on the fly, as well as set the password:

Trick to change how entropy is calculated so that Tomcat starts up quickly

The dockerServerIp parameter is replaced automatically at runtime by the Docker host IP.

```
CATALINA_OPTS=-Djava.security.egd=file:/dev/urandom
JAVA_OPTS= -Djava.rmi.server.hostname=dockerServerIp \
        -Dcom.sun.management.jmxremote.rmi.port=8088 \
        -Dcom.sun.management.jmxremote.port=8089
        -Dcom.sun.management.jmxremote.ssl=false
        -Dcom.sun.management.jmxremote.authenticate=false
```

The JMX console is configured to accept remote communication.

> ## Entropy
>
> The entropy trick in the Tomcat configuration snippet is used only on Linux platforms, but it can also improve startup on Windows machines. The default `SecureRandom` implementation is very slow, because it must wait for the OS to build up entropy— and this can take minutes. Specifying `urandom` is slightly less secure for extreme cryptography algorithms. On some systems, you may need to use the alternative syntax if you still notice significant startup times (note the extra slashes):
>
> ```
> -Djava.security.egd=file:/dev/urandom
> ```
>
> Other options are available, such as defining a physical file of random numbers. Search the internet for java.security.egd to learn more about this subject.

Last but not least, you need to configure the Arquillian Cube Extension to load the provided Docker Compose file. You also need to configure the remote adapter to set the user declared in the tomcat-users.xml file to connect to the Tomcat server and deploy the application.

Listing 8.8   Configuring the Arquillian Cube Extension and the remote adapter

```xml
<?xml version="1.0"?>;
<arquillian xmlns:xsi="http://www.w3.org/2001/XMLSchema-instance"
  xmlns="http://jboss.org/schema/arquillian"
  xsi:schemaLocation="http://jboss.org/schema/arquillian
  http://jboss.org/schema/arquillian/arquillian_1_0.xsd">;

  <extension qualifier="docker">;
    <property name="dockerContainersFile">;docker-compose.yml</property>;
  </extension>;

  <container qualifier="tomcat">;
    <configuration>;
      <property name="user">;admin</property>;
```

Sets the location of the Docker Compose file. In this case, it's located in the project's root directory.

Configures the Tomcat adapter with admin and mypass as authentication parameters to deploy

```
            <property name="pass">;mypass</property>;
        </configuration>;
    </container>;
</arquillian>;
```

This is all you need to configure. Arquillian Cube automatically takes care of where Tomcat is running and deploying the test application to the correct (remote) Docker host IP. It's important to note that most of these steps are specific to Tomcat, and that using another container might require different steps and touch different files.

> **WARNING** The `qualifier` value in arquillian.xml must be the same container name as that defined in the docker-compose.yml file. In the previous example, the container name is `tomcat` and the qualifier is also `tomcat`, which makes sense.

When you run this test, the following steps are executed:

1. Arquillian Cube reads the Docker Compose file and then builds and instantiates the specified images to the Docker host.
2. Arquillian Core deploys the microdeployment file that contains the persistence-layer classes into the Tomcat container instance running in Docker Host.
3. The test is executed when the entire test environment is set up and booted.
4. After all tests are executed, the microdeployment file is undeployed.
5. The Docker container instances are terminated and removed from the Docker host.

Note that this test now runs in its own provided testing environment that hosts the required database used in production. You don't need to install any software dependencies on your actual development environment or CI environment for each project. Docker and Arquillian Cube take care of providing the dependencies for the test automatically.

Now that you've seen how to write an integration test using Arquillian Cube, let's move on to how you can use it for end-to-end testing.

8.2.4 *Writing end-to-end tests*

Chapter 7 explained that you can validate your application from start to finish by, in theory, simulating a real-world user of your application, or at least performing the actions of a real user. In practice, these tests are usually the most difficult to write because they cover a lot of interactions—in most cases (but not always) interactions with the UI. They also require that you set up a full test environment with all possible elements the application might interact with, such as

- Server
- Databases
- Distributed caches
- Browsers

You now know that Docker, Docker Compose, and Arquillian Cube can help you prepare the environment for tests. Note that in end-to-end tests, you probably won't need to create a deployment file in your tests; you'll reuse an existing, versioned Docker image of the core of the application. For this reason, and as you saw in chapter 4, where no deployment method is provided, you'll need to use the `standalone` dependency of Arquillian Core.

Let's see what a docker-compose.yml file might look like for the same application you tested in section 8.2.3.

Listing 8.9   Docker Compose file for an end-to-end test

```
version: '2'
services:
  myservice:
    env_file: envs
    image: superbiz/myservice:${version:-latest}      ◁─┐  The image version is set using
    ports:                                                a system property or
      - "8081:8080"                                       environment variable. If it
  db:                                                     isn't set, the default value
    image: zhilvis/h2-db                                  "latest" is used, denoted by
    ports:                                                the :- symbols.
      - "1521:1521"
      - "8181:81"
```

In this file, you aren't building a new Docker container, but rather are reusing the one built during the process of building the microservice. Each time you run end-to-end tests, the Docker image bundling the microservice may be a different version; for this reason, the final image name containing the microservice is generated dynamically at testing time by setting the version using a system property or environment variable named version.

The configuration file (arquillian.xml) doesn't change from the previous use case.

Listing 8.10   Configuration file for an end-to-end test

```
<?xml version="1.0"?>;
<arquillian xmlns:xsi="http://www.w3.org/2001/XMLSchema-instance"
  xmlns="http://jboss.org/schema/arquillian"
  xsi:schemaLocation="http://jboss.org/schema/arquillian
  http://jboss.org/schema/arquillian/arquillian_1_0.xsd">;

  <extension qualifier="docker">;
    <property name="dockerContainersFile">;docker-compose.yml</property>;   ◁─┐
  </extension>;
                                      Sets the docker-compose.yml file location
</arquillian>;
```

Using multiple Docker Compose file definitions

In simple cases where a microservice isn't a consumer of another microservice, using a single Docker Compose file may do the trick. But if a microservice under test is itself a consumer of one or more microservices, you may also need to start all of these services prior to testing. This is also valid when you want to write an end-to-end test, not for a given microservice and all of its dependencies (which can be other microservices), but for the entire system.

In such cases, you can still rely on creating a single Docker Compose file containing all microservices and dependencies required for testing. But this may not be a good idea in terms of readiness, maintainability, and reflecting changes to the microservices environment.

Our opinion is that each microservice should define its own Docker Compose file to set up the testing/production environment it needs in order to run. This makes end-to-end tests easy, because you can merge all the definitions with the useful Arquillian Cube `dockerContainersFiles` property.

In the following snippet, Arquillian Cube downloads all the remote Docker Compose files and merges them into a single composition. Arquillian Cube then starts all defined containers, after which the test is executed:

```xml
<?xml version="1.0"?>;
<arquillian xmlns:xsi="http://www.w3.org/2001/XMLSchema-instance"
  xmlns="http://jboss.org/schema/arquillian"
  xsi:schemaLocation="http://jboss.org/schema/arquillian
  http://jboss.org/schema/arquillian/arquillian_1_0.xsd">;

  <extension qualifier="docker">;
    <property name="dockerContainersFiles">;        ⟵——  A list of locations
      docker-compose.yml,                                  where Docker
        http://myhub/provider1/test/docker-compose.yml,    Compose files
        http://myhub/provider2/test/docker-compose.yml     are stored
    </property>;
  </extension>;

</arquillian>;
```

As you can see, it isn't necessary to define the testing environment in a single location. Each microservice can define its own testing environment.

Finally, you can write the end-to-end tests as you learned in chapter 7, using any of the frameworks exposed there. You can enrich each test with different Docker/container environment values such as the Docker host IP, and resolve port binding values for given exposed ports:

```
@HostIp         ⟵—— Injects the Docker host IP
String ip;
                                              Resolves the binding port
                                              for exposed port 8080 of
@HostPort(containerName = "tomcat", value = 8080)  ⟵——┘ the tomcat container
```

```
int tomcatPort;
                                        Injects the IP of the
@CubeIp(containerName = "tomcat")   ◄──┘ tomcat container
String ip;
```

After injecting the Docker host IP and container binding port, you can configure any test framework used for endpoint testing against the Docker container. For example, you could configure REST Assured (http://rest-assured.io) to test a microservice that's running in the Docker host by doing something like this:

```
RestAssured.when()
           .get("http://" + ip + ":" + tomcatPort + "/myresource")
           .then()
           ....
```

This is one way to configure any testing framework by constructing the URL required. But Arquillian Cube offers tight integration with REST Assured and Arquillian Drone/Graphene, so you don't need to deal with this in every test.

8.3   *Rest API*

Because Arquillian Cube provides integration with REST Assured, you don't need to repeat the same configuration code in all the tests where REST Assured is used with Docker. Having this integration means you can inject an instance of io.restassured .builder.RequestSpecBuilder that's preconfigured with the current Docker host IP and port. (The sidebar "About port resolution" explains how the port resolution works.) The following test uses REST Assured integration:

```
@RunWith(Arquillian.class)
public class MyServiceTest {
                                        RequestSpecBuilder with
  @ArquillianResource            ◄──┘  Docker parameters predefined
  RequestSpecBuilder requestSpecBuilder;

  @Test
  public void should_be_able_to_connect_to_my_service() {
    RestAssured
      .given()                                REST Assured is configured
      .spec(requestSpecBuilder.build())   ◄──┘ with a request specification.
      .when()
      .get()
      .then()
      .assertThat().body("status", equalTo("OK"));
  }
}
```

As you can see, this test is similar to any test using REST Assured. The only difference is that now you're setting the request-specification object configured with Docker values.

About port resolution

Arquillian Cube REST Assured integration tries to automatically resolve which port is the binding port of the public microservice. By default, Arquillian Cube scans all Docker containers defined in Docker Compose files, and if there's only one binding port, it's the one that's used.

If there are several binding ports, then the `port` configuration property must be defined for the exposed port that Arquillian Cube should use to communicate with the microservice. For example, if you're using the binding configuration 8080:80, where the exposed port is 80 and the binding port is 8080, then when you set the `port` property to `80`, the extension will resolve to 8080.

To set the `port` property, you need to add it to arquillian.xml:

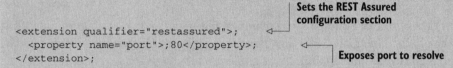

```
<extension qualifier="restassured">;
  <property name="port">;80</property>;
</extension>;
```

Sets the REST Assured configuration section

Exposes port to resolve

If there's no exposed port with the given number, then the port specified in the configuration property is also used as the binding port.

8.4   *Arquillian Drone and Graphene*

When you're running end-to-end tests that involve a browser as a frontend UI, one of the problems you may encounter is setting up the testing environment. You'll need to install all requirements on every machine where tests are run, including the required browsers (with specific versions).

As you learned in chapter 7, the de facto tool for web-browser tests is Selenium WebDriver. The Arquillian ecosystem offers Arquillian Drone and Graphene as the integration extension that uses WebDriver.

The Selenium project offers Docker images for the Selenium standalone server with Chrome and/or Firefox preinstalled. So, you effectively don't need to install a browser in the testing environment, because the browser is treated like any other test dependency managed by Docker, such as databases, distributed caches, and other services.

8.4.1   *Integrating Arquillian Cube and Arquillian Drone*

Arquillian Cube integrates with Arquillian Drone by automatically executing several cumbersome tasks:

- Starting the Docker container with the correct `browser` property for the `webdriver` extension set to `Firefox`, if not already set. The Selenium version of the image is the same as that defined in the test classpath.
- Providing a `WebDriver` that can connect to the container.
- Creating a virtual network computing (VNC) Docker container that records all test executions that occur for each test in a browser container and stores them on the local machine in MP4 format.

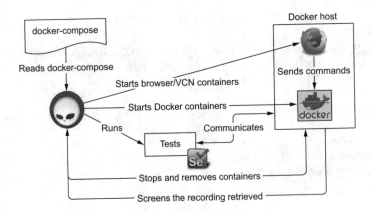

Figure 8.5   Arquillian integrations

These interactions are summarized in figure 8.5.

Table 8.2 describes the most important configuration attributes that you can define in arquillian.xml.

Table 8.2   Arquillian Cube Graphene configuration parameters

Attribute	Description	Default behavior
recordingMode	Recording mode to be used. The valid values are ALL, ONLY_FAILING, and NONE.	ALL
videoOutput	Directory where videos are stored.	Creates target/reports/videos or, if target doesn't exist, build/reports/videos.
browserImage	Docker image to be used as a custom browser image instead of the default image.	
browserDockerfileLocation	Dockerfile location to be used to build a custom Docker image instead of the default Dockerfile. This property has preference over browserImage.	

NOTE Custom images must expose port 4444 so the WebDriver instance can reach the browser. If VNC is used, port 5900 must also be exposed.

Here's an example of a typical configuration:

```xml
<?xml version="1.0"?>;
<arquillian xmlns:xsi="http://www.w3.org/2001/XMLSchema-instance"
  xmlns="http://jboss.org/schema/arquillian"
  xsi:schemaLocation="http://jboss.org/schema/arquillian
  http://jboss.org/schema/arquillian/arquillian_1_0.xsd">;

  <extension qualifier="docker">;
```

Typical Arquillian Cube configuration

```
        <property name="dockerContainersFile">;docker-compose.yml</property>;
    </extension>;

    <extension qualifier="webdriver">;                              ◄─────────┐
      <property name="browser">;${browser:chrome}</property>;                 │
    </extension>;                                                             │
                                                         Configures the browser
                                                          property from either a
    <extension qualifier="cubedrone">;                   system property or an
      <property name="recordingMode">;NONE</property>;    environment variable,
    </extension>;                                        using "chrome" as the
                                                                        default
</arquillian>;
```
Disables recording capabilities

Here, Arquillian Cube is configured to start all containers defined in the docker-compose.yml file. Notice that this file doesn't contain any information regarding browsers, because this is autoresolved by the Arquillian Cube Drone integration.

The browser is specified by setting the `browser` system property or environment variable to `firefox` or `chrome`. If it isn't defined, `chrome` is used as the default. Finally, the recording feature is disabled.

> **WARNING** At time of writing, the Selenium project offers images only for Firefox and Chrome. Creating Internet Explorer images is still a task left to the user.

The actual test shown in listing 8.11 (HelloWorldTest.java) looks similar to any Drone and Arquillian Cube test, with one slight difference. All browser commands (hence, `WebDriver`) are executed *inside* the Docker host, meaning you're governed by Docker host rules. Thus, in this test, instead of using `HostIp` to get the Docker host IP, you use `CubeIp`, which returns the *internal IP address* of the given container. This is required because the browser is running inside the Docker host, and to connect to another container in the same Docker host, you need either the host name or the internal IP address.

Listing 8.11 HelloWorldTest.java

```
@RunWith(Arquillian.class)
public class HelloWorldTest {           Uses the Drone
                                        annotation to inject the
  @Drone                     ◄──────┐   WebDriver instance
  WebDriver webDriver;              

  @CubeIp(containerName = "helloworld")   ◄───┐  Injects the internal IP of
  String ip;                                  │  the helloworld container

  @Test
  public void shouldShowHelloWorld() throws Exception {
    URL url = new URL("http", ip, 80, "/");        ◄───┐  URL to connect the browser
    webDriver.get(url.toString());                     │  to the microservice
```

```
   final String message = webDriver.findElement(By.tagName("h1")).getText();
   assertThat(message).isEqualTo("Hello world!");
}


}
```

Next, let's look at how Arquillian Cube and Arquillian Graphene are integrated.

8.4.2   *Integrating Arquillian Cube and Arquillian Graphene*

Arquillian Graphene is a set of extensions for the WebDriver API, focused on rapid development and usability in a Java environment. It strives for reusable tests by simplifying the use of web page abstractions (page objects and page fragments).

Arquillian Graphene depends on Arquillian Drone to provide an instance of Web-Driver, so everything that's valid in integration between Arquillian Cube Docker (such as recording capabilities) is also valid for Arquillian Cube Graphene.

One of the primary things that differentiates a test written in Arquillian Drone from a test written in Arquillian Graphene is that the latter test automatically resolves the host and the context of the application. In Arquillian Drone, you need to explicitly set them by calling the webdriver.get(...) method.

This autoresolution feature provided by Arquillian Graphene works only when you're running tests in container mode. (Arquillian manages the deployment file for classes that have a @Deployment method.) When you're using standalone mode (no @Deployment declaration), which may be the case in end-to-end tests, you need to configure Arquillian Graphene in arquillian.xml with the URL where the application is deployed:

```
<extension qualifier="graphene">;           Sets the URL to be used by Graphene tests
  <property name="url">;http://localhost:8080/myapp</property>;        ◄───────
</extension>;
```

The problem is that when you're using Arquillian Cube, you may not know the Docker host IP address at configuration time—only during the runtime phase. So you can't reliably set it yet!

Arquillian Cube integrates with Arquillian Graphene by providing a special keyword, dockerHost, that can be defined in the url property and is replaced at runtime by the current Docker host IP when the test environment fires up. Additionally, if the *host* part of url isn't dockerHost or a valid IP, then this host is considered to be the Docker container name and is replaced by its container internal IP.

Knowing this, the previous example can be rewritten so it's Arquillian Cube Graphene aware:

```
<extension qualifier="docker">;
  <property name="dockerContainersFile">;docker-compose.yml</property>;
</extension>;
<extension qualifier="graphene">;           Sets the URL to be used by Graphene
  <property name="url">;http://helloworld:8080/myapp</property>;        ◄───────
</extension>;
```

Based on this information, you now know the following:

- The `helloworld` part of the URL will be replaced by the container's internal IP.
- The port used should be the exposed port for the `helloworld` container.

You can now define a page object, as in any other Arquillian Graphene test:

```
@Location("/")                        Path of the page represented
public class HomePage {               by this page object

  @FindBy(tagName = "h1")
  private WebElement welcomeMessageElement;

  public void assertOnWelcomePage() {
    assertThat(this.welcomeMessageElement.getText().trim())
            .isEqualTo("Hello world!");
  }
}
```

Note that in this case, you aren't setting any information about the actual hostname, you're just setting the relative context location of this page.

Finally, the test has no changes versus a normal test. Everything is managed underneath by Arquillian Cube:

```
@RunWith(Arquillian.class)
public class HomePageTest {

  @Drone
  WebDriver webDriver;

  @Test
  public void shouldShowHelloWorld(@InitialPage HomePage homePage) {
    homePage.assertOnWelcomePage();
  }
}
```

As you can see, the host information isn't present in any test. It's resolved and provided to the environment via the arquillian.xml file. This makes the tests reusable in any environment, because you can change the base URL dynamically before executing the tests.

> **NOTE** Arquillian Cube Graphene autoresolution is required only if you're using Arquillian in standalone mode (using the standalone dependency). If you're using container mode, the URL is resolved by the deployment method, and you don't need to specify anything. In our opinion, an end-to-end test with Docker (or in general) should be written using Arquillian standalone mode; this simulates a real production environment much more closely, which is ultimately what you're trying to achieve.

8.5   *Parallelizing tests*

One of the problems you may encounter when running tests against a single Docker host is that each container running in the host must have a unique name. In general, this may not be an issue, but in some situations it can lead to a conflict:

- If you run tests defined in the same project in parallel, then, assuming they're reusing the same Docker Compose file, the same Docker host is used. This will cause a conflict because you're using the same container name for each test.
- Different projects are running tests in your CI environment and reusing the same Docker host. For example, two microservices have defined a Docker container named db, and they're building at the same time.

Workarounds are available to mitigate these problems:

- The first problem can be resolved by setting the arq.extension.docker .serverUri property in each parallel execution to use a different Docker host.
- The second problem can be resolved by using one agent/slave for each project, each of which has its own Docker host.

In conjunction with these workarounds, Arquillian Cube offers a helpful tool called the *star operator* (*).

The star operator lets you indicate to Arquillian Cube that you want to generate part of the Docker container name randomly. All generated information is automatically adapted to use the random element. The only thing you need to do is add an asterisk character (*) at the end of the container name in the Docker Compose file. Here's an example:

```
tomcat:
  image: tutum/tomcat:7.0
  ports:
    - "8081:8080"
  links:                          Sets a link to a partially
    - pingpong*                   random container name

pingpong*:                        Sets the container name
  image: jonmorehouse/ping-pong   as partially random
  ports:
    - "8080:8080"
```

Given this Docker Compose file, Arquillian Cube will substitute the * character for a UUID generated for each execution at runtime. Binding ports are changed to a random port (in the range 49152–65535). And a new environment variable with a link to the random container setting at the new host location is provided to containers; the form of this environment variable is <containerName>;_HOSTNAME.

The resulting docker-compose.yml file after Arquillian Cube has applied the changes might look like this:

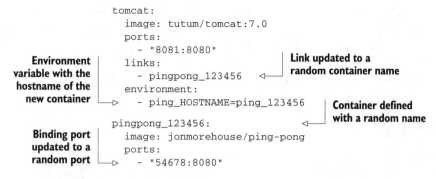

```
tomcat:
  image: tutum/tomcat:7.0
  ports:
    - "8081:8080"
  links:
    - pingpong_123456
  environment:
    - ping_HOSTNAME=ping_123456

pingpong_123456:
  image: jonmorehouse/ping-pong
  ports:
    - "54678:8080"
```

Environment variable with the hostname of the new container

Link updated to a random container name

Container defined with a random name

Binding port updated to a random port

WARNING Using the star operator will make your Docker Compose file incompatible with the `docker-compose` CLI. Also note that the `hostname` entry in DNS defined by the `links` section is also randomly generated, because the container name has been changed.

The star operator isn't an all-or-nothing solution—you can use it together with other approaches. The ideal scenario has one Docker host for each parallel execution or slave/agent.

8.6   *Arquillian Cube and Algeron*

In chapter 6, you learned about consumer-driven contracts and how they're run using the Arquillian Algeron Extension. You execute them in two steps: the first step is on the consumer side, where you start a stub HTTP server and send requests to it; and the second step is to replay and verify all interactions that occurred against a real provider. These interactions are summarized in figure 8.6.

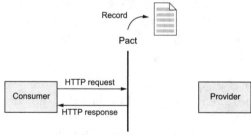

Step 1: Define consumer expectations.

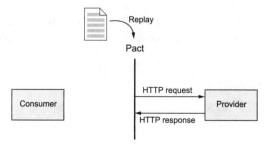

Step 2: Verify expectations on the provider.

Figure 8.6   Pact lifecycle

To run provider contract tests, you need to deploy the provider service and then replay and verify all interactions. This is where Docker and Arquillian Cube can help you, by simplifying the deployment phase of the provider service.

So far, there isn't much difference between using Arquillian Algeron with Arquillian Cube. But let's look at a quick example where a new Arquillian Cube enrichment method is introduced:

```
                                          Arquillian Cube and Arquillian
                                          Algeron annotations
@RunWith(Arquillian.class)          ◁──┘
@Provider("provider")
@ContractsFolder("pacts")
public class MyServiceProviderTest {     Enriches the URL with
                                         valid Docker values
  @ArquillianResource               ◁──
  @DockerUrl(containerName = "helloworld", exposedPort = "8080",
➡ context = "/hello")
  URL webapp;
                                    Enriches the Arquillian
                                    Algeron Target
  @ArquillianResource         ◁──┘
  Target target;

  @Test
  public void should_provide_valid_answers() {    Replays verification against
    target.testInteraction(webapp);          ◁──┘ the Docker container
  }

}
```

This test is basically the same as any other Arquillian Cube and Arquillian Algeron Pact provider, but in this case the test is enriched with a URL to access the provider. This URL is created by resolving `dockerHost` as the host part. The port part is appended by obtaining the exposed port set in the annotation for the specific container (`"helloworld"`, in this case). The annotation-defined context is then appended. For example, the resulting URL might have the value `http://192.168.99.100:8081/hello`. The rest of the test is pretty much the same as any other.

> **TIP** You can use the `@DockerUrl` annotation in any Arquillian Cube standalone test, not just when using Arquillian Algeron. But note that the enrichment test is in *standalone* mode (there's no `@Deployment` method). The `@DockerUrl` enrichment works only when you're running Arquillian in standalone mode.

Of course, you still need to define a Docker Compose file and configure Arquillian Cube. But for the sake of simplicity, and because you've seen that in previous sections, we skipped these steps.

8.7   *Using the container-objects pattern*

So far, you've seen how to "orchestrate" Docker containers using the Docker Compose file. Arquillian Cube also offers another way to define Docker containers using a Java object.

Using Java objects to define the container configuration enables you to add some dynamism to the Docker container definition, such as modifying a Dockerfile's content programmatically or modelling container attributes such as IP address, username, and password. Also, because you're creating Java objects, you can use any of the resources the language provides, such as extending definitions, injecting values from tests, or packaging values as delivery artifacts.

You can think of *container objects* as a way to model containers in a reusable, maintainable way. Because they're Java objects, nothing prevents you from reusing them across multiple projects. This reduces the amount of duplicated code, and any fixes only need to be applied in one place instead of in multiple projects.

Before we show you how to implement container objects, let's look at an example where they're useful. Suppose your microservice (or project) needs to send a file to an FTP server. You need to write an integration test validating that your business code can execute this operation correctly.

Your test must be able to execute the following operations:

- Find the hostname/IP and port where the FTP server is running.
- Define the username and password required to access the FTP server and store files.
- Assert the existence of a file on the FTP server to verify that the file is correctly sent.

One way to write this test would be to use the Docker Compose approach:

```
ftp:
  image: andrewvos/docker-proftpd
  ports:
    - "2121:21"
  environment:
    - USERNAME=alex
    - PASSWORD=aixa
```

This approach has several problems:

- You need to copy this docker-compose.yml file to all projects where you want to write an integration test using the FTP server.
- Tests need to know internal details of the Docker container, such as username and password.
- Tests contain logic specific to the Docker container, such as how to validate that a file has been copied.
- Any changes need to be propagated to all use cases.

You obviously have a good contender here for writing a container-object pattern that encapsulates all logic related to the FTP server. The following listing shows what this container object might look like (FtpContainer.java).

Listing 8.12 Container-object pattern

Defines the Cube name and binding ports

```
@Cube(value = "ftp",
    portBinding = FtpContainer.BIND_PORT + "->;21/tcp")
@Image("andrewvos/docker-proftpd")
@Environment(key = "USERNAME", value = FtpContainer.USERNAME)
@Environment(key = "PASSWORD", value = FtpContainer.PASSWORD)
public class FtpContainer {

    static final String USERNAME = "alex";
    static final String PASSWORD = "aixa";
    static final int BIND_PORT = 2121;

    @ArquillianResource
    DockerClient dockerClient;

    @HostIp
    String ip;

    public String getIp() {
        return ip;
    }

    public String getUsername() {
        return USERNAME;
    }

    public String getPassword() {
        return PASSWORD;
    }

    public int getBindPort() {
        return BIND_PORT;
    }

    public boolean isFilePresentInContainer(String filename) {

        InputStream file = null;

        try (
            file = dockerClient
              .copyArchiveFromContainerCmd("ftp", "/ftp/" + filename)
              .exec()){
            return file != null;
        } catch(Exception e){
            return false;
        } finally{
            if (null != file) {
                try {
                    file.close();
                } catch (IOException e) {
                    //no-op
                }
            }
        }
    }
}
```

Sets the Docker image

Configures environment variables to be set in the container

Enables enrichments in container objects

Encapsulates operations related to the container

As you can see in this class, a container object is a plain old Java object (POJO). This object is annotated with configuration parameters required for starting the container, such as `name` and `bind`/`expose` ports using the `@Cube` annotation, and which Docker image is mapped using the `@Image` annotation. Any Arquillian test enrichment that you've learned so far can be applied to a container object, such as `host_ip`, `host_port`, and `docker client`.

Now you've seen how to define a container object, here's how to use it in a test (FtpClientTest.java).

Listing 8.13 Using a container object in a test

```
@RunWith(Arquillian.class)
public class FtpClientTest {

  public static final String REMOTE_FILENAME = "a.txt";

  @Cube                                            The container object is
  FtpContainer ftpContainer;                       annotated with @Cube.

  @Rule
  public TemporaryFolder folder = new TemporaryFolder();

  @Test
  public void should_upload_file_to_ftp_server() throws Exception {

    // Given
    final File file = folder.newFile(REMOTE_FILENAME);
    Files.write(file.toPath(), "Hello World".getBytes());

    // When
    FtpClient ftpClient = new FtpClient(ftpContainer.getIp(),    Retrieves
            ftpContainer.getBindPort(),                          FTP properties
            ftpContainer.getUsername(),                          from the
            ftpContainer.getPassword());                         injected object
    try {
        ftpClient.uploadFile(file, REMOTE_FILENAME, ".");
    } finally {
        ftpClient.disconnect();
    }

    // Then
    final boolean filePresentInContainer = ftpContainer
      .isFilePresentInContainer(REMOTE_FILENAME);            Encapsulates operations
    assertThat(filePresentInContainer, is(true));            related to the container
  }
}
```

Using a container object in an Arquillian Cube test is as simple as declaring it as such and annotating it with `@Cube`. At execution time, Arquillian Cube inspects all test classes for fields annotated with `Cube`, reads all metainformation, and starts the defined containers. After the test is executed, the container is stopped.

As you can see, the lifecycle of a container object isn't much different from defining it in a Docker Compose file. Note that in this case, there's no need for a Docker Compose file, although you could use both approaches together if you wanted to.

Updating default values

When you're working with a POJO, you can override any part of it using normal Java language conventions. In the following example, the test overrides the name of the container, as well as the port binding configuration:

```
@Cube(value = "myftp",
       portBinding = "21->;21/tcp")           ⟵┐ Updates default values provided
FtpContainer ftpContainer;                        by the container object
```

Another feature offered by the container-objects pattern in Arquillian Cube is the possibility of not depending on a specific image. You can build your own image from a Dockerfile using the `CubeDockerFile` annotation:

```
@Cube(value = "ftp",
       portBinding = FtpContainer.BIND_PORT + "->;21/tcp")       Builds image
@CubeDockerFile("/docker")                              ⟵┐      from a
@Environment(key = "USERNAME", value = FtpContainer.USERNAME)     configured
@Environment(key = "PASSWORD", value = FtpContainer.PASSWORD)     Dockerfile
public class FtpContainer {


}
```

The `CubeDockerFile` annotation sets the location where the Dockerfile can be found, but it doesn't limit the contents of the Dockerfile. This location must be accessible by the runtime `ClassLoader`, so it must be present on the classpath.

You can also create the Dockerfile programmatically using the ShrinkWrap Descriptors domain-specific language (DSL). The following example shows how a Dockerfile can be defined using the DSL in a container object:

```
@Cube(value = "ftp", portBinding = "2121->;21/tcp")
public class FtpContainer {

  @CubeDockerFile                                      Static method for
  public static Archive<?>; createContainer() {   ⟵┘   defining a Dockerfile
    String dockerDescriptor = Descriptors.create(DockerDescriptor.class)
          .from("andrewvos/docker-proftpd")
          .expose(21)                              Creates Dockerfile content using
          .exportAsString();                  ⟵┘   the ShrinkWrap Descriptors DSL
    return ShrinkWrap.create(GenericArchive.class)
          .add(new StringAsset(dockerDescriptor), "Dockerfile");   ⟵┐
  }
}                                                     Builds an archive with
                                                      all required content
```

The method that builds the Dockerfile must be annotated with `CubeDockerFile`, and it must be public and static with no arguments. In addition, the method needs to return a ShrinkWrap `Archive` instance. The Dockerfile isn't returned directly, because in certain circumstances you might need to add extra files required for building the Docker container. This is especially true when you need to add files during container creation.

The last feature offered by the container-objects pattern is the aggregation of containers. Aggregation allows you to define container objects in other container objects. Each aggregated object contains a link to its parent, so each of the involved parties can communicate with each other.

Here's how to define an inner container object:

```
@Cube
public class FirstContainerObject {
  @Cube("inner")
  LinkContainerObject linkContainerObject;
}
```

In addition to starting both containers, Arquillian Cube creates a link between them by setting the hostname for `LinkContainerObject` to `inner`. The link can be further configured by using a `@Link` annotation:

```
@Cube("inner")
@Link("db:db")
TestLinkContainerObject linkContainerObject;
```

8.7.1 *Using a flexible container-object DSL*

Arquillian Cube also provides a generic `Container` object to generate Cube instances. Writing definitions is more efficient when you use this approach, but it's a little more difficult to reuse the code or to provide the custom operations with the custom container-object approach.

Let's look at a simple example of how to declare and start a Docker container using the `Container` DSL:

> The field is annotated with **@DockerContainer.**

```
@DockerContainer
Container pingpong = Container.withContainerName("pingpong")
                        .fromImage("jonmorehouse/ping-pong")
                        .withPortBinding(8080)
                        .build();
```

> The DSL starts with the **withContainerName method.**

```
@Test
public void should_return_ok_as_pong() throws IOException {
   String response = ping(pingpong.getIpAddress(),
                        pingpong.getBindPort(8080));
   assertThat(response).containsSequence("OK");
}
```

> Gets container information to connect

To create a generic container object, you only need to create a field of type `org.arquillian` `.cube.docker.impl.client.containerobject.dsl.Container` and annotate it with `@DockerContainer`.

You can also create a Docker network using the DSL approach:

```
                                                    The field is annotated
                                                    with @DockerNetwork.
@DockerNetwork                         ◁─┐
Network network = Network.withDefaultDriver("mynetwork").build();    ◁──┐

                                                    The DSL starts with the
                                                    withDefaultDriver method.
```

To create a network using the DSL approach, you create a field of type `org.arquillian` `.cube.docker.impl.client.containerobject.dsl.Network` and annotate it with `@DockerNetwork`.

Container objects and DSL JUnit rules

You can define generic containers using a *JUnit rule*. This way, you can use any JUnit runner such as `SpringJUnit4ClassRunner` side by side with the container object DSL. Here's how to define a Redis container:

```
@ClassRule
public static ContainerDslRule redis = new ContainerDslRule("redis:3.2.6")
                                        .withPortBinding(6379);
```

Spring Data and Spring Boot

With Spring Data, you configure the database location using environment variables. To set them in the test, you need to use a custom `ApplicationContextInitializer`. Here's an example:

```
                                                    Spring JUnit test runner
                                                    with Boot configuration
@RunWith(SpringJUnit4ClassRunner.class)        ◁─┘
@SpringBootTest(classes = Application.class,
                webEnvironment = WebEnvironment.RANDOM_PORT)
@ContextConfiguration(initializers =
        SpringDataTest.Initializer.class)      ◁─── Setup initializer to configure
public class SpringDataTest {                        environment variables

  @ClassRule
  public static ContainerDslRule redis =
      new ContainerDslRule("redis:3.2.6")
      .withPortBinding(6379);                  ◁─── Defines a Redis container
```

```
    public static class Initializer implements
            ApplicationContextInitializer
                <ConfigurableApplicationContext>; {
    @Override
    public void initialize(
            ConfigurableApplicationContext
            configurableApplicationContext) {
        EnvironmentTestUtils.addEnvironment("testcontainers",
                configurableApplicationContext.getEnvironment(),
                "spring.redis.host=" + redis.getIpAddress(),
                "spring.redis.port=" + redis.getBindPort(6379)
        );
    }
  }
}
```

> **Initializer implementation with container configuration**

Note that you must add the `org.arquillian.cube:arquillian-cube-docker-junit-rule` dependency. You don't need to add any other Arquillian dependency.

So far, you've learned how to use Docker and Arquillian Cube to set up a complex testing environment. In the next section, we'll look at how to use and deploy Docker images in Kubernetes.

8.8 Deployment tests and Kubernetes

In this chapter, you've seen how you can use Docker for testing purposes, but perhaps you're also using Docker at the production level. Docker containers on their own can be difficult to manage and maintain. Complex applications typically require booting up multiple containers on multiple machines (note that the Docker host runs on a single host). You also need a way to orchestrate all these containers and offer other features such as fault tolerance, horizontal autoscaling, distribution of secrets, naming and discovery of services across all machines, rolling updates, and load balancing. One standout tool that offers these features is Kubernetes.

Kubernetes is an open source system for managing clusters of Docker containers. It was created by Google; several other companies have contributed to it, including Red Hat and Microsoft. Kubernetes provides tools for deploying and scaling applications, as well as managing changes to existing applications, such as updating to a new version or rolling back in the case of failure or health checks. Moreover, Kubernetes was created with two important features in mind: extensibility and fault tolerance.

Following are the primary Kubernetes concepts you need to understand (figure 8.7 summarizes these concepts):

- *Pod*—The minimal unit of organization in Kubernetes. A pod is composed of one or more containers that are run on the same host machine and can share resources.

- *Service*—A set of pods and the policy by which to access them. Kubernetes provides a stable IP address and DNS name to the service, which abstracts from the pods' location. Because pods are ephemeral, their IP address can change. Services react to this change by always forwarding to the location of the required pod. Services act as a load balancer among all pod instances.
- *Replication controller (RC)*—Maintains the desired state of the cluster. For example, if you need three instances of a pod, the RC will manage the given pod and always have three instances of it running on the cluster.
- *Namespace*—A way to create a virtual cluster backed by a physical cluster.

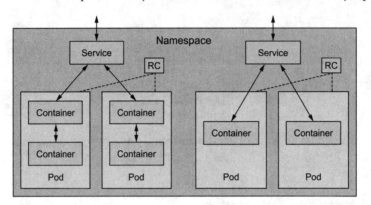

Figure 8.7 An example Kubernetes deployment

Usually, in Kubernetes, you define elements in a JSON or YAML file. For example, to define a pod, you could create the following pod-redis.json file:

```
{
  "kind": "Pod",
  "apiVersion": "v1",
  "metadata": {
    "name": "redis",
    "labels": {
      "app": "myredis"
    }
  },
  "spec": {
    "containers": [
      {
        "name": "key-value-store",
        "image": "redis",
        "ports": [
          {
            "containerPort": 6379
          }
        ]
      }
    ]
  }
}
```

This snippet defines a simple pod, using the `redis` container named `key-value-store`, exposing port number 6379 on the pod's IP address.

In Kubernetes, deploying an application/service isn't done manually but rather is programmable and automatic. This implies that you need to test that what's configured is what you expect to be deployed.

Arquillian Cube provides support for writing tests for Kubernetes. The idea behind the integration of Arquillian Cube and Kubernetes is to consume and test the provided services as well as validate that the environment is in the expected state. The integration lifecycle of Arquillian Cube and Kubernetes is summarized in figure 8.8.

> **WARNING** Only Arquillian standalone mode is supported in the integration of Arquillian Cube and Kubernetes.

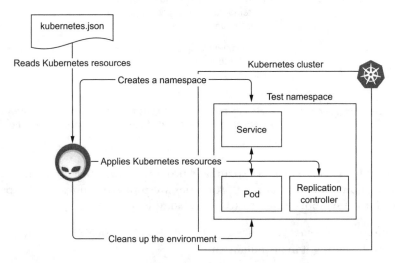

Figure 8.8   Lifecycle of Arquillian Cube and Kubernetes integration

Arquillian Cube Kubernetes creates a temporary namespace to deploy all Kubernetes resources in an isolated environment. Then it searches in the classpath for a file called kubernetes.json or kubernetes.yaml, and applies all Kubernetes resources required on that temporary namespace. Once everything is ready, it runs your tests (using a black box approach). And when testing is finished, it cleans up.

> **NOTE** Arquillian Cube Kubernetes needs to authenticate into Kubernetes. To do so, Arquillian Cube reads user information (token and password) from ~/.kube/config.

You can configure Arquillian Cube Kubernetes parameters in arquillian.xml. Table 8.3 lists some of the most useful parameters.

Table 8.3 Arquillian Cube Kubernetes parameters

Attribute	Description	Default behavior
`kubernetes.master`	URL for the Kubernetes master	
`env.config.url`	URL for the Kubernetes JSON/YAML file	Defaults to a classpath resource kubernates.json
`env.dependencies`	Whitespace-separated list of URLs pointing to more than one Kubernetes definition file	
`env.config.resource.name`	Option to select a different classpath resource	
`namespace.use.existing`	Flag that specifies not to generate a new temporary namespace, but to reuse the one that's set	
`env.init.enabled`	Flag to initialize the environment with defined Kubernetes resources (goes hand to hand with `namespace.use.existing`)	By default, creates Kubernetes resources
`namespace.cleanup.enabled`	Instructs the extension to destroy the namespace after the end of the test suite	By default, destroys namespace to keep the cluster clean

NOTE Arquillian Cube Kubernetes can read properties from environment variables. The equivalent environment properties are property names in all caps, with the dot (.) symbol converted to _: for example, KUBERNETES_MASTER.

You can configure kubernetes.master (if the KUBERNETES_MASTER environment variable isn't set), by setting it in arquillian.xml:

```
<arquillian xmlns:xsi="http://www.w3.org/2001/XMLSchema-instance"
  xmlns="http://jboss.org/schema/arquillian"
  xsi:schemaLocation="http://jboss.org/schema/arquillian
  http://jboss.org/schema/arquillian/arquillian_1_0.xsd">

  <extension qualifier="kubernetes">;
    <property name="kubernetes.master">;http://localhost:8443</property>;
  </extension>;

</arquillian>;
```

Any Arquillian Cube Kubernetes test can be enriched with the following elements:

- A Kubernetes client
- A session object containing test-session information such as the name of the temporarily created namespace
- A pod (by its ID) or a list of all pods started by the test
- An RC (by its ID) or a list of all RCs started by the test

- A service (by its ID) or a list of all services started by the test
- The URL of a service

The following test is enriched with some of these elements:

```
@RunWith(Arquillian.class)
public class ResourcesTest {

  @ArquillianResouce
  @Named("my-serivce")
  Service service;

  @ArquillianResouce
  PodList pods;

  @Test
  public void testStuff() throws Exception {
  }
}
```

Enriches the test with a
service named my-service

Enriches the test with all
pods defined in the test

In this test, all information of a Kubernetes service called `my-service` can be queried. You can also access all pods defined in the current test. In a similar way, you can get the list of services by using `ServiceList`, or a concrete pod by using `@Named` and the `Pod` object. The same goes for RC objects.

To inject a service URL, you do this:

```
@Named("hello-world-service")          ⟵── Service name
@PortForward
@ArquillianResource
URL url;
```

Moreover, as Arquillian Cube Docker does, Kubernetes integration provides tight integration with AssertJ, to provide a readable way of writing assertions about the environment. Here's a simple example of how to use this integration:

```
@RunWith(Arquillian.class)
public class RunningPodTest {

  @ArquillianResource
  KubernetesClient client;

  @Test
  public void should_deploy_all_pods() {
    assertThat(client).deployments().pods().isPodReadyForPeriod();   ⟵──
  }

}
```

Kubernetes client
enrichment

AssertJ Kubernetes integration's
assertThat method

This test asserts that the current `Deployment` creates at least one pod, which becomes available within a time period (by default, 30 seconds), and that it stays in the `Ready` state for a time period (by default, 1 second). This test is simple, but in our experience it catches most errors that may occur during deployment time on Kubernetes. Of course, this is just a start; you can add as many assertions as you need to validate that the application is deployed as required. Moreover, AssertJ Kubernetes provides custom assertions not only for `KubernetesClient` but also for pods, services, and RCs.

Arquillian Cube Kubernetes and OpenShift

Arquillian Cube Kubernetes implements some extra features to help with testing through OpenShift:

- Automatic setup of connecting to non-exported routes.
- Triggering the build job/pipeline directly from the test. This pushes the `@Deployment` artifact to a local repository and triggers an OS build for deployment.

Because OpenShift version 3 is a Kubernetes system, everything that's valid in Arquillian Cube Kubernetes is valid in OpenShift.

After this introduction to using Docker for testing purposes and which tools you can use to automate tests using Docker, let's see what you need to do to begin using them.

8.9 *Build-script modifications*

You've seen that Arquillian Cube has integrations with different technologies such as Docker, Kubernetes, and OpenShift. Each has its own dependencies, and the following sections cover how to add those dependencies to your tests.

8.9.1 *Arquillian Cube Docker*

To use Cube Docker integration, you need to add the following dependency:

```
dependencies {
  testCompile group: 'org.arquillian.cube',
              name: 'arquillian-cube-docker',
              version: '1.2.0'
}
```

To use Drone/Graphene integration, you also need to add this:

```
dependencies {
  testCompile group: 'org.arquillian.cube',
              name: 'arquillian-cube-docker-drone',
              version: '1.2.0'
}
```

Notice that in this case, you need to add Selenium, Arquillian Drone, or Arquillian Graphene dependencies, as you did in chapter 7.

To use REST Assured integration, you also need to add the REST Assured dependency:

```
dependencies {
  testCompile group: 'org.arquillian.cube',
              name: 'arquillian-cube-docker-restassured',
              version: '1.2.0'
}
```

Finally, to use AssertJ integration, add the AssertJ dependency:

```
dependencies {
  testCompile group: 'org.arquillian.cube',
              name: 'assertj-docker-java',
              version: '1.2.0'
}
```

8.9.2 *Arquillian Cube Docker JUnit rule*

To use container DSL with JUnit rule support, add the following dependency:

```
dependencies {
  testCompile group: 'org.arquillian.cube',
              name: 'arquillian-cube-docker-junit-rule,
              version: '1.2.0'
}
```

8.9.3 *Arquillian Cube Kubernetes*

To use Arquillian Cube with Kubernetes support, add this dependency:

```
dependencies {
  testCompile group: 'org.arquillian.cube',
              name: 'arquillian-cube-kubernetes',
              version: '1.2.0'
}
```

To use AssertJ integration, you also need to add this:

```
dependencies {
  testCompile group: 'io.fabric8',
              name: 'kubernetes-assertions',
              version: '2.2.101'
}
```

8.9.4 *Arquillian Cube OpenShift*

To use Arquillian Cube with specific features of OpenShift (not the Kubernetes part), add the following dependency:

```
dependencies {
  testCompile group: 'org.arquillian.cube',
              name: 'arquillian-cube-openshift',
              version: '1.2.0'
}
```

8.10   *Testing the Dockerfile for the video service*

The video service is packaged into a Docker image. To create this image, use the following Dockerfile (code/video/Dockerfile).

Listing 8.14   Video-service Dockerfile

```
FROM java:8-jdk

ADD build/libs/video-service-*.jar /video-service.jar

EXPOSE 8080
RUN bash -c 'touch /video-service.jar'
ENTRYPOINT ["java", "-Djava.security.egd=file:/dev/./urandom",
            "-jar","/video-service.jar"]
```

As you can see, nothing special happens here. The output of the Spring Boot artifact is copied inside the image, and when the image is instantiated, the service is also started.

Next, you create a Docker Compose file to automate the building of the image (code/video/c-tests/src/test/resources/arquillian.xml).

Listing 8.15   Docker Compose file

```
<?xml version="1.0"?>;
<arquillian xmlns:xsi="http://www.w3.org/2001/XMLSchema-instance"
            xmlns="http://jboss.org/schema/arquillian"
            xsi:schemaLocation="http://jboss.org/schema/arquillian
  http://jboss.org/schema/arquillian/arquillian_1_0.xsd">;


    <extension qualifier="docker">;
        <property name="machineName">;dev</property>;
        <property name="dockerContainers">;          ◁─┐  Builds and defines
            videoservice:                                │  dependencies of
              build: ../.                                │  the service
              environment:
                - SPRING_REDIS_HOST=redis
                - SPRING_REDIS_PORT=6379
                - YOUTUBE_API_KEY=${YOUTUBE_API_KEY}
              ports:
                - "8080:8080"
              links:
                - redis:redis
            redis:
              image: redis:3.2.6
        </property>;
    </extension>;

</arquillian>;
```

Finally, you can write the test to validate that the image can be built and the container instantiated (code/video/c-tests/src/test/java/book/video/VideoServiceContainerTest.java).

Listing 8.16 Validating the image and the container

```
@RunWith(Arquillian.class)
public class VideoServiceContainerTest {


    @ArquillianResource
    DockerClient docker;

    @Test
    public void should_create_valid_dockerfile() {
        DockerJavaAssertions.assertThat(docker).container
            ("videoservice").hasExposedPorts("8080/tcp")
            .isRunning();
    }

}
```

> **Validates the Docker container properties** ← (annotation pointing to the `hasExposedPorts("8080/tcp")` line)

This test uses Docker AssertJ integration. Although it isn't mandatory, we recommend using it to maintain your test's readability.

When executing this test, Arquillian Cube instructs the Docker host to build and run the given image. If the image can be built, the test verifies that ports that should be exposed are still exposed (nobody has changed them in the Dockerfile) and finally verifies that the container is running.

> **TIP** You don't need to build the image every time. Instead, you can create the image once in the CD build and then reuse it for each kind of test.

Exercise

You should now be able to use Docker to set up a testing environment to run your tests. Using the video-service example, write a simple end-to-end test using REST Assured.

Summary

- You can use Docker for testing purposes by using it to set up test environments. You can also use it to test applications that use Docker in production.
- You can write tests for the UI using Docker and Selenium/Arquillian Graphene so that everything, including the browser, is containerized.
- The container-object pattern lets you create containers programmatically.
- Docker doesn't force you to use any specific language or framework. This means you can use Arquillian Cube to test any application written with any language, as long as it's Dockerized. This is a perfect match for a microservices architecture, where each microservice may be coded in a different language.

- If a microservice depends on an external service, you shouldn't set up the testing environment using the real external service (doing so could make your tests flaky); you can use service virtualization to simulate external services. Because WireMock is an HTTP server, you can containerize it and use it in Docker. This way, you can use Docker to test microservice(s) and cut dependencies at the level you need, and simulate the responses with a WireMock/Hoverfly container.

Service virtualization

9

This chapter covers

- Appreciating service virtualization
- Simulating internal and external services
- Understanding service virtualization and Java

In a microservices architecture, the application as a whole can be composed of many interconnected services. These services can be either internal services, as in members of the same application domain, or external, third-party services that are totally out of your control.

As you've seen throughout the book, this approach implies that some changes are required when continuous application testing is part of your delivery pipeline. Back in chapter 7, we observed that one of the biggest challenges faced when testing a microservices architecture is having a clean test environment readily available. Getting multiple services up, running, and prepared is no trivial task. It takes time to prepare and execute tests, and it's highly likely that you'll end up with several flaky tests—tests that fail not due to code issues, but because of a failures within the testing environment. One of the techniques you can adopt to fix this is service virtualization.

9.1   *What is service virtualization?*

Service virtualization is a technique used to emulate the behavior of dependencies of component-based applications. Generally speaking, in a microservices architecture, these dependencies are usually REST API–based services, but the concept can also be applied to other kinds of dependencies such as databases, enterprise service buses (ESBs), web services, Java Message Service (JMS), or any other system that communicates using messaging protocols.

9.1.1   *Why use service virtualization?*

Following are several situations in which you might want to use service virtualization:

- When the current service (consumer) depends on another service (provider) that hasn't been developed yet or is still in development.
- When provisioning a new instance of the required service (provider) is difficult or too slow for testing purposes.
- When configuring the service (provider) isn't a trivial task. For example, you might need to prepare a huge number of database scripts for running the tests.
- When services need to be accessed in parallel by different teams that have completely different setups.
- When the provider service is controlled by a third party or partner, and you have a rate-limited quota on daily requests. You don't want to consume the quota with tests!
- When the provider service is available only intermittently or at certain times of the day or night.

Service virtualization can resolve all these challenges by simulating the behavior of the required service. With service virtualization, you model and deploy a *virtual asset* that represents the provider service, simulating the parts required for your test.

Figure 9.1 shows the difference between provisioning a real environment and a virtualized one for running tests. On the left, you can see that writing a test for service A requires that you boot up service B, including its database. At the same time, you might also need to start *transitive* services such as services C and D. On the right side, you can see that service B and all of its dependencies are replaced by a virtualized version that emulates the behavior of service B.

It's important to note that this diagram isn't much different than the one you saw when you learned about mocking and stubbing in chapter 3; but rather than simulating classes, you're simulating service calls. Streamlining that thought, you can imagine service virtualization as mocking at the enterprise level.

Service virtualization shouldn't be used only for testing optimal path cases, but also for testing edge cases, so that you test the entire application (negative testing). Sometimes it's difficult to test edge cases against real services. For example, you might want to test how a client behaves with low-latency responses from the provider, or how it acts when characters are sent with a different character encoding than expected.

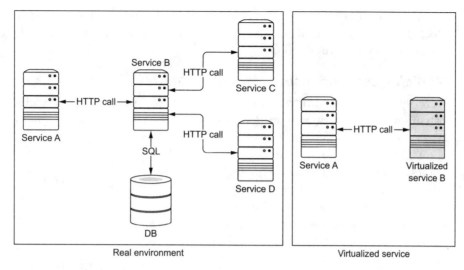

Figure 9.1   Real versus virtualized services

Think back to the Gamer application—you can't ask igdb.com and youtube.com to shut down their APIs for an afternoon while you perform negative testing. (Well, you could, but don't hold your breath waiting for an answer!) In such cases, it should be apparent why service virtualization is so useful.

9.1.2   When to use service virtualization

The book has presented many different kinds of tests, from unit tests to end-to-end tests. When is service virtualization useful?

- *Unit tests*—You're unlikely to need service virtualization for unit tests. In 99% of cases, using traditional mock, dummy, and stub techniques will be enough.
- *Component tests*—This is where service virtualization shines: you can test how components interact with each other without relying on external services.
- *Integration tests*—By their nature, integration tests are run against real services. In test cases, this might be a problem (such as edge cases, third-party services, and so on), so you might opt for service virtualization.
- *Contract tests*—When testing a contract against a provider, you might need service virtualization to simulate dependencies of the provider service.
- *End-to-end tests*—By definition, end-to-end tests shouldn't rely on service virtualization, because you're testing against the real system. In some rare cases where you relay on flaky third-party services, service virtualization might still be a viable solution.

As you can see, virtual assets are replaced by progressively more real services as you move to more functional tests.

In chapter 4, we discussed the concept of simulating external services with Wire-Mock. In this chapter, we'll introduce a new tool called *Hoverfly*, which is designed specifically for service virtualization.

9.2 *Mimicking service responses with Hoverfly*

Hoverfly (https://hoverfly.readthedocs.io) is an open source, lightweight, service-virtualization proxy written in the Go programming language. It allows you to emulate HTTP and HTTPS services. As you can see in figure 9.2, Hoverfly starts a proxy that responds to requests with stored (canned) responses. These responses should be exactly the same as the ones the real service would generate for the provided requests. If this process is performed correctly, and if the stored responses are accurate for the real service, Hoverfly will mimic the real service responses perfectly, and your tests will be accurate.

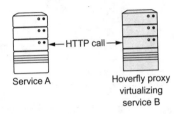

Figure 9.2   Hoverfly proxy

NOTE *Hoverfly Java* (https://hoverfly-java.readthedocs.io) is a Java wrapper for Hoverfly that abstracts you away from the actual binary and API calls, and also provides tight integration with JUnit. From this point on, when we talk about Hoverfly, we mean the Java wrapper.

9.2.1 *Hoverfly modes*

Hoverfly has three working modes:

- *Capture*—Makes requests against real services as normal. Requests and responses are intercepted and recorded by the Hoverfly proxy so they can be used later.
- *Simulate*—Returns simulated responses for the provided requests. Simulations might be loaded from different kinds of sources such as files, classpath resources, or URLs, or programmatically defined using the Hoverfly domain-specific language (DSL). This is the preferred mode for services under development.
- *Capture or simulate*—A combination of the other two modes. The proxy starts in capture mode if the simulation file doesn't exist, or in simulate mode otherwise. This mode is preferred when already developed services or third-party services are available.

Figure 9.3 shows a schema for capture mode:

1 A request is performed using a real service, which is probably deployed outside of the machine where the test is running.
2 The Hoverfly proxy redirects traffic to the real host, and the response is returned.
3 The Hoverfly proxy stores a script file for the matching request and response that were generated by the real service interaction.
4 The real response is returned to the caller.

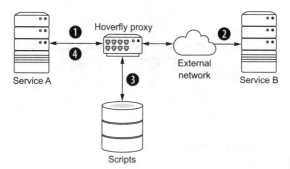

Figure 9.3 Hoverfly capture mode

Figure 9.4 illustrates simulate mode:

1 A request is performed, but instead the call being routed to the real service, it's routed to the Hoverfly proxy.
2 The Hoverfly proxy checks the corresponding response script for the provided request.
3 A canned response is replayed back to the caller.

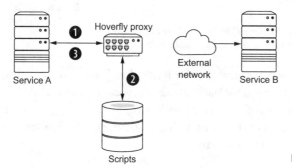

Figure 9.4 Hoverfly simulate mode

Hoverfly and JVM proxy settings

Hoverfly Java sets the network Java system properties to use the Hoverfly proxy. This means if the client API you're using to communicate with other services honors these properties, you don't need to change anything to work with Hoverfly. If that isn't the case, you need to set `http.proxyHost`, `http.proxyPort`, `https.proxyHost`, `https.proxyPort`, and, optionally, `http.nonProxyHosts` to your client proxy configuration.

When this override is in place, all communication between the Java runtime and the physical network (except `localhost` by default) will pass through the Hoverfly proxy. For example, when using the `okhttp` client, which honors network system properties, you might do this:

```
URL url = new URL("http", "www.myexample.com", 8080, "/" + name);
Request request = new Request.Builder().url(url).get().build();
final Response response = client.newCall(request).execute();
```

> **(continued)**
> Because the proxy settings are now overridden, the request is performed through the
> Hoverfly proxy. Depending on the selected configuration mode, the request will either
> be sent to www.myexample.com or simulated.

9.2.2   *JUnit Hoverfly*

Let's look at some examples of how to use Hoverfly with JUnit.

JUNIT HOVERFLY SIMULATE MODE

Hoverfly comes in the form of a JUnit rule. You can use either @ClassRule for static
initialization, or @Rule for each test. We recommend using @ClassRule, to avoid the
overhead of starting the Hoverfly proxy for each test method execution. Here's an
example:

```
import static io.specto.hoverfly.junit.core.SimulationSource.defaultPath;
import io.specto.hoverfly.junit.rule.HoverflyRule;
```

```
@ClassRule
public static HoverflyRule hoverflyRule = HoverflyRule
                .inSimulationMode(defaultPath("simulation.json"));
```

Reads simulation.json from the default Hoverfly resource path

Here, the Hoverfly proxy is started, and it then loads the simulation.json simulation
file from the default Hoverfly resource path, src/test/resources/hoverfly. After that,
all tests are executed, and the Hoverfly proxy is stopped.

In addition to loading simulations from a file, you can specify request matchers
and responses using the DSL, as shown here:

```
import static io.specto.hoverfly.junit.core.SimulationSource.dsl;
import static io.specto.hoverfly.junit.dsl.HoverflyDsl.service;
import static io.specto.hoverfly.junit.dsl.ResponseCreators.success;
import static io.specto.hoverfly.junit.dsl.ResponseCreators.created;

import io.specto.hoverfly.junit.rule.HoverflyRule;
```

```
@ClassRule
public static HoverflyRule hoverflyRule =
HoverflyRule.inSimulationMode(dsl(                    Starts Hoverfly using
    service("www.myexample.com")                     the DSL method
        .post("/api/games").body("{\"gameId\": \"1\"}")
        .willReturn(created("http://localhost/api/game/1"))

        .get("/api/games/1")
        .willReturn(success("{\"gameId\":\"1\"}", "application/json"))
));
```

Sets the host where the connection is to be made

Creates a request and a response for a POST method

Creates a request and a response for a GET method

Request-field matchers

Hoverfly has the concept of *request-field matchers*, which let you use different kinds of matchers in the DSL elements. Here's an example:

Matches the URL using a wildcard

```
service(matches("www.*-test.com"))        ←──┐  Matches the request path
        .get(startsWith("/api/games/"))   ←──   that starts with /api/games/
        .queryParam("page", any())        ←──┐
                                             Matches the page query
                                             parameter with any value
```

JUnit Hoverfly capture mode

Starting Hoverfly in capture mode is the same as it is in simulate mode, but you use `inCaptureMode` to indicate that you want to store the interaction:

```
@ClassRule                                            Starts Hoverfly in
public static HoverflyRule hoverflyRule               capture mode, and
    = HoverflyRule.inCaptureMode("simulation.json");  ←── records the result
```

In this example, Hoverfly is started in capture mode. This effectively means the traffic is redirected/routed to the real service, but now these interactions are recorded in a file located by default at src/test/resources/hoverfly/simulation.json.

JUnit Hoverfly capture or simulate mode

This mode is the combination of both previous modes, using capture mode if no previously recorded file is present. The generated files can then be added to your version control to complete the test case for others to use without the real service. Here's an example:

```
@ClassRule
public static HoverflyRule hoverflyRule
    = HoverflyRule.inCaptureOrSimulationMode("simulation.json");
```

9.2.3　Configuring Hoverfly

Hoverfly ships with defaults that may work in all cases, but you can override them by providing an `io.specto.hoverfly.junit.core.HoverflyConfig` instance to the previous methods. For example, you can change the proxy port where the Hoverfly proxy is started by setting `inCaptureMode("simulation.json", HoverflyConfig.configs()`
`.proxyPort(8080))`.

By default, all hostnames are proxied, but you can also restrict this behavior to specific hostnames. For example, `configs().destination("www.myexample.com")` configures the Hoverfly proxy to only process requests to www.myexample.com.

Localhost calls are *not* proxied by default. But if your provider service is running on localhost, you can configure Hoverfly to proxy localhost calls by using `configs()`.`proxyLocalHost()`.

CONFIGURING SSL

If your service uses Secure Sockets Layer (SSL), Hoverfly needs to decrypt the messages in order to persist them to a file in capture mode, or to perform the matching in simulate mode. Effectively, you have one SSL connection between the client and the Hoverfly proxy, and another between the Hoverfly proxy and the real service.

To make things simple, Hoverfly comes with its own self-signed certificate that must be trusted by your client. The good news is that Hoverfly's certificate is trusted automatically when you instantiate it.

You can override this behavior and provide your own certificate and key using the `HoverflyConfig` class: for example, `configs().sslCertificatePath("ssl/ca.crt")`.`sslKeyPath("ssl/ca.key")`. Note that these files are relative to the classpath.

CONFIGURING AN EXTERNAL INSTANCE

It's possible to configure Hoverfly to use an existing Hoverfly proxy instance. This situation might arise when you're using a Docker image hosting a Hoverfly proxy. Again, you can configure these parameters easily by using the `HoverflyConfig` class: for example, `configs().remote().host("192.168.99.100").proxyPort(8081)`.

9.3 *Build-script modifications*

Now that you've learned about service virtualization and Hoverfly, let's look at the involved dependencies. Hoverfly requires only a single group, artifact, version (GAV) dependency definition:

```
dependencies {
    testCompile "io.specto:hoverfly-java:0.6.2"
}
```

This pulls in all the required transient dependencies to the test scope.

9.4 *Using service virtualization for the Gamer application*

As you've seen throughout the book, in the Gamer application, the aggregator service communicates with three services to compose the final request to the end user with all information about games, as shown in figure 9.5. Let's write a component test for the code that connects to the comments service.

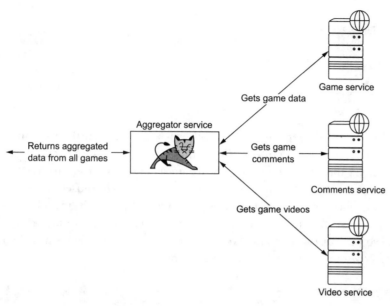

Figure 9.5 The aggregator service

In the following listing (code/aggregator/cp-tests/src/test/java/book/aggr/CommentsGatewayTest.java), the comments service is deployed in (pre)production at comments.gamers.com, and you'll use capture or simulate mode so that initial requests are sent to the real service. All subsequent calls will be simulated.

Listing 9.1 Testing the CommentsGateway class

```
public class CommentsGatewayTest {

    @ClassRule
    public static HoverflyRule hoverfly = HoverflyRule
        .inCaptureOrSimulationMode("simulation.json"); /

    @Test
    public void shouldInsertComments()
        throws ExecutionException, InterruptedException {

        final JsonObject commentObject = Json.createObjectBuilder()
            .add("comment", "This Game is Awesome").add("rate",
                5).add("gameId", 1234).build();

        final CommentsGateway commentsGateway = new CommentsGateway
            ();
        commentsGateway.initRestClient("http://comments.gamers.com")
        ;

        final Future<Response>; comment = commentsGateway
            .createComment(commentObject);
```

Instantiates the Hoverfly rule

Makes the call to the real host

```
        final Response response = comment.get();
        final URI location = response.getLocation();

        assertThat(location).isNotNull();                    Asserts that the
        final String id = extractId(location);               location is valid
        assertThat(id).matches("[0-9a-f]+");          ◁─┘
    }
```

The big difference between this and the other test cases is that the first time you run this test, the request is sent to the comments service deployed at comments .gamers.com via the Hoverfly proxy, and requests and responses are recorded. The src/test/resources/hoverfly/simulation.json file is created because it doesn't yet exist. The next time you run the test, communication is still proxied through the Hoverfly proxy, but because the file now exists, the canned responses are returned.

In case you're curious (we know you are), the recorded file looks like the next listing (src/test/resources/hoverfly/simulation.json).

Listing 9.2 Simulation file with canned responses

```
{
  "data" : {
    "pairs" : [ {
      "request" : {
        "path" : {
          "exactMatch" : "/comments"
        },
        "method" : {
          "exactMatch" : "POST"
        },
        "destination" : {"exactMatch" : "comments.gamers.com"},
        "scheme" : {
          "exactMatch" : "http"
        },
        "query" : {"exactMatch" : ""},
        "body" : {
          "jsonMatch" : "{\"comment\":\"This Game is Awesome\",
                          \"rate\":5,\"gameId\":1234}"
        }
      },
      "response" : {
        "status" : 201,
        "encodedBody" : false,
        "headers" : {
          "Content-Length" : [ "0" ],
          "Date" : [ "Thu, 15 Jun 2017 17:51:17 GMT" ],
          "Hoverfly" : [ "Was-Here" ],
          "Location" : [ "comments.gamers.com/5942c915c9e77c0001454df1" ],
          "Server" : [ "Apache TomEE" ]
        }
      }
    } ],
```

```
      "globalActions" : {
        "delays" : [ ]
      }
    },
    "meta" : {
      "schemaVersion" : "v2"
    }
  }
```

Summary

- Service virtualization isn't a substitute for contract tests but something to use with them, mostly in provider-validation scenarios.
- Service virtualization is used for removing the flakiness of tests that depend on external and potentially unreliable services.
- A virtual asset is the service you're simulating.
- You can use service virtualization to emulate unfinished services in addition to existing services, thus allowing rapid development in parallel teams.
- Hoverfly Java takes care of all network redirections and lets you get on with writing the test.

Continuous delivery
in microservices

10

This chapter covers

- Using microservices in a continuous-delivery pipeline
- Executing tests on the pipeline
- Understanding the coded pipeline
- Building the Jenkins pipeline
- Deploying services with certainty

We hope this book has broadened your insight and expanded your skill set for developing tests for a microservices architecture. The purpose of these tests is to enable changes to any service with the certainty that no regression has been introduced when you refactor, fix bugs, or add a new feature.

The questions now are when to execute the tests, where to execute them, and how the tests are related to the deployment of the production service. In this chapter, you'll see how the traditional continuous delivery (CD) pipeline has evolved to serve a microservices architecture, and how to build a pipeline programmatically that focuses on test execution.

We'll assume that you have some experience with CD of your applications, and perhaps some basic use of Jenkins (https://jenkins.io) as a CD server. There are several other good build-automation servers out there, such as Travis CI (https://travis-ci.org) and Bamboo (www.atlassian.com/software/bamboo), but we had to pick one to focus on, and we chose Jenkins. The principles described in this chapter more or less apply to whichever CD server you may end up choosing.

We'll also assume that you're using some kind of source control or source code management (SCM) server, such as Git (https://git-scm.com) or SVN (https:// subversion.apache.org), to manage your source code. If not, then you're wicked, and your source code will die with your hard drive! Seriously, we wouldn't wish that on anyone.

10.1 What is continuous delivery?

Continuous delivery is a methodology that revolves around releasing software faster and more frequently. This methodology helps reduce the cost, time, and risk of delivering changes that will potentially affect the user experience. Because delivery of the application is performed continuously and with incremental updates, it's easier to capture feedback from the end user and react accordingly.

The main concept in CD is the *deployment pipeline.* As the name suggests, it's a set of steps or procedures through which the application must pass in order to be released for production. The deployment pipeline may be changed depending on the process you choose to follow when releasing the application. For example, some companies might have a manual testing/exploratory test phase before release. Others might go one step further and apply *continuous deployment* to the pipeline, releasing every change to production automatically on a successful build. *Continuous delivery*, on the other hand, is put in place only to ensure that every change is *potentially* releasable at any time (performing the actual release is a manual decision).

The most common, generic deployment pipeline is shown in figure 10.1. Typically, a deployment pipeline includes the following four primary phases:

1 *Commit stage*—The first part of the release process, triggered after a team member commits something to the SCM server. This stage is composed of the compilation process, unit (and significant other) test executions, code-quality analysis, and building the artifact deliverable. Ideally, the commit stage shouldn't take more than 10 minutes.

2 *Automated acceptance tests*—Automated tests are executed that are deemed to be slow because they employ several parts of the system under test (for example, automated UI testing).

3 *User acceptance tests*—Users test the application to make sure it meets their expectations. Some of these tests may be automatic (for example, capacity testing), but other manual tests, such as exploratory testing, can also be employed. Quality gates are commonly defined for code analysis, such as test coverage,

metric collection, and measurement of technical debt; the umbrella term for this is *definition of done (DoD)*.

4 *Release*—Based on all feedback from each stage, key users decide to release to production or drop the version. This is the final acceptance test or criteria.

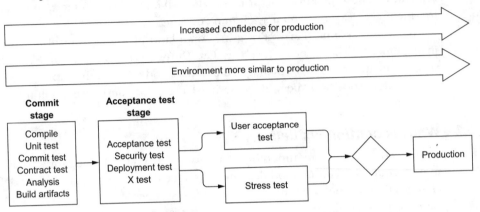

Figure 10.1   A typical deployment pipeline

Now that you're familiar with the basics of CD, let's move on to how the microservices architecture fits in.

10.2 *Continuous delivery and the microservices architecture*

Microservices should have the following characteristics when they're deployed:

- Each microservice should be a small, independent deployment unit. Deploying microservices together in the same process is not considered a best practice.
- Business features should be deployed independently. It's important to note that this implies that each microservice should provide backward compatibility where changes have occurred in the public API, usually by versioning the API.

These characteristics affect the deployment pipeline. Because each microservice should be deployed independently, you need to create a new pipeline for each micro-service. Figure 10.2 shows an overview.

The main advantages of using this approach for creating the deployment pipeline are as follows:

- The pipeline is smaller and only contains steps for a single microservice.
- The pipeline is easier to set up, because there are fewer integrations with third-party systems.
- You receive feedback more quickly, because there are fewer tests to execute. You're executing tests from a single microservice, not the entire application.

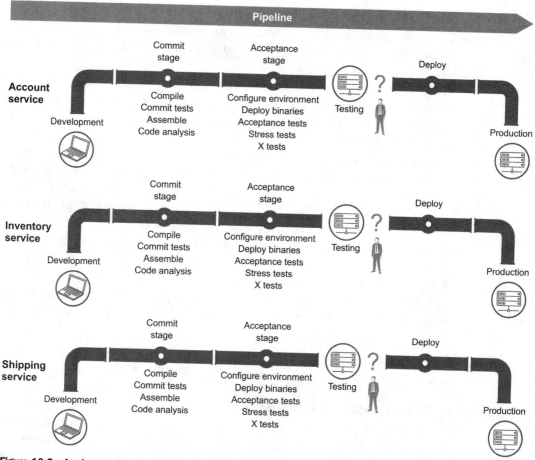

Figure 10.2   A microservices architecture deployment pipeline

But there are also some disadvantages that you need to be aware of:

- Each microservice might be developed using a different technology stack. This means each deployment pipeline might require different tools for each stage, making the code less reusable and more complex to maintain.

- A microservice is the combination of the application, the server where it runs, the databases it needs, and any other required infrastructure. This means the process for deploying microservices may vary greatly from one microservice to another. For example, deploying a SQL database schema isn't the same as deploying a NoSQL database schema.

- Even if a microservice is well tested with unit tests, component tests, contract tests, service virtualization, and so forth, you still have the uncertainty of deploying a new piece of the system independently into an already running system. It's normal to ask questions like, "Can old consumers communicate with new providers?" and "Will the new service be able to consume data from other providers (both old and new)?"

To mitigate the risks of these drawbacks, you can follow these strategies:

- Define the pipeline in the same repository as the project's source code. This ensures that the pipeline is created and maintained by the same team that's developing the microservice.
- Use a blue/green deployment approach. This means you create a complete cluster with each new release. Then run some automated tests or use an exploratory testing approach to validate that everything works as expected. After that, switch to the new cluster.
- Use canary releases (to coin a term used by coal miners). With this approach, a new microservice is deployed to only a few nodes at a time. A few real users (preferably internal users) use the system against the new microservice for a defined period. During this time, you can monitor the results of the selected users' interactions to ensure that the new service is behaving as expected.
- Create a rollback strategy that's easy and fast to apply to any given microservice, so in case of failure, you can roll back to the previous state as soon as possible.
- Release often. Releasing often means releasing fewer features at once, which in turn means you're changing the system one step at a time. This implies it's more difficult to completely break the system. More important, it's easier to detect where problems are.

As you can see, release automation in a microservices architecture has the same requirements as any other application: being able to deploy with certainty and speed.

10.3 *Orchestrating continuous delivery*

You've seen that a CD pipeline is composed of several stages, each of which may contain several steps. The code implementing each step is usually located with your build tool. For example, the *commit stage* is composed of the *compile, test, code quality,* and *package* steps, as shown in figure 10.3. When you're using the Gradle build tool, commands executed in the commit stage are, respectively, `gradle compileJava`, `gradle :test`, `gradle check`, and `gradle assemble`.

Figure 10.3   Commit stage example

You wouldn't want to call these commands manually every time you wanted to execute the commit stage, or any other stage, for that matter. You need a way to orchestrate the calls for all these commands and run them in the correct order to optimize the process. (The test and static-code-analysis steps can be performed in parallel.)

The *continuous integration* (CI) server coordinates all the steps that define the pipeline, manages the build process, and provides the magic for deploying the application. In addition to managing the release process, the CI server also offers a central place to retrieve all feedback from pipeline execution, such as test failures, artifact deployments for each environment, and hanging the build process for manual interaction.

10.3.1 *Working with Jenkins*

You need a CI server to manage the entire build. As we mentioned earlier, in our opinion, Jenkins is the most widely used server for managing the deployment pipeline that meets all the requirements for integrating with the full range of systems.

Jenkins is a cross-platform, CI/CD server. It provides various means to define your deployment pipeline, and it integrates well with a large number of testing and deployment technologies.

Here are just some of the many available integrations:

- *Code and commit*—Git, GitHub, Mercurial, Visual Studio, Eclipse, and Nexus
- *Build and config*—Maven, Gradle, Docker, Chef, Ant, Vagrant, Ansible, and AWS
- *Scan and test*—Gerrit, Sauce Labs, Sonar, Gatling, JUnit, FitNesse, and Cucumber
- *Release*—uDeploy, Serena, and MidVision
- *Deployment*—AWS, Docker, OpenShift, Kubernetes, OpenStack, GCE, and Azure

As you can see, Jenkins covers all the steps you might require for implementing any deployment pipeline. Let's look at how to define a deployment pipeline with code using the Jenkins pipeline.

10.3.2 *The Jenkins pipeline*

The *Jenkins pipeline* is a group of plugins designed to help you implement continuous integration/delivery/deployment pipelines into Jenkins. Using the Jenkins pipeline, you can define your delivery pipeline *as code* in your project, rather than relying on the point-and-click UI of the past.

Normally, this definition lives in the same SCM repository as your service. This is perfect for a microservices architecture, because you're keeping together everything related to the service.

A coded pipeline offers several benefits. Because it's code and you can treat it as such, you can do the following:

- Automatically create pipelines for all branches and pull requests
- Perform code reviews and iterative improvement of the pipeline
- Keep an audit trail, because changes are also committed to the SCM
- Enable collaboration, because everyone can see and edit the code

The de facto filename for coding the pipeline in Jenkins is *Jenkinsfile*, and it's usually checked into a service's SCM repository in the root directory. Jenkinsfile is a text file that contains all the steps required to deliver a service/project via the *Pipeline* DSL.

As of version 2.5, the Jenkins pipeline supports two discrete syntaxes to define the pipeline: the *declarative pipeline* and the *scripted pipeline*. Under the covers, both are implemented as Groovy DSLs.

THE DECLARATIVE PIPELINE

The declarative pipeline presents a simplified, opinionated syntax for authoring the deployment pipeline. This simplification restricts flexibility and extensibility; but, on the other hand, it makes the deployment pipeline easy to write and read. In our experience, the declarative approach is sufficient for almost all cases.

All declarative pipelines must be enclosed in a `pipeline` block. Each block must only consist of *sections, directives,* and *assignment statements.*

Here's an example Jenkinsfile:

```
pipeline {
    agent any
    stages {
        stage('Commit Test') {
            steps {
                sh './gradlew check'
            }
        }
    }
    post {
        always {
            junit 'build/reports/**/*.xml'
        }
    }
}
```

Stages are where all the work is done.

Executes the pipeline in any available Jenkins agent (a Jenkins process)

Steps to execute within a stage

Shell directive command

The section executed after build (post-build steps)

Directive to archive the test results

The root element must be `pipeline`, which encloses all the stages for the current pipeline. The `agent` directive specifies where the entire pipeline or specific stage will be executed.

The any option states that the pipeline should be executed on any available node. You can also specify nodes with a specific label or a specific Docker image.

Next, you define a list of stages. Each stage is related to the stages of your deployment pipeline, such as commit stage, acceptance-test stage, and so on. Each stage is composed of several steps that are responsible for performing the work.

At the end of the execution, the `post` directive is set to always register `junit` results. The `post` directive can be used in top-level `pipeline` blocks and in each `stage` block. Note that `post` supports conditional blocks such as `always`, `failure`, `success`, `changed`, and `unstable` that set whether `post` actions should be executed.

Let's look at some other minimalistic examples of declarative pipelines before we explain the scripted pipeline. The following Jenkinsfile allocates a new Docker container based on a Maven image. The workspace is added to the image, and then the steps are run inside it:

```
pipeline {
    agent {
        docker 'maven:3-alpine'
    }
    stages {
        stage('Example Build') {
```

Docker image on which the build is to be executed

```
        steps {
            sh 'mvn -B clean verify'          ◁─┐  Shell command executed
        }                                        │  within the container
    }
  }
}
```

You can also interact with users in a Jenkinsfile, as shown in this example:

```
stage('Deploy - Staging') {
        steps {
            sh './deploy staging'
            sh './run-smoke-tests'
        }
}
post {                                              Sends an email in the
    failure {                                       event of a failure
      mail to: 'team@example.com',          ◁─
            subject: "Failed Pipeline: ${currentBuild.fullDisplayName}",
            body: "Something is wrong with ${env.BUILD_URL}"
    }
}

stage('Sanity check') {                                   Waits for
        steps {                                           user input
            input "Does the staging environment look OK?"   ◁─┘
        }
}
```

This Jenkinsfile has two stages: one for deploying the service and one for checking the state of the build. There's also an error-handling routine. If an error occurs, an email is sent to the team, informing them of the failure. The second stage waits for approval from any user: the deployment pipeline is paused until a user clicks the Proceed button.

The script directive

The `script` step takes a block of scripted pipeline code and executes it in the declarative pipeline:

```
script {
  def zones = ['EMEA', 'US']
  for (int i = 0; i < zones.size(); ++i) {
    echo "Deploying service to ${zones[i]} datacenter"
  }
}
```

`script` blocks of nontrivial size or greater complexity should be implemented as a shared library.

THE SCRIPTED PIPELINE

So far, you've seen how to use the Jenkins declarative pipeline to define pipelines. Although this will probably cover most use cases, if you want more control or need to perform more-complex operations, then the *scripted pipeline* is the best approach. All the steps covered by the declarative pipeline are also valid for the scripted pipeline.

The scripted pipeline is effectively a general-purpose DSL built with Groovy. This means most of the features that are valid in the Groovy language are available in the scripted pipeline.

Here's a Jenkinsfile that shows an example of the scripted pipeline in use.

Listing 10.1   Jenkinsfile

```
                Selects the node to run
stage ('Compile') {
    node {                        <—— Checks out the code
        checkout scm      <——          from the SCM
        try {
            sh "./gradlew clean compile"
        } catch (ex) {
Safe flow       mail to: 'team@example.com',
control with        subject: "Failed Pipeline: ${currentBuild.fullDisplayName}",
try/catch           body: "Something is wrong with ${env.BUILD_URL}"
        }
    }
}
stage ('Deploy') {
    node {
        if (env.BRANCH_NAME == 'master') {
            echo 'Proceed with deployment'
        } else {
            echo 'Only master branch can be deployed'
            currentBuild.result = "UNSTABLE"     <—— Changes the build result
        }
    }
}
```

You can see that this Jenkinsfile looks more like a Groovy script than a pure pipeline.

In a scripted pipeline, you define stages and nodes. A *node* is the agent where the pipeline stage will be executed. You can begin coding the pipeline either using steps such as sh, checkout, and mailto, or using Groovy structures such as try/catch and if/else.

This is just a taste of how to code a deployment pipeline, to get you on the right track—covering the full Jenkins pipeline would require an entire book. To learn more, you can read the documentation at https://jenkins.io/doc.

10.3.3 *Deploying with certainty*

In chapter 6, you learned that *consumer-driven contracts* aren't just a design process of your service's API, but also a way to split the dependencies of a service so they're tested in isolation. The contract is tested first against a consumer, and subsequently against the providers of that consumer.

This is a big advantage over end-to-end tests in a microservices architecture, where trying to write end-to-end tests can be complicated due to the environmental preparation. Moreover, because of the complexity of the running environment (lots of interconnected services, networks, different databases, and so forth), these tests are candidates for being flaky or nondeterministic.

If you don't use end-to-end tests, how can you deploy a new service independently and with the certainty that nothing is broken? The answer is to run contract tests during the deployment pipeline against a matrix of environments.

In chapter 6, you learned that the first step is to write a contract. Then, you test that contract against the *head* (current development) versions of the consumer and providers so you know they're compatible with each other. As least, this is the methodology on a developer machine.

During the CD phase, where services are deployed independently of each other (and there may be both consumers and/or providers), this methodology isn't enough. There's no reliable way to answer the following questions:

- Is the head version of a consumer compatible with the production version of the provider?
- Is the head version of a provider compatible with the production versions of its consumers?

You need to go one step further in contract testing and also verify the contracts against the production environments.

DEPLOYING A NEW CONSUMER

Before deploying a new consumer to production, it's important to verify the contract generated by a consumer against the head version of its provider. This is also true of the production version of the provider. You need to ensure that when a new consumer hits production, the current providers already in production will still be able to receive input and produce output for that input.

> **NOTE** Contract tests are permitted to fail against the head version, but not against the production version. Although we suggest that you fix this scenario, it isn't a blocker for deploying the consumer to production—at least, until the head version is promoted to production.

DEPLOYING A NEW PROVIDER

Before deploying a new provider to production, you need to verify that the head versions of contracts still work for consumers that the provider depends on. Again, this is true of the production contract versions. You need to ensure that when a new provider hits production, the consumers that are already deployed to production are still able to communicate with it.

NOTE Contract tests are permitted to fail against the head versions, but not those in production. Again, we suggest that you fix this, but it's not a blocker for deploying the provider to production.

10.4   *Jenkins*

Jenkins provides a huge variety of plugins to support all the stages of the CD process. Jenkins is distributed in several formats, including a WAR file, a platform-dependent installer, and a Docker container. We're guessing that if you've made it this far, you've already installed Java. But in case you haven't, let's look at how to download, install, and perform an initial setup for Jenkins from a WAR file (a self-contained executable archive that only needs Java to run).

NOTE At the time of writing, the latest version of Jenkins was 2.114. Please check for and install the latest version of Jenkins—this project is released often.

Generated password

Before opening a browser to access the Jenkins console, pay special attention to the console output, similar to the following snippet.

```
INFO:

**************************************************************
**************************************************************
**************************************************************

Jenkins initial setup is required. An admin user has been created and a password generated.
Please use the following password to proceed to installation:

eb1ebb04089c44aaa95b63fc1b087391
```

Initial password

The first time Jenkins starts, a default password is generated. You need to copy or make a note of this password, because it's required the first time you access the Jenkins web console, to create the initial admin account.

Follow these steps:

1 Download Jenkins from https://jenkins.io/download (see figure 10.4). Select the generic Java package (.war) download link, and save the file locally.
2 Open a terminal, and move the downloaded jenkins.war file to a final destination where you'd like the service to run: for example, `mv ~/Downloads/jenkins.war /opt/jenkins`.

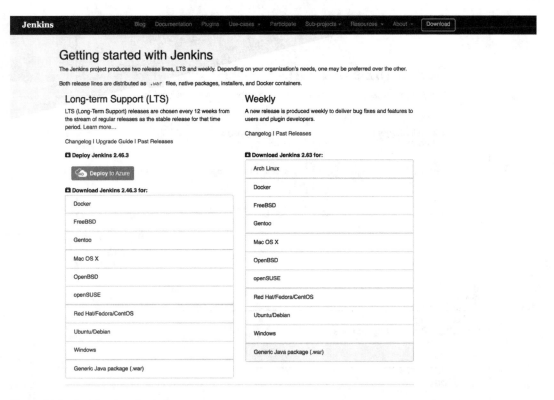

Figure 10.4   Jenkins download site

3 Start Jenkins by running `java -jar jenkins.war`. After a few seconds, Jenkins will be up and running.

4 Open a browser and access http://localhost:8080, where you're prompted to provide your new default administrator password.

5 After you enter the new password, you're presented with a screen where you can choose to install suggested plugins or manually select which plugins to install. For the sake of simplicity, and because it's a pretty good start for most cases, click Install Suggested Plugins, as shown in figure 10.5. Jenkins will download and install the most commonly used plugins in the Jenkins ecosystem, including the Jenkins Pipeline plugin. Figure 10.6 shows the plugin installation window.

6 When all plugins have been installed, you're presented with a screen to create the first admin user, as shown in figure 10.7.

The installation and setup are complete, and you can begin defining your first Jenkins pipeline job.

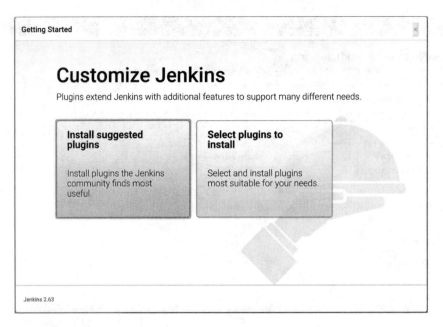

Figure 10.5   Customizing Jenkins

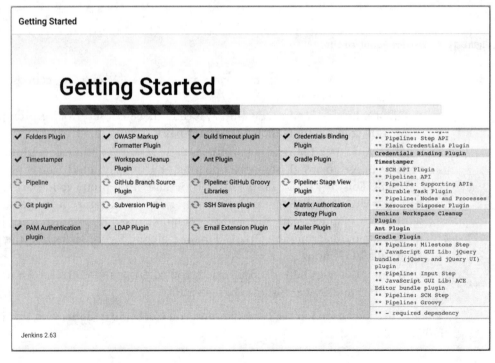

Figure 10.6   Plugin installation

Getting Started

Create First Admin User

Username: |

Password:

Confirm password:

Full name:

E-mail address:

Jenkins 2.63   Continue as admin   Save and Finish

Figure 10.7 Creating the admin user

10.4.1 *Defining a pipeline*

To create a pipeline, follow these steps:

1 Click the New Item link on the Jenkins main page, and add a name for the item (for example, game-service).

2 Select the Multibranch Pipeline type. This option creates a group of pipeline projects for each detected branch within the (yet to be specified) project (see figure 10.8).

3 With the item created, you can configure the pipeline job. The most important part of the configuration is the Branch Sources section, where the project location is defined. Click Add Source, and then select the Git option. You'll be presented with the block shown in figure 10.9.

4 Add the full Git URL for the project to the Project Repository field, and click Save to complete the process of registering a new item.

At this point, Jenkins will detect all branches in the configured repository. If the branch contains a Jenkinsfile file, Jenkins will use that file to schedule a new build for the branch.

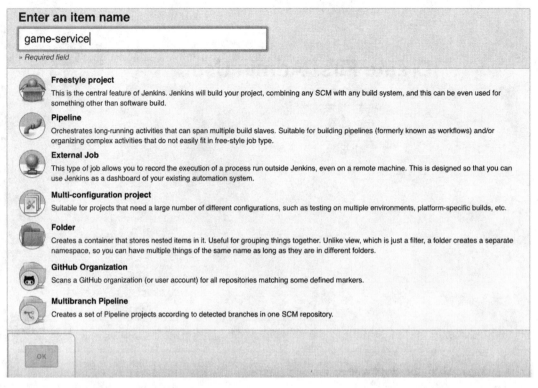

Figure 10.8   New multibranch pipeline item

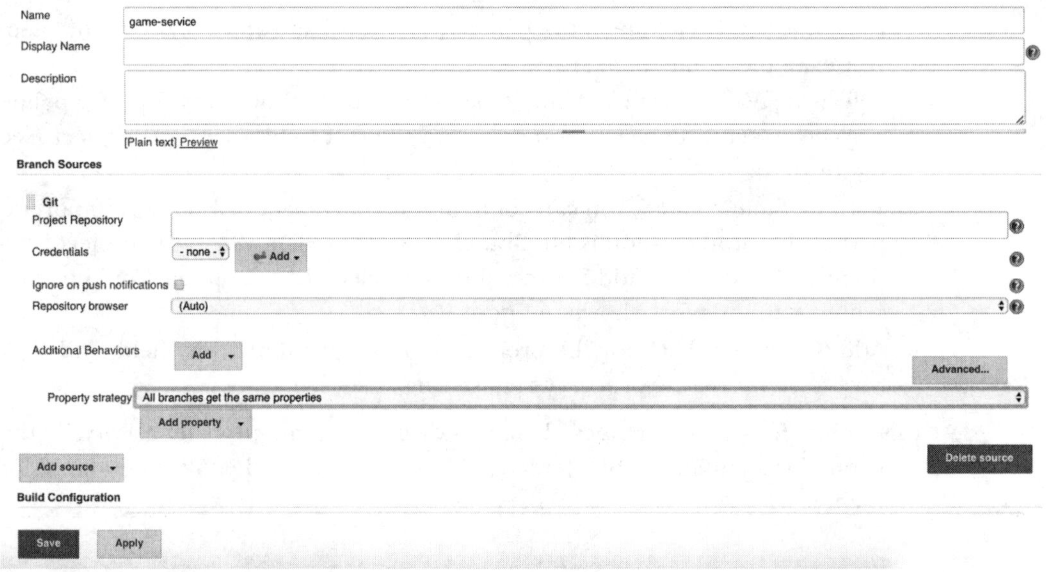

Figure 10.9   Item configuration block

Blue Ocean

Blue Ocean is, at the time of writing, a plugin available for Jenkins that improves the Jenkins user experience by reducing the complexity and increasing the visual clarity of a pipeline. It isn't installed by default, so you need to install it via the Jenkins Plugin Manager. Here are some notable features:

- Visualization of CD pipelines for fast, easy checking of a pipeline's status
- A pipeline editor for creating pipelines using a visual process
- Personalization to meet the role-based needs of the team
- Pinpoint precision, showing exactly the point in the pipeline that requires attention
- Native integration for branch and pull requests

Creating a new job in Blue Ocean is simple: navigate to http://localhost:8080/blue, click New Pipeline, and fill in the required information.

New pipeline

Under the covers, Jenkins detects available Jenkinsfiles and schedules builds accordingly.

10.4.2 Example of a Jenkins pipeline

Section 10.2.3 discussed running contract tests so as not to break the environment when a new service is released. The idea is to run contract tests against the head and production versions, to ensure that all services will be able to communicate with each other after the new release.

Let's see how to use Jenkins and the scripted pipeline to release a *consumer* with certainty. The following example skips the steps related to the compile and test phases, and focuses on the contract part of the *consumer* delivery pipeline:

```
stage('Consumer Contract Tests') {           Sets the publishContracts
  withEnv(['publishContracts=true']) {       environment variable to true
    sh "./gradlew :contract:test"
  }                                            Executes the contract tests
}
```

The consumer contract tests (stored in the `contract` module) are run, and the resulting contracts are published to the contracts repository. This happens because the following arquillian.xml file evaluates the `publishContracts` environment variable to make the Arquillian Algeron extension (http://arquillian.org/arquillian-algeron) publish the created contracts:

```
<extension qualifier="algeron-consumer">;
  <property name="publishConfiguration">;
    <!-- Information about repository-->;
  </property>;
  <property name="publishContracts">;${env.publishcontracts:false}</property>;
</extension>;
```

In this stage, contract tests are running on the consumer side, validating that a new consumer version can communicate with latest contract versions.

Before deploying this new consumer to production, you need to ensure that the providers of the specified consumer are compatible with this new contract. The following Jenkinsfile snippet depicts how to validate the latest contract against the head provider and against the current production provider.

Listing 10.2   Validating the latest contract

```
def headResult, productionResult
stage('Provider Contract Tests') {           The head and production
                                             contract validations are
  parallel (                                 run in parallel.
    headRun : {
      headResult = build job: 'comments-service',
        parameters: [string(name: 'commentsserviceurl', value: '')],
          propagate: false
      echo "Contract test against head Comments Service" +
          "${headResult.result}"
    },
    productionRun : {                                        Passes the
      productionResult = build job: 'comments-service',      production
        parameters: [string(name: 'commentsserviceurl',      location as a
                    value: 'commentsservice:8090')],          parameter
          propagate: false
      echo "Contract test against production Comments Service" +
          "${productionResult.result}"
```

```
    }
  )
}

if (productionResult.result != 'SUCCESS') {          The build fails on a
  currentBuild.result = 'FAILURE'          ◄────────  production provider failure.
  echo "Game Service cannot be deployed to production" +
    "Comments Service is not compatible with current GameService."
} else {
  def lineSeparator = System.lineSeparator()
  def message = "Do you want to Deploy Game Service To Production?" +
  "${lineSeparator} Contract Tests against Production" +
  "${productionResult.result} ${lineSeparator} Contract Tests against" +
  "HEAD ${headResult.result}"

  stage('Deploy To Production?') {     ◄────  If production is OK,
    input "${message}"                       requests to deploy
    deploy()
  }
}
```

This stage validates that the latest contract is also valid for the head and production versions of the provider, in this case, the comments service. Validation of both versions is performed in parallel. Because the provider's validation contract resides in the provider project, the build needs to be triggered.

For the production run, the service location is defined as a build parameter. After the provider version is successfully validated against the latest contract, the user is prompted to deploy the new consumer to production.

> **TIP** Depending on your software release model, the pipeline script is likely to vary from project to project. For this reason, we encourage you to visit https://jenkins.io/doc/book/pipeline and learn in depth how the Jenkins pipeline fits into various scenarios.

Summary

- Each service should be deployed independently.
- A coded pipeline simplifies deployment and encourages the delivery of a service to be treated as part of the service project.
- Be sure to deploy to production with certainty, using contract tests against production versions.
- Jenkins covers all your needs for implementing continuous delivery in a microservices architecture.

appendix
Masking multiple
containers with
Arquillian Chameleon

Testing against several containers (WildFly, Glassfish, Tomcat, and so on) or even switching between different modes (managed, remote, or embedded) invariably results in a bloated pom.xml file. You'll encounter the following problems:

- You need to register a specific dependency for each container and mode that you want to test against, which also requires several profiles.
- In the case of a managed container, you need to download, install, and possibly configure the application server.

Chameleon containers (https://github.com/arquillian/arquillian-container-chameleon) can quickly adapt to your needs without requiring additional dependency configuration. To use this approach, do as you usually would in Arquillian, but add a Chameleon container to pom.xml instead of an application server–specific artifact:

```
<dependency>
  <groupId>org.jboss.arquillian.junit</groupId>
  <artifactId>arquillian-junit-container</artifactId>
  <scope>test</scope>
</dependency>
<dependency>
  <groupId>org.arquillian.container</groupId>
  <artifactId>arquillian-container-chameleon</artifactId>
  <version>1.0.0.Beta2</version>
  <scope>test</scope>
</dependency>
```

Then, add this configuration to arquillian.xml:

```
<container qualifier="chameleon" default="true">
  <configuration>
    <property name="chameleonTarget">
    wildfly:9.0.0.Final:managed</property>
    <property name="serverConfig">standalone-full.xml</property>
  </configuration>
</container>
```

Selects the container, version, and mode

Specific properties of the adapter

This example tells Arquillian to use WildFly 9.0.0 in managed mode. When running a test, Chameleon checks whether the configured container is installed; if it isn't, Chameleon downloads and installs it. Then, Chameleon registers the required underlying adapter on the classpath. After that, the container is started, and the test is executed normally.

Notice that any properties that are set are passed to the underlying adapter. This effectively means that with Chameleon, you can use any property that's valid in the adapters.

You can read more about Arquillian Chameleon and the advantages of using it at https://github.com/arquillian/arquillian-container-chameleon.

index

RELATED MANNING TITLES

Microservices Patterns
With examples in Java
by Chris Richardson

ISBN: 9781617294549
477 pages, $49.99
September 2018

Microservices in Action
by Morgan Bruce and Paulo A. Pereira

ISBN: 9781617294457
395 pages, $49.99
September 2018

Modern Java in Action
Lambda, streams, functional and reactive programming
by Raoul-Gabriel Urma, Mario Fusco,
   and Alan Mycroft

ISBN: 9781617293566
550 pages, $54.99
August 2018

The Java Module System
by Nicolai Parlog

ISBN: 9781617294280
400 pages, $44.99
August 2018

For ordering information go to www.manning.com